BUTCHER Burbridge

Union General Stephen Burbridge and His Reign of Terror Over Kentucky

BUTCHER *Burbridge*

Union General Stephen Burbridge and His Reign of Terror Over Kentucky

Bryan S. Bush

Acclaim Press
MORLEY, MISSOURI

Acclaim Press

ACCLAIM PRESS, INC.
Your Next Great Book
P.O. Box 238
Morley, MO 63767
(573) 472-9800
www.acclaimpress.com

Designer: Ron Eifert
Cover Design: Emily K. Sikes

Publishing Rights: Acclaim Press

Library of Congress Catalog No. 2007943951

ISBN-13: 978-0-9798802-5-4
ISBN-10: 0979880254

Printed in the United States of America
First Printing:
10 9 8 7 6 5 4 3 2 1

Additional copies may be purchased from
Acclaim Press.

Contents

Introduction 7

His Early Days in Kentucky 15

The Kentucky Campaign of 1862 34

The Vicksburg Campaign 40

The Bayou Teche Campaign 63

Taking Command In Kentucky 70

Morgan's Last Raid and the Battle of Cynthiana 86

His Controversial Reign Begins 108

The Saltville Massacre 142

The Great Hog Swindle and Election of 1864 150

Political Relations Break Down 168

A Career Comes to an End 180

Leaving the State and a Legacy 192

References 202

Index 204

Introduction

One of the most vilified men during the Civil War in Kentucky was Kentucky-born Union (Brevet) Major General Stephen Gano Burbridge, and Kentucky historians continue to cast him negatively. Burbridge had a meteoric rise as a military commander, starting as a colonel of the 26th Kentucky Union infantry and becoming a major general by 1863. He fought well at Arkansas Post and Champion's Hill during the Vicksburg Campaign and received the praise of Union General William T. Sherman. Burbridge also received the thanks of President Abraham Lincoln for his victory over Confederate General John Hunt Morgan's forces at Cynthiana, Kentucky.

Burbridge's problems arose when he became military commander of Kentucky in January of 1864. He issued an order in which, for every Union soldier killed by a guerilla, four Confederate prisoners would be taken to the spot and shot. His brutal tactics to stop guerilla warfare in Kentucky alienated Unionists in the state and moved Kentucky away from the Unconditional Unionist Party, who supported Abraham Lincoln and toward the Democratic Party. Burbridge has also been accused of fixing the 1864 state and presidential elections and of being involved in the Great Hog Swindle of 1864.

Burbridge's policies toward guerillas did not differ from those of Union General William T. Sherman, and Sherman actually influenced Burbridge's policy decision toward guerillas. Not only did Union General William T. Sherman influence Burbridge's decisions, but so did the Reverend Robert Breckinridge, Secretary of War Edwin Stanton, Kentucky Governor Thomas Bramlette, and the Radicals. While Burbridge commanded a brigade in Kentucky in early 1862, he made friends with powerful radicals who later helped him secure his position as military commander in Kentucky and influenced his decisions on how to govern the state. While Burbridge fought in the Vicksburg campaign, he became friends with Union General William T. Sherman, who also influenced Burbridge's decisions as military commander in Kentucky. Governor Thomas Bramlette's friendship with Burbridge influenced his decisions in dealing with guerillas, but the friendship with

Burbridge ended when Burbridge recruited and armed ex-slaves and slaves to fight in the Union army and his decision to disarm the state guard. After the Great Hog Swindle of 1864, Governor Bramlette pushed Lincoln to remove Burbridge from command.

The thesis of this book will deal with the military career of Stephen Gano Burbridge and the factors that eventually led to his downfall as military commander of Kentucky and his eventual ostracism from Kentucky.

In 1907, Kentucky historian Captain Thomas Speed's book *Union Cause in Kentucky* was the first to deal with Burbridge's handling of guerilla warfare. Speed supported Burbridge's actions. He wrote that Burbridge had a "fine reputation as a soldier in the field, and no officer was more highly regarded."[1] Speed wrote that the active guerilla warfare in Kentucky gave Federal officers problems and so much trouble that Burbridge had to deal with the guerillas and their supporters and sympathizers with "great severity."[2] Burbridge's handling of guerillas and their supporters brought the wrath of the Confederate element in Kentucky. Speed wrote that the Confederate element in Kentucky never realized that the Union side was rightfully in control in Kentucky, but acted as though they believed Kentucky was a Confederate state and the Unionists were intruders. Burbridge denied he had done anything wrong.

The principal complaint against Burbridge was that he put into practice retaliatory measures and caused men to be shot for the killing of Unionists by guerillas. Speed pointed out that retaliation was practiced on both sides. According to Speed, Burbridge was practicing retaliation and was acting under the orders of his superiors.[3] Speed stated that Burbridge only executed guerillas, not Confederate soldiers, but every guerilla captured by Union soldiers claimed to be in the Confederate army.

According to Speed, every Federal officer in control was made out to be unworthy for some reason by Kentuckians. Abuse was heaped upon all Union officers without discrimination, and "these ill-tempered criticisms of the war period have been duly reiterated by the writers of history."[4] Speed claimed that guerillas acted under the authority of the Confederate government and there were no Union guerillas. Confederate guerillas made war on the Unionists and Union soldiers. Speed blamed Kentucky Governor Thomas Bramlette for holding responsible all rebel sympathizers for guerillas raids. He held Governor Bramlette responsible for ordering all military

1 Thomas Speed, *Union Cause in Kentucky* (New York & London: G. P. Putnam's Sons, 1907), 243.

2 Ibid., 243.

3 Ibid., 245.

4 Ibid., 245.

commanders in the state to arrest and hold responsible rebel sympathizers when guerilla outrages were perpetrated.[5] He stated that Governor Bramlette ordered military commanders to arrest five of the most prominent and active rebel sympathizers in the vicinity for any outrage on a loyal citizen. The sympathizers were held as hostages for the safe return of loyal citizens.[6] Burbridge only acted under Bramlette's orders. Speed felt that partisan rangers and guerillas were one and the same and authorized by the Confederate government to harass Union forces. He pointed out that no records showed guerilla bands roving Kentucky were authorized by the Union government. According to Speed, there were no Union guerillas. Speed gave the impression that when Burbridge executed a Confederate prisoner of war, he was justified in the execution, since all guerillas in the state were sanctioned by the Confederacy. Speed was one of the few supporters of Burbridge.

In 1924, E. Merton Coulter published *The Civil War and Readjustment in Kentucky*. Coulter dealt with Burbridge's military command in Kentucky. He wrote that Burbridge was the "most bitterly hated of all Kentuckians."[7] During the state elections of 1864, Burbridge sent an order to every sheriff in the 2nd District to forbid Alvin Duvall's name to appear on the poll books. Duvall was standing for re-election and had been on the bench since 1856 and had been chief justice. Military officers and the Unconditional Union Party wanted their candidate, Mortimer M. Benton, elected, and the surest way was to order Duvall's name off the election ballot. Duvall was forced to flee the state. The Democrats nominated George Robertson, a former chief justice, and telegraphed his name on the morning election to the polling places. Before the military authorities could do anything about Robertson's name on the election ballot, he won the election. Burbridge's army had intimidated and demoralized the people that only 11,000 votes were cast out of a possible 45,000.[8]

Coulter wrote that a wave of arrests swept the state for the purpose of removing objectionable candidates, such as Joshua Bullitt, chief justice, accusing him of being involved in the "Knights of the Golden Circle" and "The Sons of Liberty."

During the Presidential election of 1864, Burbridge stated that the utmost importance for Kentucky's future rested on President Abraham Lincoln's winning the state. Burbridge used "patronage to win over the luke-warm and when he could by honorably bestowing a favor make a vote for Mr. Lincoln he did

5 Ibid., 248.

6 Ibid., 249.

7 E. Merton Coulter, *The Civil War and Readjustment in Kentucky*, (Chapel Hill: University of North Carolina Press, 1921 reprint 1966), 392.

8 Coulter, 184-185.

so." Burbridge sent state claims commissioners to begin settling with loyal slave holders whose blacks had gone into the Federal army. Burbridge stated: "Now gentlemen, you all want pay for your horses and niggers and corn and your hogs. Be cautious what record you make."[9] Coulter stated that only those supporting Lincoln would be given the trade permit, which was required by the military authorities to carry on trade.[10] There were 54,000 fewer votes cast than in the 1860 election. George B. McClellan received 61,478 votes, Lincoln received 25,592 votes. Burbridge and Reverend Robert Breckinridge "sedulously worked to create the impression that the test of loyalty, which meant payment for slaves and property seized and freedom from arrest and persecution, would be determined by the way a person voted–if he voted at all."[11]

Coulter stated that Burbridge arrested John Houston for no other reason than his opposition to Lincoln's election. Burbridge claimed that he arrested Houston because he was disloyal and had been reviling the administration. Burbridge stated, "When the civil authorities make no efforts to suppress disloyalty, the military must and will."[12]

Coulter quoted a series of questions that were originally printed in the *Cynthiana News* to Burbridge such as: "Does not the ghost of Walter Ferguson haunt Mr. Burbridge?" "Can he forget the appeals the ladies of Lexington made to him in behalf of this youth, and how he spurned them from his presence and doomed him to an infamous death? Can he have forgotten so early how he sent young Jameson and Reese of Harrison County to eternity for no other reason than that they were rebel soldiers? Has the death of Thornt Lafferty passed out of his mind? And many others we could mention. If he has let him be assured the people have not filled their places yet; and that their homes are desolate and dreary today on account of their absence, and that their memory is fresh and green in the hearts of Kentucky."[13]

In 1954, Kentucky historian Thomas Clark wrote *A History of Kentucky*, in which he wrote that guerilla warfare became the most "disturbing factor"[14] in Kentucky's Civil War history. Clark wrote that during the war, both Union and Confederate armies left a large number of stragglers and deserters to forage and pillage at will. Guerillas attacked Union troops and civilians. According to Clark, Burbridge's Order Number 59, in which four guerilla prisoners would be killed for every loyal Union person killed by guerillas led to confusion of

9 Coulter, 185.
10 Ibid., 185.
11 Ibid., 187-188.
12 Ibid., 187.
13 Coulter, 392-393.
14 Thomas Clark, *A History of Kentucky* (Lexington: The John Bradford Press, 1954), 327.

Confederate prisoners with the outlaws and many innocent men paid a "dear price for crimes of which they knew nothing."[15]

Clark stated that one of the most "dastardly tricks imposed upon Kentucky during the war" was Burbridge's Great Hog Swindle of 1864.[16] On October 28, 1864, Burbridge ordered in a dispatch that all Kentucky hog farmers sell their surplus hogs to the United States government. Burbridge became "so solicitous"[17] as to assure his Kentucky friends that there would be no chance of losing their pork in Confederate raids. Union Major H. C. Symonds was in charge of the hog trade, and Burbridge allowed him to close both the Cincinnati market and the Ohio River to the hog trade, preventing the hog farmers in Kentucky from selling their hogs to anyone else but the Union government. Governor Thomas Bramlette suspected foul play and asked Lincoln to revoke Burbridge's order.

In 1962, Robert McDowell published *City of Conflict: Louisville in the Civil War*, in which the author confronted several of Burbridge's orders. In June 1864, Union General William T. Sherman wrote to Burbridge that guerillas were not soldiers, but "wild beasts, unknown to the usages of war."[18] He ordered Burbridge to "arrest all males and females who had encouraged or harbored guerillas and robbers and you may cause them to be collected in Louisville, and when you have enough–say 300 or 400–I will cause them to be sent down the Mississippi, through their guerilla gauntlet and by a sailing ship send them to a land where they can take their negroes and make a colony, with laws and futures of their own."[19] According to McDowell, Burbridge set about collecting plenty of rouges, guerillas, rebel sympathizers, and political prisoners and a few innocent victims at the military prison in Louisville. On July 16, 1864, Burbridge issued Order Number 59 which stated that "Rebel sympathizers living within five miles of any scene of outrage committed by armed men not recognized as public enemies by the rules and usages of war [guerillas] will be liable to be arrested and sent beyond the limits of the United States. So much of the property of rebel sympathizers as may be necessary to indemnify the government or loyal citizens for losses incurred by the acts of such lawless men will be seized and appropriated for the this purpose. Whenever an unarmed Union citizen is murdered, four guerillas will be selected from the prisons in the hands of the military authorities and publicly shot to death in the most convenient place near the scene of outrage.[20]

15 Clark, 328.

16 Ibid., 346.

17 Ibid.

18 Robert McDowell, *City of Conflict: Louisville in the Civil War*, (Louisville: Louisville Civil War Roundtable Publishers, 1962), 160.

19 Ibid., 160.

20 Ibid., 165.

According to McDowell, retribution, harsh and brutal, fell on the guilty and innocent. In many instances legitimate prisoners of war were shot. Every guerilla who was caught claimed to be a regular Confederate soldier and most of them had forged or stolen papers to prove it, but some of the guerillas who were caught and executed were legitimate soldiers in the Confederate army.

According to McDowell, the execution of four alleged guerillas at Jeffersontown, whether innocent or guilty, was an "arbitrary and tyrannical abuse of power."[21] The men had not been given a trial and their rights had been ignored. Burbridge's "barbaric" retaliatory measures only succeeded in arousing sympathy for guerillas. McDowell wrote that since guerillas knew that they were to be executed they abandoned any self restraint and their actions became more desperate and vicious.[22]

In 1971, Louis DeFalaise wrote an article for the *Kentucky Historical Society* entitled "General Stephen Gano Burbridge's Command in Kentucky," in which the author recognized two different types of guerillas. The first were detached units of the Confederate army and the second type of guerilla were brigands, native Kentuckians and deserters from the Confederate army, who used the war for an excuse to loot and pillage. DeFalaise stated that part of Burbridge's command took part in lawlessness and he tried to put a stop to the lawlessness in his command. Governor Thomas Bramlette originally supported Burbridge, but the friendship eroded into bitter animosity. Burbridge's superior, Union General William T. Sherman hated the press because he felt that the newspapers printed nonsense and rumors and ordered Burbridge to "check this (type of reporting) as much as possible."[23] Burbridge ordered that the *Cincinnati Enquirer* be banned in his district.

Sherman influenced Burbridge's actions. He ordered Burbridge to punish Confederate troops who had broken their parole with severe treatment. Burbridge's faithful adherence to Sherman's instructions led to satisfaction among his superiors.

Burbridge wanted to use black men as soldiers, which gave rise to resentment from the people of Kentucky who did not want to "keep step to the 'music of the Union' alongside of Negro soldiers."[24] Many Kentuckians, especially slave owners, saw the recruitment of black soldiers as an insult and degradation. Governor Thomas Bramlette agreed. Burbridge's solution was to compensate slave owners and train the black soldiers outside the state.

---

21 Ibid., 180.

22 Ibid., 180.

23 Louis DeFalaise, "General Stephen Gano Burbridge's Command in Kentucky," (*Kentucky Historical Society*, 69, Issue 2, April 1971) 106.

24 DeFalaise, 107.

Burbridge's policy as military commander of Kentucky was twofold: the suppression of any disloyalty of sentiment that might weaken Kentucky's attachment to the Union, and the suppression of the guerillas. In late July and early August 1864, under Sherman's order, Burbridge arrested many prominent citizens. He forbade candidates to run for public office who might not be staunch Unionists.[25]

When implementing his guerilla policy, Burbridge was influenced by two factors, his superior General William T. Sherman and the radicals in Kentucky led by Robert Breckinridge. According to DeFalaise, Breckinridge used his influence with Burbridge to make him act in the harshest way possible toward any Southern sympathizer.

DeFalaise felt that Burbridge was a man who had some "talent but was thrust into too great a command where his judgment could not meet the exigencies of the test."[26] Throughout his career radical Unionists advised Burbridge. Dr. Robert Breckinridge and his radicals kept Burbridge in power. DeFalaise could not help to wonder if Burbridge was the source of the minority status the Republican Party held far into the twentieth century.[27]

In 1975, Lowell Harrison published *The Civil War in Kentucky*, in which the author agreed with other authors that Kentucky's Union authorities in their efforts to suppress guerilla activities led to a repressive and partially unconstitutional program that aroused civilian resentment. Harrison felt that General Burbridge lacked the experience and tact needed for the job of enforcing the anti-guerilla provisions. Harrison stated that in Burbridge's zeal to enforce the laws, he antagonized many of the staunch Unionists in the state. Only after prolonged efforts by the governor and the state legislature did President Lincoln remove Burbridge.[28]

In 1986, James Ramage published *Rebel Raider: The Life of Confederate General John Hunt Morgan*, in which he described Burbridge as "an extremist who expressed himself through action. Ignoring public opinion and refusing to temper his enthusiasm with wisdom or mercy, he ruled Kentucky with a provocative, arbitrary hand." To Kentuckians, Burbridge "became one of the most detested individuals in the war. His reign of terror "was one of the bloodiest violations of human rights in the Civil War." Ramage stated that Burbridge executed Confederate civilians and soldiers who were not guilty of any crime. His

25 Ibid., 109.
26 Ibid., 124.
27 Ibid., 127.
28 Lowell Harrison, *The Civil War in Kentucky* (Lexington: The University Press of Kentucky, 1975), 76-78.

executions "left courthouse laws throughout the state stained with blood."[29]

In 1995, Odis Lee Harris wrote an article in *The Kentucky Explorer* entitled "Union General Burbridge Brought Hate and Terror to His Kentucky," in which the author stated that Burbridge took "drastic and cruel actions"[30] to subdue guerilla warfare in Kentucky. In doing so, he "made enemies of state citizens and made no attempt to conciliate the disaffected. He antagonized moderate Union men by his seemingly arbitrary severity. He made matters worse for himself by suppressing the Home Guards and disbanding state troops raised to resist guerillas."[31]

According to Harris, Burbridge's Order Number 59 resulted in the execution of guerillas, Confederate army prisoners whose only crime was fighting for the Confederate army, and Kentucky citizens who openly criticized President Abraham Lincoln and opposed the Union army's occupation of Kentucky, or were reported to have done so.[32]

Harris's article covered Burbridge's control of the state and presidential elections of 1864, and the Great Hog Swindle of 1864. Harris stated that Burbridge's harsh treatment brought "terror to state citizens." Burbridge's hog sale policy "helped fan the flames of hatred" that the majority of the people of Kentucky felt for him. As for Burbridge's treatment of guerillas, Harris stated that his actions were no worse than Union General William T. Sherman or Confederate General Nathan Bedford Forrest.

Although Harris criticizes Burbridge for his actions in the article, he stated that Burbridge "deserves a better place in history than the one given him. His military operations in Kentucky were successful, overall, in promoting the Union cause."

In 2005, Marshall Myers wrote an article for *Kentucky's Civil War: 1861-1865*, entitled "Union General Stephen Gano Burbridge: The Most Hated Man in Kentucky," in which the author mentioned Burbridge's inference with the state and Presidential elections of 1864, the Great Hog Swindle of 1864, and Order Number 59. According to Myers, Burbridge was largely responsible for turning Kentucky toward the Southern attitude in her sympathies after the war.[33]

---

29 James Ramage, *Rebel Raider: The Life of General John Hunt Morgan*, (University of Kentucky Press, Lexington, Kentucky 1986), 212-213.

30 Odis Lee Harris, "Union General Burbridge Brought Hate and Terror to His Kentucky," The Kentucky Explorer, Feb. 1995.

31 Harris, 2.

32 Ibid., 2.

33 Jerlene Rose, Editor, *Kentucky's Civil War: 1861-1865*, "Union General Stephen Gano Burbridge: The Most Hated Man In Kentucky," Marshall Myers, 144.

Chapter 1
Early Days in Kentucky

On August 19, 1831, Robert Burbridge and Eliza Ann Barnes brought Stephen Gano Burbridge into the world. Stephen Burbridge came from a military family. His father, Captain Robert Burbridge, had served in the War of 1812 and his grandfather served as a Captain in the American Revolution. He attended Georgetown College. Georgetown College was the first Baptist College founded west of the Allegheny Mountains. In 1858, Stephen Burbridge attended the Kentucky Military Institute. The Kentucky Military Institute was one of Kentucky's foremost military institutes.

After attending the Kentucky Military Institute, Stephen Gano Burbridge studied law and acquired a law degree, but did not practice his profession. He instead became a farmer in Logan County, Kentucky.[34] As Burbridge made his living as a farmer, conditions in the country deteriorated, and, on December 20, 1860, South Carolina became the first state to secede from the Union. Kentucky quickly adopted its stance on secession. On January 21, 1861, the Kentucky legislature introduced a series of resolutions. The first declared that "the General Assembly had heard with profound regret of the resolutions of the States of New York, Ohio, Maine, and Massachusetts, tendering to the President, men and money to be used in coercing sovereign States of the South into the Federal government." The second resolution stated that the Governor of Kentucky should inform these States that if they sent armed troops to the South for the purpose of forcing the States of the South into the Federal government, "the people of Kentucky, uniting with their brethren of the South, will as one man resist the invasion of the soil of the South at all hazards and to the last extremity." Both resolutions were passed. The following passage was later added, which stated that "we deplore the existence of a Union to be held together by the sword, with laws to be enforced by standing armies." [35]

34 Louis DeFalaise, "Gen. Stephen Gano Burbridge's Command in Kentucky," *Kentucky Historical Society*, 69 (April 1971), 2), 101.

35 Evans, Clement, *Confederate Military History Extended Edition: A Library of Confederate States History Written by Distinguished Men of the South*, (Wilmington, NC: Broadfoot Publishing Company, 1988), 18.

On April 4, 1861 a new state arsenal at Frankfort, Kentucky, was provided for by the legislature and $19,400 was allotted to buy machinery and labor to repair state arms. The state was gearing for war.

On April 12, 1861, the Civil War began when Confederate General P. G. T. Beauregard fired upon Fort Sumter, in the Charleston, South Carolina, harbor. Fort Sumter, commanded by Union General Robert Anderson, surrendered to the Confederates. Kentucky declared its neutrality. Three days later Lincoln called for 75,000 troops and the Secretary of War informed the Governor of Kentucky Beriah Magoffin that four regiments of militia should be raised for the Union. Magoffin wrote back to Secretary of War Simon Cameron that "Kentucky will furnish no troops for the wicked purpose of subduing her sister Southern states."[36] Kentucky Senator John J. Crittenden, who had just retired from the Senate and was a member of the Union State Central Committee, urged for neutrality. He gave a lecture in Lexington, Kentucky in which he said, "If the President should at any time hereafter assume the aspect of war for the overrunning and subjugation of the seceding States through the full assertion therein of the national jurisdiction by a standing military force, we do not hesitate to say that Kentucky should promptly unsheath her sword in behalf of what will then have become a common cause. Such an event . . . could have but one meaning, a meaning which a people jealous of their liberty would be keen to detect, and which a people worthy of liberty would be prompt and fearless to resist. When Kentucky detects this meaning in the action of the government, she ought, without counting the cost, to take up arms at once against the government. Until she does detect this meaning, she ought to hold herself independent of both sides, and to compel both sides to respect the inviolability."[37] It was clear that Kentucky wanted neutrality. After a large meeting in Louisville, Union leader John Crittenden and Democratic leader Senator John C. Breckinridge clasped hands with the assurance from both that Kentucky would forever be neutral.

But neutrality was slowly falling apart. Throughout the state, individuals and groups left to join the Confederacy in Virginia or Tennessee. On April 20, 1861, two companies from Louisville, under the command of Captains Ben Anderson and Fred Van Osten, left for New Orleans and were later joined by Captain Jack Thompson's company and became the 3rd Kentucky battalion. On April 25, Captain Joe Desha and 100 men from Harrison County, along with three companies from Louisville under Captains John Pope, J. B. Harvey and M. Lapielle, left the state to join the Confederate army. They were joined in Nashville by two

36 Evans, *Confederate Military History*, 19.

37 Ibid., 19.

companies from southwest Kentucky under Captains Edward Crossland and Brownson. Others joined the Union army in Indiana or Ohio.[38]

In April 1861 Kentucky took out loans to pay for arms. The money was to be used "for arming the State for self defense and protection, to prevent aggression or invasion from either the North or South, and to protect the present status of Kentucky in the Union."[39]

Kentucky Governor Beriah Magoffin refused the Confederate call for troops from Kentucky, but many Kentuckians joined the Confederacy anyway. On May 15, 1861, a Confederate regiment was formed at Harper's Ferry, Virginia, under Colonel Blanton Duncan. Buckner maintained that the Kentucky State Guard was to remain neutral in this conflict and protect Kentucky from both factions, but, since many of the State Guard were pro-Southern in sentiment, large numbers of the Guard resigned and joined the Confederacy. The Kentucky legislature ordered the organization of the enrolled militia into companies, to be called Home Guards, for home and local defense.[40]

In May 1861, a supply of 5,000 muskets with bayonets and a quantity of ammunition was sent by the U.S. War Department to Cincinnati for distribution to "faithful and reliable Union men in Kentucky." Each man was to pay one dollar for each weapon. Garrett Davis of Kentucky sent these arms for the Home Guard with 1,500 arms going to the counties of Fleming and Mason, 200 to Boyd, 200 to Greenup, 100 to Montgomery, 100 to Bath, 100 to Clark, 100 to Madison, 200 to Fayette, 200 to Scott, 300 to Bourbon, and 500 to the city of Covington. The arms were delivered on May 18, 1861, and two days later Governor Magoffin issued an armed neutrality proclamation, and warned both Confederate and Union to stop the acts of war on Kentucky soil. The Confederacy immediately recalled its recruiting agents from the state.[41]

On May 6, 1861 the state legislature provided for the arming of the state under supervision of five commissioners, who were Governor Magoffin, Dr. J. B. Peyton, General Peter Dudley, George Wood, and Samuel Gill. An appropriation of $75,000 was made for the purchase of arms and accouterments to be distributed to the State Guard and the Home Guards. Power mills were erected, and the state was given control over state arsenals and arms. The State guard was to be trained in camps and neither the militia nor the state arms were to be used against the Union or Confederate states, unless they were protecting

38 The Kentucky Department of the Military, *Military History of Kentucky*, (The American Guide Series, The Works Projects Administration, 1939), 153; E. Merton Coulter, *The Civil War and Readjustment in Kentucky*, (Chapel Hill: University of North Carolina Press, 1921), Chapter 1.

39 *Military History of Kentucky*, 153.

40 Ibid., 154-155.

41 Ibid., 155.

the state from unlawful invasion. The arms and ammunition were only to be used for the defense of the state. Magoffin appointed Scott Brown as Adjutant General and M. D. West quartermaster general of the State Militia.[42]

On May 16, 1861, the committee on Federal relations in the House of Representatives reported the following resolutions:

> Considering the deplorable condition of the country and for which the State of Kentucky is in no way responsible and looking for to the best means of preserving the internal peace and securing the lives, liberty and property of the citizens of state; therefore, Resolved, by the House of Representatives, that this State and the citizens thereof should take no part in the civil war now being waged, except as mediators and friends to the belligerent parties; and that Kentucky should, during the contest, occupy the position of strict neutrality.[43]
>
> Resolved, that the act of governor in refusing to furnish troops or military force upon the call of the executive authority of the United States under existing circumstance is approved."[44]

The preamble and the resolutions passed. Governor Magoffin again stated his stance that Kentucky must remain neutral. He warned all States both Union and Confederate that he forbade "any movement upon the soil of Kentucky, or the occupation of any port, post or place whatever within the lawful boundary and jurisdiction of this State, by any of the forces under the orders of the States aforesaid for any purpose whatever, until authorized by invitation or permission of the legislature and executive authorities of this State previously granted."[45]

In June 1861, the state held their elections. The people of Kentucky elected men in Congress and the Legislature who were pro-Union. During this same month, Tennessee seceded. That would totally change the way Kentucky would hold its neutrality position. Kentucky had enjoyed its neutrality up to this point because both sides saw the state as an important buffer state. For the Confederacy, the state guarded 700 miles of the Ohio River front and made the State a safe frontier in which the armies of the South could organize free from molestation. For the North, the State made the Tennessee line instead of the Ohio line the limit of the Southern advance and gave time for organization and for the

42 Ibid., 155-156.

43 Coulter, *The Civil War and Readjustment in Kentucky*, Chapter III.

44 Ibid., Chapter III.

45 *Confederate Military History*, 22.

ultimate occupation of Kentucky when the necessity should arise or the conditions prove favorable. When Tennessee officially seceded, the line had changed. Both sides became suspicious of Kentucky's real motives and purposes. Northern cities denounced Kentucky's neutrality as nothing more than a device of the secessionists for holding Tennessee border safe from invasion. The Southerners saw Kentucky's neutrality as "hypocritically and treacherously to deceive the Confederate States and allow the despot, Lincoln, to cover Kentucky soil with his mercenaries and from that cover to invade Tennessee."[46]

During the months of June and July, members of the Kentucky militia and State Guard left the state to enlist in either the Confederacy or the Union army. The men heading for the Union enlisted at Camp Clay, across the Ohio River from Newport, or at Camp Joe Holt, in Indiana. In Louisville the "Union Club" was formed, which was a secret organization that raised over 1,000 men and armed them with arms secretly purchased from Washington through the agency of Lieutenant William Nelson and Joshua Speed. Early in July Camp Boone was established for the Kentucky Confederate enlistments. Camp Boone was located in Montgomery, Tennessee, just over the Kentucky border.[47]

In July Camp Dick Robinson was established in Garrard County, by Brigadier General William Nelson, in direct violation of Kentucky's neutrality. This camp was to expedite Union recruiting in eastern Tennessee. Both Nelson and Garrett Davis worked for Adjutant General L. Thomas in recruiting Union troops. On July 1, 1861, Thomas wrote to Nelson to muster into service five regiments of infantry and one of cavalry in east Tennessee and one regiment of infantry in west Tennessee. The ordnance bureau would send 10,000 arms, six pieces of field artillery, two smooth bore and two rifle bore cannon and two mountain howitzers and ample supplies of ammunition to be carried through Kentucky into eastern Tennessee for the distribution among the Home Guards. He was also to muster into service three regiments of infantry from southwest Kentucky. On July 14, 1861, Nelson reported back to Adjutant General L. Thomas that he had appointed Speed Fry to be Colonel of the First Regiment of infantry; Theophilus Garrard was made Colonel of the Second; Thomas Bramlette was made Colonel of the Third; and Frank Wolford was Lieutenant Colonel of the cavalry regiment. Thirty companies of infantry and five of cavalry would soon be raised. This was in direct violation of Kentucky's neutrality.[48]

On August 19, 1861, Governor Magoffin asked Lincoln for the removal

46 Stanley Horn, *The Army of the Heartland-The Army of Tennessee 1861-1862*, (Baton Rouge & London: Louisiana State University Press, 1967, reprint 1983).

47 *Military History of Kentucky*, 159.

48 *Confederate Military History*, 25-27.

of Camp Dick Robinson, but the request was denied. Lincoln stated, "I do not believe it is the popular wish of Kentucky that this force shall be removed beyond their limits, and with this impression I must decline to so remove it."[49] Magoffin wrote to Confederate President Jefferson Davis telling him that a "military force has been enlisted and quartered by the United States authorities within this State."[50] He also told Davis that he had also written Lincoln and asked for the troops to be removed from Kentucky. He was worried about the build-up of Confederate troops along the Southern frontier. He wanted an assurance that the Confederate States would respect Kentucky's neutrality. Davis wrote Magoffin back on August 28, 1861, saying that the Confederacy "neither intends nor desires to disturb the neutrality of Kentucky. The assemblage of troops in Tennessee to which you refer had no other object than to repel the lawless invasion of that State by the forces of the United States, should their government attempt to approach it through Kentucky without respect for its position of neutrality."[51] He went on to say: "But neutrality to be entitled to respect must be strictly maintained between both parties; or if the door be opened on the one side to aggression of one of the belligerent parties upon the other, it ought not to be shut to the assailed when they seek to enter it for purposes of self defense."[52]

On August 16, the U.S. War Department established the Military Department of Kentucky, and native Kentuckians were put in command. Union General Robert Anderson, who had lost his command at Fort Sumter in April of 1861, was given command of the Department of the Cumberland, which consisted of Kentucky and Tennessee. While Kentucky struggled with her neutrality, Stephen Burbridge decided to take action into his own hands and form a Union regiment of his own. On August 19, 1861, the Federal government accepted Burbridge's regiment and he became commander of the 26th Kentucky Union Volunteer Infantry.

By early September the Union army made its move toward the occupation of Kentucky. Major General Robert Anderson moved his headquarters from Cincinnati to Louisville. William "Bull" Nelson was commissioned a Brigadier General. The troops raised at Camp Dick Robinson were placed under the command of Brigadier General George Thomas. The Union forces began a shift of troops from Cairo to Columbus, Kentucky. On September 2, 1861, Union troops occupied Belmont, Missouri, across the river from Columbus. General John Fremont put General Ulysses S. Grant in command of the forces

49 Ibid., 29-30.
50 Ibid.
51 Ibid.
52 Ibid., 29-30.

in southeastern Missouri and made it known that he wanted to take Columbus, Kentucky, because it was a strategic location on the Mississippi river. Columbus was located on the Mississippi below the bluffs called "Iron Banks." The "Iron Banks" could command the river and the surrounding countryside for miles. Ships would have to slow down to get past the bend in the river which the "Iron Banks" commanded, and cannons could easily stop the traffic along that particular part of the Mississippi.[53]

On September 3, Confederate General Leonidas Polk ordered Confederate General Gideon Pillow to fortify Columbus, Kentucky, which violated Kentucky's neutrality and provided the North the justification to invade Kentucky. Polk justified his action by saying that the Union army had already broken Kentucky's neutrality.

On September 4, Governor Harris learned of Pillow's invasion into Kentucky and the seizure of Columbus. Harris was trying hard to get Kentucky into the Confederacy. He had just sent three Tennessee citizens to Frankfort, Kentucky, as commissioners, in hopes to get the Kentucky government to side with the Confederacy. Harris immediately telegraphed Polk and Jefferson Davis to withdraw the troops.

The next day President Jefferson Davis told Secretary of War Leroy Walker to telegraph Polk to withdraw the troops from Kentucky and explain his actions. Davis sent a telegram to Harris telling him that the action was unauthorized. On September 4, Polk sent a telegram to Davis saying that he was keeping his troops in Kentucky. On September 5, Davis telegraphed Polk: "Your telegram received. The necessity must justify the action." It is of some interest to note that this statement can have several interpretations. It can mean the necessity does justify the action or the necessity had better justify the action.[54]

The seizure of Columbus was a huge Confederate blunder. The invasion of Kentucky by the Confederates enraged Kentucky's legislature, as well as Governor Magoffin. The seizure of Columbus also alienated many citizens in Kentucky. The Confederates were viewed as the aggressors, offsetting whatever advantage Columbus may have had in providing the defense of the river ways. On September 7, the House of Representatives of the Kentucky Legislature ordered the U.S. flag to be hoisted on the State Capitol in Frankfort.[55] On that same day Brigadier General U.S. Grant, along with 5,000 men from Fort Holt,

---

53 Stanley Horn, *The Army of Tennessee*.

54 Steven Woodworth, *No Band of Brothers: Problems of the Rebel High Command* (University of Missouri Press, Columbia and London, 1999), 14-17.

55 *Military History of Kentucky*, 163.

which was located on the Kentucky shore opposite Cairo, Illinois, entered the city of Paducah.

On September 15, Confederate Gen. Albert Sidney Johnston arrived in Nashville, Tennessee. He had resigned his commission in the old army and the command of the department of the Pacific at San Francisco. He was assigned by the Confederacy to command Department Number 2, which embraced the States of Tennessee, Arkansas, and that part of the State of the Mississippi west of New Orleans, Jackson, and Great Northern and Central Railroad. His command also included the military operations in Kentucky, Missouri and Kansas, and the Indian country immediately west of Missouri and Arkansas. Johnston appointed Buckner as Brigadier General. He was assigned to command the forces at Camp Trousdale and Camp Boone.[56]

Three days later, on September 18, the Kentucky legislature passed resolutions which constituted a declaration of war on the Confederacy. The resolutions passed over the veto of Governor Magoffin. On that same day on September 18, General Buckner led his 4,500 troops to occupy Bowling Green, Kentucky. He also sent 500 men to Munfordville, Kentucky, instructing them to build fortifications around the city. On that same day, Gen. Albert S. Johnston arrived to inspect the progress of the fortifications at Columbus.

Confederate Gen. Albert Sidney Johnston's defensive line stretched from Columbus, Kentucky, and Fort Donelson and Fort Henry in western Kentucky to Bowling Green, Kentucky, in the middle of the state, to the Cumberland Gap, in eastern Kentucky. Union forces in Louisville, Kentucky, began to test Johnston's line. On October 21, the 7th Kentucky Infantry commanded by Col. Theophilus Garrard and the 33rd Indiana were attacked by two regiments of Tennessee volunteers commanded by Colonels Newman and Bowler, supported by two Mississippi regiments and two Alabama regiments under the command of Brig. General Felix Zollicoffer. The Confederates lay in waiting until the Union forces advanced. The Confederates chased after the surprised and retreating Federals, but were met by the fire of Col. Frank Wolford's dismounted Kentucky cavalry, who supported the Union right flank. After an hour's fight, the Confederates withdrew, leaving between 100 and 300 dead and wounded on the battlefield. Four companies of the 14th Ohio reinforced the Federal line. At 4:00 p.m., the Confederates attacked but failed to dislodge the Union troops. On October 22, the Confederates retreated under the cover of night. Federals losses were four killed and 18 wounded.[57]

56 *Confederate Military History*, 36-38.

57 Beach, Damien, *Civil War Battles, Skirmishes, and Events in Kentucky* (Different Drummer Books, Louisville, Kentucky, 1995), 27.

On October 23, 1861, Gen. William "Bull" Nelson, with the 16th Kentucky Infantry routed some Confederate cavalry at Hazel Green, Henderson County, capturing 38 men. On that same day, Union forces comprised of the 2nd Ohio and Konkel's battery and Langlin's cavalry routed Captain May's Confederate cavalry in West Liberty, Morgan County, Kentucky.

On October 29, 1861, Stephen Gano Burbridge had his first test of the 26th Kentucky Infantry in Woodbury and Morgantown, Kentucky. On October 29, Colonel John H. McHenry, Jr. received information that 140 Confederate cavalry were encamped at Woodbury, Kentucky. He reported his information to Burbridge that Confederate forces were in force on the south side of the Green River and about to attack Colonel McHenry, Jr.

Confederate Captain Thomas Lewers's Mississippi Cavalry scouted the country adjacent to Morgantown, the ferries, and the bend of the Green River, near Woodbury, with the purpose of viewing Union movements. On October 29, Captain Lewers sent out a scout party, under the command of Lieutenant Bondurant, in the direction of Morgantown.[58] Colonel McHenry and Lieutenant Bondurant were on a collision course.

Burbridge rode out to join Colonel McHenry's force. Burbridge's force comprised of 125 infantry, 100 cavalry, and two 6-pound cannons, under Captain Somerby. After a march of 30 miles over rough roads, Burbridge reached Colonel McHenry, Jr.'s camp. Colonel McHenry and Colonel Burbridge marched in the direction of Morgantown and camped 14 miles from Hartford and near Cromwell, on the Green River, and sent out his scout to ascertain the position and strength of the Confederates.[59]

A small portion of Captain Breathitt's company of cavalry, under Colonel John McHenry, with his force crossed the river and proceeded to Morgantown, where they encountered the Confederate's pickets under Captain Lewers, and in the engagement Colonel McHenry lost Private Granville Allen, of Company D, 17th Kentucky Cavalry, but wounded several of the pickets, all of whom made their escape.[60]

In the meantime, Burbridge ordered Captain Netter to join his command at Cromwell, but failing to make the junction, he crossed the river and passed Morgantown in the direction of the Confederate's retreat and about one mile from the town came upon the Confederate pickets, who had been reinforced to 60 men by

58 O.R. Series I, Vol IV Chapter XII October 29-31, 1861, Skirmishes at and near Woodbury and Morgantown, Kentucky. Report of Captain Thomas Lewers, Mississippi Cavalry.

59 O.R. Series I, Vol IV Chapter XII October 29-31, 1861, Skirmishes at and near Woodbury and Morgantown, Kentucky. Report of Col. S. G. Burbridge, Kentucky Volunteers.

60 Beach, 28.

Confederate Lieutenants Doniphan and Brown, and with 20 men the battle began, in which Captain Netter killed six Confederates, without a single loss.

While Captain Netter fought the Confederate pickets, Burbridge moved the main body of his force over a mountainous and circuitous route, some 20 or 30 miles up the river to Woodbury, and found the Confederates, under Captain Lewers, camped on a summit commanding the surrounding area. The Confederates immediately formed into line of battle, but were thrown into confusion by a few rounds from one of Somerby's six-pounders. A detachment of Confederate cavalry was below the summit at the ferry flat, which was the only means of transport across the river. On the opposite side and in possession of the ferry were the Confederate pickets. Union Lieutenant Ashly engaged the Confederate pickets at the ferry, and the Confederates who were not killed were driven back and the ferry captured. Captain Belt, with 85 men, entered the battle, supported by Captain Shacklett, with 25 men and Captain Porter with 25 Home Guards. While under Confederate fire the entire time, Colonel Burbridge ordered Captain Belt, Captain Shacklett, and Captain Porter over the river with one piece of artillery. Burbridge's small arms fire played "upon the enemy destructively."[61]

According to Burbridge, the entire operation was a success. Captain Belt took the Confederate's position, which overlooked their encampments. Burbridge ordered a few shells into the Confederate's tents, and Captain Belt's men charged with bayonets, with the Confederates scattering in confusion, leaving behind them 50 killed and many wounded. A number of small arms and shotguns were captured, and four or five horses were taken, along with two prisoners. Burbridge ordered all of the Confederates tents, baggage train, magazines, etc., destroyed.[62]

Burbridge learned that the Confederates, after reinforcing, were about to cut off Colonel McHenry's retreat, so he marched double-quick and proceeded to join McHenry, one and a half miles west of Morgantown. Burbridge made a stand, but the Confederates decided not to attack the Federal forces. He fell back, crossed his forces over the river, and camped at Cromwell's Ferry. While at Cromwell's Ferry, 150 Home Guards joined Burbridge's forces, but he noted that the Home Guards disappeared at the approach of danger.[63]

In the after-battle report, Colonel Henry thanked Colonel Burbridge for his promptness and zeal in Burbridge's quick response to his appeal for help. He also thanked Burbridge for his "bravery, discretion, and energy displayed

61 Ibid.
62 Ibid.
63 Ibid.

by him in routing the enemy from Woodbury."[64] The defeated Confederates under Captain Lewers met Major James Hagan's Mississippi Cavalry, with reinforcements. Major Hagan rode toward Morgantown. Major Hagan decided to pursue Burbridge's force. As he approached Morgantown, Hagan learned that Burbridge's force was still in position on the ground occupied by Captain Lewers. After leading a reconnaissance, Hagan learned that Burbridge had left Captain Lewers' former position. Hagan entered Morgantown without opposition. Then he decided to head back to camp at Bowling Green, Kentucky.

On January 12, 1862, Colonel Burbridge wrote to Union General Thomas Crittenden asking for a leave of 20 days. He wrote that he needed the 20 days because he had business at home of great importance involving the amount of eight or ten thousand dollars. He had to personally be present or he ran the danger of losing the money. His family had been compelled to leave their home in Logan County, and, since he had not seen his family for four months, they needed his attention. Crittenden granted his request.[65]

While Burbridge left for Logan County to attend to his family and business, Confederate General Albert Sidney Johnston's defensive line quickly crumbled before his eyes. The first crack in Johnston's defensive line came in eastern Kentucky. In November 1861 Confederate General Felix Zollicoffer's force advanced west into Kentucky with 4,000 men, to strengthen control in the area around Somerset, Kentucky. He found a strong defensive position at Mill Springs and decided to make this his winter quarters. He fortified the area, especially both sides of the Cumberland River. Union Brigadier General George Thomas received orders to drive the Rebels across the Cumberland River and break up Confederate Major General George B. Crittenden's army. Thomas left Lebanon and slowly marched through rain soaked country, arriving at Logan's Crossroads on January 17, where he waited for Brigadier General Alfred Schoeph's troops from Somerset to join him. Major General George Crittenden, Zollicoffer's superior, had arrived at Mill Springs and taken command of the Confederate troops. He knew that Thomas was in the vicinity and decided that his best defense was to hit the Federals first. At dawn, on January 19, 1862, the Rebels attacked Thomas at Logan's Crossroads. Unbeknownst to the Confederates, some of Schoeph's troops had arrived and reinforced the Union troops which now numbered around 4,000 men. Initially, the Rebel

64 O.R. Series I, Vol IV Chapter XII October 29-31, 1861, Skirmishes at and near Woodbury and Morgantown, Kentucky. Report of Col. John H. McHenry, Jr., Colonel Kentucky Volunteers.

65 Letter from Colonel Stephen Gano Burbridge to General Thomas Crittenden, January 11, 1862, Compiled Service Records of Volunteer Union Soldiers from the State of Kentucky, National Archives, 1934, Microfilm 397, Roll 375.

attack forced the 10th Indiana to retire, but during the battle General Zollicoffer was killed. Zollicoffer was nearsighted and rode up to a Union officer. The officer, Colonel Speed Fry, shot Zollicoffer dead. After Zollicoffer was killed, Crittenden took over and rallied his men to attack. Crittenden's men were armed with flintlock rifles that did not shoot well in the rain, and his men began to retreat. The Federals were equipped with percussion capped rifles. Union counterattacks on the Confederate right, led by Colonel Samuel P. Carter's brigade, and the left, led by the 9th Ohio Infantry, were successful, forcing the Confederates from the field. Crittenden had to abandon twelve cannon and large quantities of stores in Beech Grove, and then crossed the Cumberland River headed toward Knoxville. Crittenden lost 439 men. Federal losses were 232. The Battle of Mill Springs, along with one at Middle Creek, broke whatever Confederate strength there was in eastern Kentucky.[66]

The next crack in Confederate General Albert Sidney Johnston's defensive line came at Fort Henry and Fort Donelson. Fort Henry and Fort Donelson were in the middle of the South's defense line stretching from Columbus, Kentucky, to Bowling Green, Kentucky, then southward to the Cumberland Gap. Loss of the forts would allow the North invasion routes by land and by water. In November of 1861, the forts were commanded by Confederate General Lloyd Tilghman. Fort Henry, located above a bend in the Tennessee River, commanded a stretch of river three miles long, but the fort had obvious weaknesses. The fort was built on low ground and subject to flooding, and overshadowed by hills on both sides of the river. Though he had eleven of Fort Henry's seventeen guns facing the river, Tilghman still felt that the fort could not stand an attack. He sent most of his men to Fort Donelson, only ten miles away, keeping 100 artillerymen with him to serve the guns.

On January 30, 1862, Union General Henry Halleck, commander of the Department of Missouri, gave Union General Ulysses S. Grant permission to seize Ft. Henry. Grant commanded 17,000 infantry on board transport boats, and Flag Officer Andrew Foote commanded seven gunboats. On February 3, 1862, Grant unloaded his infantry from the transports onto land just outside the range of the guns at Fort Henry. On February 6, Brigadier General Charles Smith seized the heights above the fort and Brigadier General John McClernand advanced to cut off the escape route. The gunboat Cincinnati attacked Fort Henry and knocked out two of Captain Jesse Taylor's most important guns, a 6 inch rifled cannon, and a 128-pound cannon. Taylor then lost two more guns, both thirty two-pounders. With only four guns still serviceable at Fort Henry,

66 Bryan Bush, *The Civil War Battles of the Western Theater*, (Paducah: Turner Publishing, 1998, reprint, 2000), 19-20.

General Lloyd Tilghman and Captain Taylor surrendered to Andrew Foote. By the time Grant's infantry arrived, the Battle of Fort Henry was over.

Grant focused his attention on Fort Donelson. Halleck sent Grant 10,000 reinforcements. Confederate General Albert Sidney Johnston, at Bowling Green, decided to give up his position and retire to Nashville. Johnston left 5,000 men at Fort Donelson and placed Brigadier Generals John Floyd, Gideon Pillow, and Simon Buckner in command. On February 12, Grant's force approached Fort Donelson. On February 14, Foote's gunboats arrived and twelve army transports with 10,000 men on board came into view. General Wallace arrived with troops from Fort Henry. Three divisions were formed under Lew Wallace, McClernand, and General Smith. At 3:30 p.m., Foote's gunboats attacked, but were repulsed by the shore batteries. Foote was wounded in the battle, and the St. Louis, the Pittsburg, Carondelet, and the Louisville were severely damaged.

The Confederates decided to attack the Federals the next day and then make their escape from Fort Donelson. Gideon Pillow was to attack McClernand, and Buckner was to leave the 13th Tennessee infantry in the trenches to the right, facing General Smith's division, and move the bulk of his men to the center. Once Pillow rolled the Federal troops back, Buckner would strike the hinge and hold the door open while Pillow's division marched out safely. Buckner would follow, fighting a rear guard action to make sure the army escaped. The attack began at daylight, and the battle went well for the Confederates at first; they were close to a victory. Their escape route was open, and they had managed to drive off McClernand and Wallace's divisions. By 1:00 p.m., Grant had arrived on the scene and realized what the Confederates were trying to do, and immediately ordered Wallace and McClernand to counterattack. Grant also ordered Foote's gunboats to fire, and Smith to take the fort by attacking the Confederate right. The troops under Captain Jack Slaymaker rushed the Confederate earthworks and Buckner's 30th Tennessee fell back. The Federals brought guns to bear on the entrenchments. Pillow ordered a retreat back into the fort. At 1:00 a.m., the generals left Buckner to surrender the garrison, while Floyd and Pillow would escape with Nathan Bedford Forrest's cavalry. On February 16, 1862, Buckner surrendered to Grant. Grant took 12,000 to 15,000 prisoners, 2,000-4,000 horses, 48 cannon, seventeen heavy guns, and large quantities of commissary stores. The capture of the forts forced the Confederates to evacuate Nashville and Columbus. General Albert Sidney Johnston lost his grip on southern Kentucky and lost virtually all of middle and western Tennessee.[67]

---

67 Bryan Bush, *The Civil War Battles of the Western Theater* (Paducah: Turner Publishing, 1998, reprint 2000), 29-30.

After the disaster of Forts Henry and Donelson, Confederate General Albert Sidney Johnston continued to fall back through Tennessee until he reached Corinth, Mississippi. The Union army followed in pursuit. By the third week of March 1862, Union General Ulysses S. Grant moved up the Tennessee River and landed at Pittsburg Landing to prepare for an attack on Corinth. Union General Don Carlos Buell's Army of the Ohio occupied Nashville. Colonel Burbridge and the 26th Kentucky belonged to the 14th Brigade, under Colonel W. Smith, Fifth Division, under the command of Brigadier General Thomas Crittenden, Buell's Army of the Ohio. On March 16, Union General Henry Halleck ordered Buell to march to Savannah, Tennessee, located nine miles from Pittsburg Landing. Confederate General Albert Sidney Johnston decided to attack Grant at Pittsburgh Landing before Buell could reinforce Grant. On April 6, 1862, Johnston attacked Grant's forces and caught him by surprise. At 5:00 a.m. on Sunday, April 6, 1862, Union Major James Powell of the 25th Missouri and 300 men scouted the area, and collided with Confederate Major Aaron Hardcastle's 3rd Mississippi Infantry Battalion, the advance guard of Wood's brigade, Hardee's Corps. The Confederates began to fire, and the Federals under Powell stood their ground as reinforcements were brought up. Jesse Appler of the 53rd Ohio, deployed his men, but soon fell back before the massive Confederate onslaught. Cleburne then began to advance, his goal being to seize the crossroads at Shiloh Church. Braxton Bragg moved up to support William Hardee. Grant called for Buell's troops, who had arrived in Savannah the day before, and were on the east bank of the river. Grant also called for Lew Wallace to get his men ready to move out. At 9:00 a.m., Grant rode from his headquarters to the front. By 10:00 a.m., the Confederates had driven through the camps of three Union divisions, sending the surprised blue-clad soldiers reeling back toward the river. Union General Benjamin M. Prentiss's division was pushed back almost a mile. The Confederates stopped at Prentiss' camp and began to eat the food that Prentiss's men had been cooking for their breakfast. That gave Prentiss time to take up a good defensive position on high ground along a sunken road. About 1,000 men formed along the road, which was about a mile behind their original position. Other units formed on either side of Prentiss: Hurlbut sent two brigades on his left, and W.H.L. Wallace aligned three brigades on Prentiss's flanks, two on Prentiss's right and one to his far left, beyond Hurlbut. To the right of Wallace were two brigades of McClernand's division and then Sherman's division. These troops made a desperate attempt to slow the Confederate advance. Union General Ulysses Grant looked over the new line and ordered Prentiss to "maintain that position at all hazards."

Cheatham's division advanced upon the new Federal line, and when they came within 150 yards, the Federals unleashed their artillery. At 30 yards, Union Colonel William Shaw and his 14th Iowa fired at the oncoming Confederates. The Confederate line fell back. On Cheatham's extreme right, Union Brigadier General Jacob Lauman's brigade of Hurlbut's division took on the Confederates. His men opened fire on the Rebels at 100 yards, but the Confederates approached until they were within 10 yards of the 31st Indiana before they were stopped. The Rebel troops under Braxton Bragg continued crashing and screaming through the woods, toward the Federal position. Bragg ordered the 4th, 13th, and the 19th Louisiana and the 1st Arkansas to attack the Federals on the sunken road. Charge after charge, 12 in all, were made against Prentiss's position, and each was repulsed with great slaughter. "It's a hornet's nest in there!" cried the Rebels, recoiling from the blasts of canister and case shot and the fire from the 8th Iowa's eight hundred rifles. By 2:30 p.m., after two hours of fighting, the Confederates were no closer to taking the Federal lines at the Hornet's Nest than they were at the Sunken Road, and the Confederate onslaught began to grind to a halt. There were massive problems on the field. There was no overall Confederate commander and no coherent plan of attack. The Confederates had 17,000 men against Grant's 4,000 men under Prentiss, but the Confederate troops were sent in piecemeal. Orders were given and then countermanded by different generals. At some points along the line Confederate companies halted because there were no further orders for them. Beauregard was in the rear and did not know what was going on at the front and only sent men where he heard fighting. Corps commanders reduced themselves to small unit commanders.

A Confederate attack led by General Albert Sidney Johnston broke through Union troops in the Peach Orchard on Prentiss's left, led by the Kentucky troops under General John C. Breckinridge, and the Rebels pushed back the troops on his right, leaving what was left of Prentiss's division without support. Johnston led the Kentucky Confederate troops toward the Peach Orchard, but about halfway there he was struck in the leg by a bullet that severed a major artery, and the blood was flowing into his boot. Johnston soon became disoriented and dismounted. He had a field tourniquet in his pocket, but his officers did not know how to use it, and earlier in the battle he had sent his personal surgeon, Dr. Yandell, away to tend to the wounded soldiers. General Johnston soon bled to death.

After Albert Sidney Johnston's death, General P.G.T. Beauregard took command of the Rebel forces. Beauregard was obsessed with the Hornet's Nest also. He could have gone to the flanks and driven the Federals right into the river at Pittsburg Landing, but he chose not to. Beauregard soon massed the largest assembly of cannon in the War up to that point, 62 in all, and he aimed them at point blank range at the Hornet's Nest and the Sunken Road. At about 4:00 p.m., he began a bombardment with shell and canister that was like "a mighty hurricane sweeping everything before it." The Hornet's Nest exploded under the fire, but Prentiss and his men held on, their lines bending back into a horseshoe shape as more and more pressure was applied to their flanks. By 5:30 p.m., they were completely surrounded and being attacked on all sides. Unable to do any more to obey Grant's order to hold his position, Prentiss ordered cease-fire and surrendered his remaining 2,200 men at 6:00 p.m. However, his gallant defense had given Grant the time he needed to construct a new line to the rear. Grant's new line ran inland at a right angle from the river above Pittsburg Landing northwest toward Owl Creek. The line was three miles long and strongly defended. Colonel J.D. Webster grouped cannon on the left of the line while Sherman and McClernand protected a road that ran north parallel to the Tennessee River. Lew Wallace arrived at 7:00 p.m. and set up at the far right of the new line. Colonel Jacob Ammen's brigade, from Buell's corps arrived. The division commander, Brigadier General William Nelson and his men followed Ammen's brigade across the river and took their positions on Grant's new line.

The Confederates had been fighting for 12 hours and were exhausted and hungry, having not eaten since 3:00 a.m. Many of the Confederates refused to go on and sat down in the abandoned Federal camps, and began to eat. Most believed they had won a great victory and thought they had beaten most of the Union forces.

Bragg and Polk tried to rally the men for one more attack before darkness set in. Bragg, on the left, could only gather Chalmers' troops and John Jackson's men, who were already out of ammunition. Bragg's two divisions tried to rush the new line, but Federal artillery ripped Bragg's men to pieces. Polk and Hardee, on the right, fought with Sherman's and McClernand's troops, but were not successful in capturing any of them. As twilight settled, Beauregard suspended the assault on the Federals, and recalled Polk and Bragg.

During the night, Union General Don Carlos Buell's Army of the Ohio arrived at Pittsburg Landing, including the 26th Kentucky Infantry. Colonel Nathan Bedford Forrest's cavalry scouted the Federal lines. Forrest reported to Hardee that Grant had about 45,000 men, against their 20,000 Confederates. Grant decided that he would attack the Confederates the next day.

On April 7, the Union forces rolled forward at about 7:30 a.m., and the outnumbered Confederates were pushed back. Grant took back most of the ground he had lost the previous day. Cleburne put up some resistance around Shiloh

Church, leading an attack on Sherman's men, but his soldiers became entangled in the thick undergrowth, and soon his lines were decimated by the Federals. Confederate Brigadier General Sterling A. M. Wood tried to hold Shiloh Church, but his left was crumbling and as his flanks became exposed to Federal fire, and he pulled back. At 2:30 p.m., Beauregard ordered a withdrawal to Corinth. An hour later, the Confederates began to withdraw. The Union troops were just as exhausted as the Confederates and did not pursue them.

On April 7, Colonel William Smith was commander of the 14th Brigade, which was comprised of the 26th Kentucky, 14th Wisconsin, and the 13th Ohio, moved out from Pittsburg Landing at 6 a.m., toward the front and placed in position alongside General William Nelson's division, which was already engaged. The 14th Wisconsin was on the right, the 13th Ohio on the left and the 26th Kentucky in the center. The 11th Kentucky was held in reserve and placed 200 yards in the rear of the center of the line of battle, in a position covered by the crest of a hill. Two companies of skirmishers, one from the 11th and one from the 26th Kentucky, were deployed to the front. The skirmishers engaged the Confederates in an open field on their front of the right of the line. The Confederate skirmishers retired. A lull in battle occurred for about an hour, when the brigades skirmishers encountered the Confederates and a furious attack opened on the brigade's entire front. The right recoiled, while the left and center stood their ground. The 26th Kentucky was sent forward to support the right, and a heavy crossfire to their front was opened from Bartlett's batter, which was in position on the brigade's right. The Confederates yielded, when a running fight broke out, which extended for about one mile to their front, where they captured a battery and shot the horses and many of the cannoneers.[68]

The brigade's line turned into a column of attack, and at the head of the column stood a few heroic men, when the Confederates returned to the attack with three fresh regiments. The Confederates drove the brigade back to the first position occupied early in the attack, when the brigade rallied and moved forward toward the battery. Reaching a ravine to the right, and about 600 yards from the battery, the brigade halted and awaited the assistance of Mendenhall's battery, which was brought into action on a knoll within half a mile of the Confederate's battery, which Mendenhall silenced. The brigade advanced and captured the Confederate battery for a second time, and succeeded in holding the battery, despite the efforts of the Confederates to repulse the brigade. One of the guns was at once turned upon the Rebels, and Mendenhall's battery was advanced to nearly the same position and opened fire upon the flank of the

68 O.R. Series I, Vol. X/1 April 6-7, 1862-Battle of Pittsburg Landing or Shiloh, Tennessee. Report No. 123 Col. William Smith, 13th Ohio Infantry, commanding 14th Brigade.

Confederate's column, which was retiring before General Alexander McCook's division on the brigade's right. The brigade had been fighting for five hours.[69]

The 13th Ohio and 26th Kentucky had "determined valor"[70] during the fight even though some of their officers and men exhibited a "laggard discharge of their duty."[71] Colonel William Smith commented that the 13th Ohio and 26th Kentucky "bore themselves as true soldiers and efficient officers through the danger of the day."[72] The brigade lost 23 killed, 156 wounded, and nine missing, for a total of 188 men.

On April 11, 1862, General Halleck arrived at Pittsburg Landing and removed General Grant from field command. Although Colonel Burbridge rejoined his command, he did not fight in the Battle of Shiloh. Health problems prevented him from participating in the battle. On April 24, 1862, Colonel Burbridge wrote to Major General Don Carlos Buell stating that he had sent through division and brigade commanders detailing the condition of his regiment. He stated that his regiment was exceedingly small, because of the men who were absent or absent without leave because of their illnesses. He suggested that the best means to make the regiment efficient was to send the regiment either to Kentucky or Tennessee in place of some other regiment who was anxious to commence active campaigning and furnish the 26th Kentucky an opportunity to recruit and build up the regiment's health and numbers and prepare for the field. His application for the regiment to be sent back to Kentucky or Tennessee to recruit and re-cooperate was signed by the officers and the men of the regiment.[73]

Colonel Burbridge also stated that his health was exceedingly bad and failing him daily. In Kentucky or Tennessee, where the life would not be quite as hard, he thought that he could recover his health. He desired to remain with his men and he did not want to resign, but only if he was permitted to take his regiment to some locality where their health and his would improve and strengthen the command. He added that his brigade commander visited the regiment and knew about the poor condition of the regiment and suggested for the removal of the regiment from the field.[74]

---

69 O.R. Series I, vol. X/1 April 6-7, 1862-Battle of Pittsburg Landing or Shiloh, Tennessee. Report No. 123 Col. William Smith, 13th Ohio Infantry, commanding 14th Brigade.

70 O.R. Series I, vol. X/1 April 6-7, 1862-Battle of Pittsburg Landing or Shiloh, Tennessee. Report No. 123 Col. William Smith, 13th Ohio Infantry, commanding 14th Brigade.

71 Ibid.

72 Ibid.

73 Letter from Colonel Stephen Burbridge to Major General Don Carlos Buell, April 24, 1862, Compiled Service Records of Volunteer Union Soldiers from the State of Kentucky, National Archives, 1934, Microfilm 397, Roll 375.

74 Ibid.

Burbridge stated that if he remained he would be forced because of his health and the health of his family to tender his resignation, as would several of his officers in his command. He stated that his health declined every day.[75]

On April 28, 1862, on the field at Shiloh, Burbridge wrote to the commander of the 14th Brigade, 5th Division. He stated that he tendered his resignation as Colonel of the 26th Kentucky. He stated that he had to resign because his health had been "so exceedingly bad for three months past that I have been unable to do duty."[76] He wrote that he went home on leave of absence, but he still came back debilitated and unable to assume command of the regiment. His health was growing worse daily and there seemed to be no prospect that he would regain his health and strength sufficiently to perform military service. If he did not go home and stayed in camp, he would never recover from his illness. He felt there was no other alternative than to resign from the army. The surgeon of the 26th Kentucky, J. M. Bailey, certified that Colonel Burbridge had been afflicted with dyspepsia and chronic sore throat for six weeks and grew worse daily.[77]

By late May, Union General Henry Halleck personally organized the army into a 100,000-man force, with 200 cannon. On May 28, Halleck arrived on the outskirts of Corinth. Confederate General Beauregard, outnumbered two to one, tried to trick Halleck into thinking that Confederates had more men than they actually had, by sending trains in and out of Corinth. Each time the train arrived, the townspeople and soldiers would give a great cheer as if a new train load of soldiers had arrived into Corinth. The ruse worked well and bought Beauregard enough time to safely escort his men out of town. On May 30, the Federals entered a deserted Corinth and seized the Memphis and Charleston railroad. Confederate President Jefferson Davis said "this railroad was the vertebra of the West," and now it was in Federal hands.

Major General Don Carlos Buell did not accept Burbridge's resignation. Burbridge's health improved and by June 22, 1862, he resigned as commander of the 26th Kentucky to accept the commission as a brigadier general. He returned to Kentucky.

---

75 Ibid.

76 Letter from Colonel Stephen Burbridge to Brigadier General Van Cleave (?) April 28, 1862. Compiled Service Records of Volunteer Union Soldiers from the State of Kentucky, National Archives, 1934, Microfilm 397, Roll 375.

77 Ibid.

Chapter 2

The Kentucky Campaign of 1862

On July 31, 1862, Confederate General Braxton Bragg and Major General Edmund Kirby Smith met in Chattanooga, Tennessee, to plan their invasion of Kentucky. Both generals were hoping to bring Kentucky into the fold of the Confederacy. Bragg had high hopes for Kentucky. Kentucky Confederate Calvary Gen. John Hunt Morgan promised that Braxton Bragg would be able to pick up 100,000 men if he entered Kentucky. Bragg was also looking for badly needed supplies. On August 13, 1862, Edmund Kirby Smith was the first to enter the state and was very much supported by the locals, as large crowds came out to greet him. At Lexington, Kentucky, Smith was greeted with Confederate flags waving as he entered the town.

While General Edmund Kirby Smith took Lexington, Burbridge wrote on August 22, 1862, to Doctor Gano (?) from the Galt House in Louisville, Kentucky, stating that the Senate petitioned for Burbridge to have a brigade in Kentucky and that he hoped he would get the brigade.[78]

On August 28, Confederate Gen. Braxton Bragg, commander of the Army of Mississippi, entered the state in areas where Union support was very high. He was hoping to link up with Smith and then both armies were to march on Louisville. They were trying to get to Louisville before Union General Don Carlos Buell's Army of the Ohio arrived from Knoxville, Tennessee. Bragg was never able to link up with Smith, and on September 14 through 17, he ended up fighting at Munfordville, Kentucky. The battle delayed Bragg long enough to allow Don Carlos Buell to arrive in Louisville first. While in Louisville, Buell picked up recruits and brought his army to 58,000 men. Bragg had about 15,000 men and Smith had the main army of about 25,000.

Buell secured Louisville and was awaiting Bragg. Buell's job was on the line, and he knew that he had to win a victory, or else. Buell originally did not want the job of commanding the Army of the Ohio, but the commanding

78 Stephen Burbridge to Doctor (Gano), August 22, 1862, Stephen Gano Burbridge Collection, Microfilm (one reel), University of Kentucky Special Collections and Digital Programs, Lexington, Kentucky.

officer before him, General Bull Nelson was killed in the lobby of the Galt House in Louisville by Union General Jeff Davis. Buell got the job by default and was unaware of the true size of Bragg's army.

On September 29, 1862, Special Order Number 40 ordered Brigadier General Burbridge from Cincinnati, Ohio, to report for duty to Brigadier General A. J. Smith, commanding U.S. forces in Covington, Kentucky.

During the summer of 1862, Kentucky was going through one of its worst droughts ever. Both armies were looking for water sources. Bragg had heard that there was water at the Chaplin River, Doctor's Creek, Bull Run, and Wilson Creek in Perryville, Kentucky. Bragg arrived in Perryville first. William Hardee, along with Simeon Buckner's Division came, in from the west along the Springfield road on October 6. They were falling back from Bardstown, Kentucky, and were hoping to settle in at Harrodsburg, Kentucky. Hardee stopped for water in Perryville, thinking that the Union army under Buell was to the north, and was confused when he saw heavy numbers of Union troops traveling along the Springfield Pike. Hardee asked for support and was given two divisions from Leonidas Polk's corps, Patrick Cleburne's and Anderson's. At 3:00 a.m. on October 7, Anderson moved out with Patrick Cleburne following. Polk commented that the Union force approaching Hardee was not large. He was very wrong.

The Yankee force converging at Perryville was three corps strong, a total of 60,000 men. General Buell's plan had been to keep the Rebels guessing as to where his force was, hoping to prevent Bragg and Smith from linking up. The strategy worked.

Buell moved northeast from Louisville with his main force, while launching a feint toward Frankfort, with troops led by Joshua Sill and supported by Dumont. These 20,000 men were to confuse Bragg as to the real direction of Buell's army. Bragg swallowed the bait and was sure that Buell was going to attack Harrodsburg.

The Union army approached Perryville on three roads. On the Federal left, moving by the Mackville Road, was the three division corps of Major General Alexander McCook. On the Federal right flank, advancing on Perryville via the Lebanon Road, was the corps of Major General Thomas Crittenden, also comprised of three divisions. Occupying the center was the corps of Major General Charles Gilbert, moving toward Perryville on the Springfield road. Gilbert arrived before McCook and Crittenden.

The Federals would have to fight the Rebels to get the water since the Rebels already had the water sources secured. Confederate General William Hardee deployed his forces, and after positioning two of Buckner's three brigades between the Harrodsburg Pike and the Chaplin River, sent St. John Liddell to occupy Peter's Hill, where the Turpin house was located.

On October 7, Buell was less than five miles from Perryville. On October 8, 1862, Confederate General Braxton Bragg attacked Union General Don Carlos Buell's forces. A four-hour battle erupted, in which the First Corps, under Union Gen. Alexander McCook, was pushed back almost a mile and half. Bragg won a tactical victory, but the battle was a strategic victory for the Union, because Bragg would pull out that night from Perryville, and move toward Harrodsburg. Total casualties from the battle amounted to 7,407; 4,211 Union and 3,196 Confederate.

While the battle raged in Perryville, General Burbridge became commander of the First Division, Army of Kentucky. While he commanded a division in Kentucky, he became obsessed with strict military discipline and also had to deal with Kentucky Union officers who brought their slaves into camp with them.

Kentucky was a slave-holding state, but also devoted itself to the Union, which made for a delicate situation for General Burbridge. On October 8, 1862, Burbridge wrote to Union General A. J. Smith in Covington, Kentucky, reporting that he had sent out 300 men under Captain Lesslie, of the 4th Indiana Cavalry, with instructions to move to the front and ascertain if the Confederates were near. Captain Lesslie proceeded as far as Williamstown with his command and divided his force into three commands sending them in the direction of Cynthiana, Big Eagle Bridge, and Owenton. They all returned, bringing prisoners. They heard of no large Rebel force on the railroad at any point. Captain Lesslie went up the pike as far as Big Eagle Bridge, but found no Rebel force and continued to Owenton.

After making a junction with the force sent to Williamstown, he found at the Owenton Ponds three Confederate regimens of infantry, 600 cavalry, and two pieces of artillery, which had just arrived there from the direction of Frankfort, making about 2,500 men. Burbridge ordered Captain Lesslie not to engage the Confederates, so Lesslie returned without attacking the large Confederate force. Burbridge wanted permission to capture the Confederate force. He had two captains of the 10th Kentucky Cavalry under arrest for refusing to obey orders while on scouting duty and also had two pickets under arrest, who left their post and went to the front. He asked General A. J. Smith what to do with them. He claimed that court-martials were too slow. According to Burbridge, he never saw so much demoralization in his life. He claimed that the 10th Kentucky Cavalry did not have a true military officer in the regiment. He stated that if he had some good cavalry he could do good service. He suggested mounting the 18th Kentucky Infantry. After talking with a man from Georgetown, Kentucky, Burbridge learned that there was no force at Frankfort, but Confederate Generals Humphrey Marshall and Edmund Kirby Smith were at Lexington, and General John Breckinridge, Simon Buckner, and Braxton Bragg were at Frankfort at the inauguration of the Confederate Governor Richard Hawes, but all had retreated to Versailles after burning bridges on Union General Don Carlos Buell's approach. Buell fell back to Shelbyville. He reported that huge numbers of Union refugees were coming into his camp running from Rebel conscription.[79] Burbridge was correct in his information, except General John C. Breckinridge was actually still in Knoxville.

Burbridge asked permission from General A. J. Smith to move the 118th Ohio and a squadron of cavalry of the 10th Kentucky, to his headquarters. He claimed that neither regiment was doing well in Independence, Kentucky, and that if they stayed in Independence they would be no better than a mob until the regiments were put under a strict military discipline. He asked for more cavalry. Burbridge reported that the Confederates were evacuating Lexington and concentrating at Camp Dick Robinson or Harrodsburg.[80]

Once Bragg linked up with Edmund Kirby Smith, Bragg made for the Cumberland Gap and crossed back into Tennessee. Union General Don Carlos Buell reported to General Henry Halleck that he would not follow Bragg's army, because the roads were too rough and the country barren and devoid of supplies and food.

On October 13, 1862, Burbridge wrote to General Smith that there were no rebel forces at Georgetown, Covington, or Frankfort. He asked that the Federal cavalry under General Granger or General Wright to be placed under his command. He asked for one more battery and two more mounted howitzers, with small light guns. He wanted another full regiment of cavalry. He also needed government funds. He had been paying the expenses of spies out of his private funds. He needed a division train for transporting provisions and ammunition. He asked if he should issue rations to the black men in his camp and furnish transportation for women and children. He asked what kind of vouchers he should give to the Union men in the Federal service who had slaves in his camp.[81] Burbridge wrote to General Smith that he considered the issue of slaves in camp "a delicate matter."[82]

On October 29, 1862, Burbridge wrote to his uncle Harry that the manner in which some of his troops were acting was very discouraging to him. He wrote that he had left the division at Williamstown. The division was in fine

79 O.R Series I, Vol XVI/2, General S. G. Burbridge to General A. J. Smith, October 8, 1862.
80 Ibid.
81 O.R Series I, Vol XVI/2, General S.G. Burbridge to General A. J. Smith, October 13, 1862.
82 Ibid.

condition and ready to march through the country of his birth. He assured his Uncle Harry that he protected every citizen. He wrote that General Gilmer promised him to issue an order which removed all blacks in camp and prevent the soldiers from stealing, but Gilmer failed to issue the order. He blamed the officers in the division for not controlling their men. Burbridge wrote that he has been changed from division to division and at last assigned to a brigade, which he did not consider justice. He ordered all the blacks who belonged to the Union soldiers to be out his camps. He wrote that he had to arrest several officers first but he wrote that "a little firmness is all that is necessary."[83] He wrote that while he conducted his own command, other officers allowed their men to "steal all they want."[84] Burbridge had been threatened with having charges preferred against him, but he had arrested every officer that had spoken of it. He claimed that he wanted a better command to where he could do the state some service. As a brigade commander he claimed he could do little in protecting the citizens of his state. He spoke to several friends, and they all wanted him in Kentucky. He wrote that, "Mr. Davis of Paris wishes me to have Command of Kentucky or a Division in the State, where I can do more for the loyal men of the State knowing them all."[85] He wrote that Dr. Gano had a talk with some of the Union men on the subject of his being commander in Kentucky. He wrote that "Mr. Davies, William and Brutus Clay of Paris and Judge Buckner, Tom Clay and others of Lexington will do what they can to make sure Burbridge is commander in Kentucky. We ought to have one of our state men in command here, and, if the citizens have confidence in me, I would like to have the place. You will find that the officers and men want me."[86] He wrote that uncle Harry should come up to see him, and if uncle Harry or any of his Union friends have lost their slaves, he can get them without any trouble.[87]

Although Burbridge had made powerful friends in Kentucky among the Radical Unionists, and hoped that he would become the district commander in Kentucky, the Union army had other plans. He would have to wait a whole year before he commanded Kentucky. As 1862 came to an end, the Union army needed Burbridge elsewhere. Union General Ulysses S. Grant gathered his forces for the upcoming Vicksburg Campaign. Union General William T. Sherman ordered General A. J. Smith's division, along with General Burbridge's brigade

---

83 Letter from Stephen G. Burbridge to Uncle Harry, October 29, 1862, Stephen Gano Burbridge Letters, 1862-1865, Microfilm, University of Kentucky Special Collections and Digital Programs, Lexington, Kentucky.

84 Ibid.

85 Ibid.

86 Ibid.

87 Ibid.

to join his forces in Memphis. For the next year, Burbridge would fight in the upcoming Vicksburg Campaign. His fighting and commanding abilities would gain him respect with General Sherman and his peers and increase his image as a competent military commander. His growing friendship with General Sherman would play a major role when Burbridge returned to Kentucky in early 1864.

Chapter 3

The Vicksburg Campaign

December 20, 1862-Janaury 3, 1863.
Expedition from Milliken's Bend to Dallas Station and Delhi, La.

By early November 1862, Union General Ulysses S. Grant began his movement against Vicksburg, Mississippi. He moved south from the Tennessee border along the tracks of the Mississippi Central Railroad and planned to move through Mississippi, until he reached Jackson. Once he arrived in Jackson, he would cut the railroad line between Jackson and Vicksburg and flank Vicksburg. Grant ordered Union General William T. Sherman's 30,000 men to the mouth of the Yazoo River, just north of Vicksburg. His troops would attack Chickasaw Bluffs, while Grant moved south. Sherman collected his forces in Memphis, and by December 12, 1862, he began his preparations for the Vicksburg Campaign.

When Burbridge arrived at Memphis, he became part of the First Division, under the command of Brigadier General A. J. Smith. Sherman ordered a large fleet of steamboats from St. Louis and Cairo, including Admiral David Porter's gunboat fleet, to Memphis, to cooperate in his movement toward Vicksburg. On December 19, the troops at Memphis boarded the steamboats and headed for Helena, Arkansas. On December 23, 1863, General Sherman sent a letter to all his divisional commanders, including General A. J. Smith. Sherman stated that that their object was to secure the navigation of the Mississippi River and its main branches and to hold them as military channels of communication and for commercial purposes. The Confederates held Vicksburg to Baton Rouge, and was able to connect communications and routes of supply east and west. He wrote that General Banks had reinforced General Butler in Louisiana and moved north. General Grant, with the 13th Corps, moved south and planned to advance down the high ridge between the Big Black and the Yazoo and meet Sherman at the Yazoo. Before any actual battle with the enemy, Sherman would gather his forces at Gaines Landing,

Arkansas, and proceed to Milliken's Bend and dispatch a brigade to the Vicksburg and Shreveport Railroad with the purpose to destroy the railroad and cut off the Confederate route of supply and then head for the Yazoo. He planned to land his entire force on the Mississippi side and reach the point where the Vicksburg & Jackson Railroad crosses the Big Black. He would then attack Vicksburg by land, while the gunboats attacked the city by water.[88]

On December 25, 1862, Sherman reached Milliken's Bend. Sherman ordered Burbridge's brigade to the southwest to break up the railroad leading from Vicksburg toward Shreveport, Louisiana. Sherman left General A. J. Smith's division at Milliken's Bend to await the return of General Burbridge, while he proceeded with three divisions to the mouth of the Yazoo and up river to Johnston's plantation and land General Steele's division above the mouth of the Chickasaw Bayou. According to Sherman's orders, Burbridge landed and marched two miles and came across the Lake Providence and Tallulah telegraph, which he destroyed. Burbridge reached Dallas and ordered Lieutenant Whilldin, with a detachment of the 6th Missouri Cavalry under the command of Major Montgomery, to proceed to Delhi. The men and horses were completely exhausted from chasing the Rebel cavalry, which had been hovering around his brigade's flank all day. Burbridge proceeded with orders to destroy the Vicksburg, Shreveport, and Texas Railroad. A detachment was sent to Quebec under the command of Captain D.W.C. Shockley, in which the railroad was destroyed for half a mile. A bridge and about 100 yards of trestlework were burned, and the crossing of the Tallulah was completely destroyed. Captain Shockley encountered Rebel pickets, some of which he captured, and, after accomplishing his mission, he turned to Dallas. Burbridge concentrated his forces at Dallas.[89]

Burbridge found 400 cavalry and four pieces of artillery on his left flank, but Captain Blount's 17th Ohio Battery dispersed the Confederate forces. Burbridge burned a large quantity of cotton, corn, and forage and destroyed a large section of trestle work, a bridge, and the depot at Dallas. At Bear Lake, he found a large quantity of cotton marked "C.S.A." which had been taken by the Confederate government in lieu of taxes. Burbridge burned the cotton.[90]

When Burbridge's Union cavalry reached Delhi, they found teams in the

88 William Tecumseh Sherman, Memoirs of General W. T. Sherman (The Library of America: New York, New York, 1990), 310-311.

89 O.R. Series I Vol. XVII/1 December 20, 1862-Janaury 3, 1863, Operations against Vicksburg, Miss. Report No. 6, Report of Brig. Gen. Stephen Gano Burbridge, U. S. Army Commanding First Brigade, First Division, of expedition from Milliken's Bend to Dallas Station and Delhi, La.

90 Ibid.

act of removing a large quantity of brown cotton. A large quantity of the brown cotton was burned, together with the depot and its contents. They also found a full supply of medicines, drugs, instruments, and the appliances of a medical staff, all of which were burned. About a mile from Delhi, a trestle extending across the Tallulah was destroyed. The mail was captured and about a quarter of a million yards of muslin was burned.[91]

The command returned to their transports on December 26, 1862, having made a march of 75 miles in 36 hours, including a cavalry dash 30 miles farther. During Burbridge's expedition, he managed to capture a large number of horses, and 100 mules; he destroyed a telegraph line, and damaged the Vicksburg, Shreveport, and Texas Railroad to a point where the railroad could not be repaired for several months. All the saw-mills on the route were burned.[92]

Major General William T. Sherman, commanding the Army of Tennessee, indorsed Burbridge's report stating that he "fully and completely carried out his instructions and has deprived the enemy in Vicksburg of the use of one of his chief avenues of supply."[93]

On December 27, General A. J. Smith, along with Burbridge's brigade, landed below General M. L. Smith's division, near Chickasaw Bayou. General Sherman ordered General A. J. Smith to take a road from Johnston's plantation which led directly to Vicksburg, but the road had many obstacles including numerous bayous and swamps. The road ended at the foot of the Vicksburg Bluff, opposite the strong forts. By December 28, Sherman realized General A. J. Smith could not cross the obstacles.

On December 29, Sherman placed all his troops into position to attack Chickasaw Bluffs. At his signal, a Union heavy artillery fire opened up along the whole line, with the Confederates replying with their batteries. The Union infantry opened fire, especially on Union General A. J. Smith's front and in front of Union General George Morgan. The Union troops crossed the bayou to the foot of the hills, but a cross fire of artillery forced them to fall back, leaving 500 wounded Union soldiers on the battlefield. The attack failed. Sherman took heavy causalities and accomplished nothing.

On January 2, all of Sherman's troops boarded ships and left Chickasaw Bluffs. Sherman received a message that General McClernand arrived with orders from the War Department to command the expeditionary force on the Mississippi River. He advised McClernand that Confederate reinforcements had arrived at Vicksburg and that Grant should be near. McClernand told

---

91 Ibid.
92 Ibid.
93 Ibid.

Sherman that General Grant was not coming to help Sherman and that his depot at Holly Springs was captured by Confederate General Earl Van Dorn. Grant fell back to Holly Springs and Lagrange. Sherman realized any attempt to attack on the Yazoo was hopeless. On January 3, Sherman fell back to Milliken's Bend. The next day General McClernand assumed command of the Army of the Mississippi. Sherman asked McClernand if he could take Arkansas Post and Fort Hindman.[94]

Battle of Arkansas Post

In 1685, the French established Arkansas Post, a village located on elevated ground 50 miles above the mouth of the Arkansas River, about 120 miles northwest of Vicksburg, Mississippi, or 117 miles below Little Rock, Arkansas: the state capital. Fort Hindman, a square full-bastioned fort, was built within the village, upon the bank of the river, at the head of a bend resembling a horseshoe. The exterior sides of the fort, between salient angles, were each 300 feet in length; the faces of the bastions two-sevenths of an exterior side and the perpendiculars one-eighth. The parapet was 18 feet wide on the top; the ditch was 20 feet wide on the ground level, and eight feet deep, with a slope of four feet base. A banquette for infantry was constructed around the interior slope of the parapet; also three platforms for artillery in each bastion and one in the curtain facing north. On the southern face of the northeastern bastions was a casemate 18 feet by 15 feet wide and seven and a half feet high in the clear, the walls of which were constructed of three oak timbers sixteen inch square, and the roof with an additional revetment of iron bars. One of the shorter sides of the casemate was inserted in the parapet and was pierced by an embrasure three feet eight inches on the inside and four feet six inches in the outside, the entrance being in the opposite wall. This casemate contained a nine inch Columbiad. A similar casemate was constructed in the curtain facing the river, containing an eight-inch Columbiad, and still another nine inch Columbiad was mounted in the salient angle of the southeastern bastion on a center pintle barbette carriage. All of these guns commanded the river below the fort. Beside these guns were four three-inch Parrots guns and four 6-pounder iron smooth bore guns mounted on field carriages on the platforms in the fort which also contained a well-stored magazine, several frame buildings, and a well. The entrance to the fort, secured by a traverse, was on its northwestern side, and from the salient angle of the northwestern bastion extended a broken line of rifle pits westerly for 720 yards toward the bayou, intersected by wooden traverses. Along the line of rifle pits six field pieces were mounted,

94 Sherman, 321.

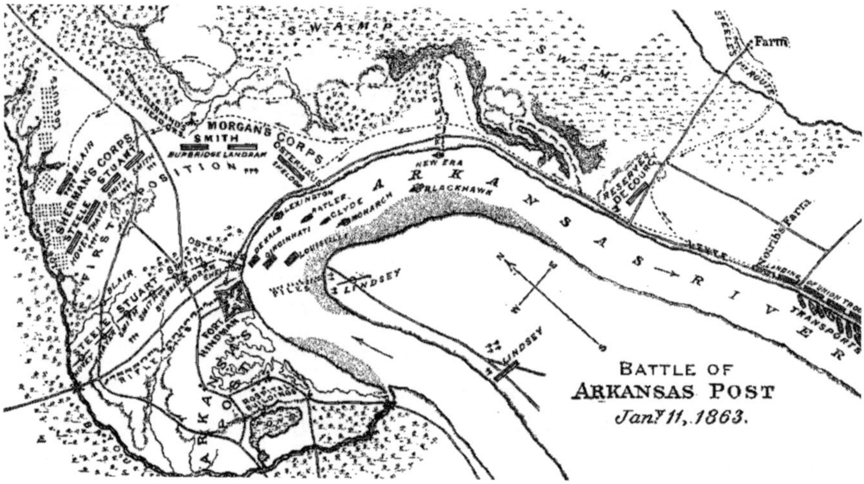

of which three were rifled. Below the fort occurred rifle pits and a levee. The levee exposed a convex line which was pierced for ten guns and lined on the inside by rifle pits. The second line of rifle pits, with intervals left for six guns, extended across the high land from the river to the swamp, its near approach being obstructed by an abatis of fallen timber and still nearer the fort was a deep ravine entering the river at right angles and extended inland in different arms in front of the left of the Union line. In front of the center of the line was an open field. The second line of rifle pits expanded into a dry plateau extending to the swamp on the east and northeast and to the bayou and river on the west and south. This plateau, crossed by the Brownsville and Little Rock road, embraced the Rebels cantonment. The fort and surrounding outer works had 5,000 men, under the command of Colonel John Dunnington, who was in charge of the fort and Brigadier General Thomas Churchill, who commanded the men in the mile long trenches.[95]

Union General John McClernand decided to capture Arkansas Post. Union Major General William T. Sherman gave permission for McClernand to take the fort. McClernand enlisted the help of Admiral David Porter and his fleet of gunboats to help him in his task of taking the Confederate fort. McClernand has several reasons for capturing Fort Hindman. The first reason was the necessity of opening and securing communication by the Mississippi River between a point near Vicksburg and Memphis, which was obstructed near the mouth of the Arkansas by armed detachments sent from Arkansas Post. After the Vicksburg expedition had been left unsupported by the retirement of

95 O.R. Series I, Vol. XVII/1 Jan. 4-17, 1863, Expedition against Arkansas Post, or Fort Hindman, Arkansas, and operations in that vicinity. No 1-Report of Maj. Gen. John McClernand, U.S. Army, commanding expedition of operations January 4-17, with congratulatory orders.

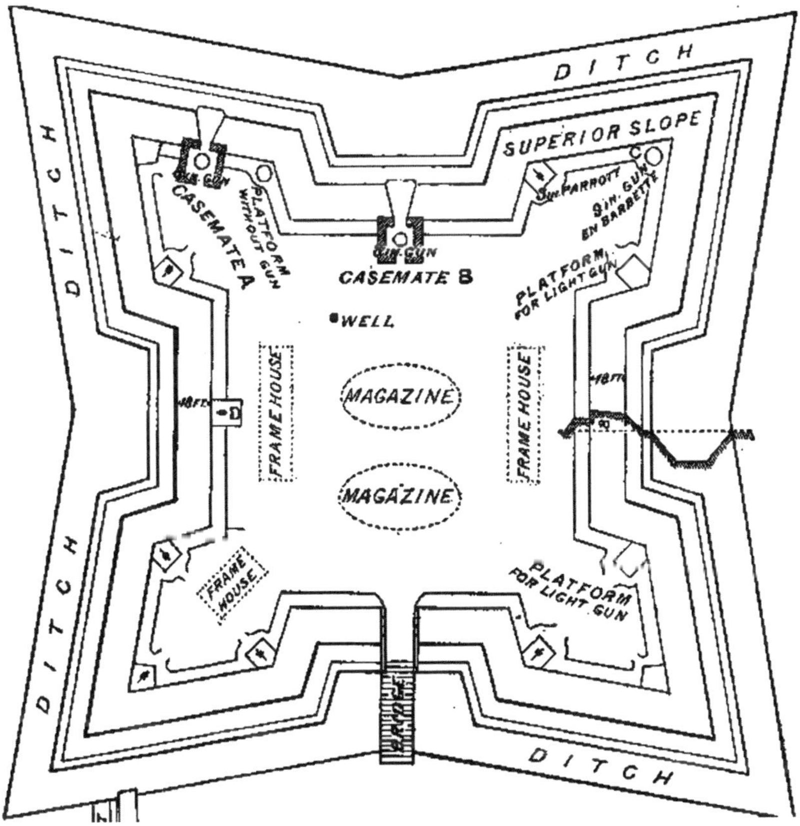

Above: View of the construction of Fort Hindman. Below: Side view of the construction of the casemate at the Battle of Fort Hindman.

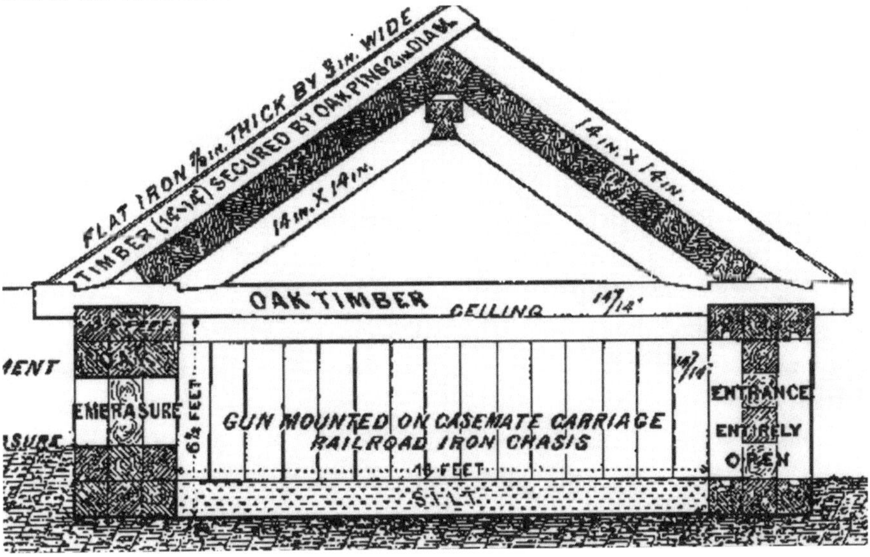

Casemate at Fort Hindman.

General Grant's army from Oxford to Holly Springs, and after the repulse of the expedition under General Sherman near Vicksburg, McClernand surmised that it would have been criminal to have renewed the attack upon Chickasaw Bluffs, without any kind of support or cooperation. The retirement of Grant's army left Confederate General Sterling Price's army at Grenada at Liberty to reinforce the garrison at Vicksburg, which was done to such an extent as to give the Confederates, independently of their works, a large numerical superiority over the Union forces. Union General Nathaniel Banks had not been heard from, nor was it believed that he could reach Port Hudson and Vicksburg before McClernand returned from his expedition. Had McClernand not embarked on the Arkansas Post expedition, his forces would have rusted in comparative idleness at Milliken's Bend. Vicksburg cannot be reduced by a frontal attack, unsupported by cooperation from the rear, except by a large land and naval force and after great delay. According to General McClernand, the golden moment for the reduction of Vicksburg was allowed to pass unimproved.[96]

On January 8, 1863, McClernand's 50 transports and Porter's 13 gunboats left Milliken's Bend, and passed the mouth of the Arkansas River in order to deceive the Confederate scouts. They sailed into the White River and followed a tributary into the Arkansas. On January 9, the transports began unloading 30,000 Union infantry three miles downriver from Fort Hindman, while Porter's gunboats steamed father ahead and drove the Rebels defenders a mile and half from the fort. By January 10, all the Union soldiers had been landed and

96 Ibid.

began to close in on the fort. Burbridge's first division was one of the infantry units landed near Fort Hindman. His brigade comprised of the 60th, 16th, and 67th Indiana Infantry; the 83rd and 69th Ohio, and the 23rd Wisconsin.

On January 10, at midnight, Burbridge's entire command, including the 17th Ohio Battery, moved up the road to follow Sherman's corps. After finding the route impracticable, they returned and were ordered to follow the road leading up the river bank, which the brigade did until they reached the first line of outer works of Fort Hindman, which had been evacuated. Burbridge turned to the right through the swamps until they came to within a half mile of the fort. Porter's gunboats approached to within 400 yards of the fort and shelled the fort for two hours.

About sunset, Smith ordered Burbridge to throw his brigade into battle. He found that, owing to a misapprehension of orders, only one regiment, the 60th Indiana, commanded by Colonel R. Owen, had followed. Burbridge immediately sent back orders for the rest of the brigade to move up, and, becoming impatient, he rode back himself and brought them up at the double quick. He ordered the 60th and 16th Indiana to the right and front with the 23rd

Union troops storm and capture Fort Hindman at Arkansas Post, Arkansas, under the command of General Stephen G. Burbridge, on January 11, 1863.

Wisconsin, under Colonel J. J. Guppey, in their rear as a reserve, with orders to the former two regiments to skirmish well to their front. He ordered the 67th Indiana, under Colonel Emerson, and the 69th Ohio, Colonel Vance, on the left, and the 83rd Ohio, Lieutenant Colonel Baldwin, in their rear, with the same instructions as those given to the right of the brigade.

On January 11, at daylight, Burbridge moved his command to the right directly in front of the fort and in rear of an open field, across which he was ordered to make the assault. He formed his command in two lines, with the 60th Indiana on the right, the 16th Indiana, center, and the 83rd Ohio, on the left, with orders to feel their way to the edge of the open field, across which was the fort about 400 yards away. He placed three pieces of Captain Blount's 17th Ohio battery on his left, having some earthworks thrown up for the battery's protection and ordered the 96th Ohio to protect the guns.

At 1:00 p.m., Colonel Parsons, aide to General McClernand, came with orders that the Confederates were retreating, and Burbridge should be ready to storm the works. At 1:30 p.m., Porter's gunboats approached the fort and began shelling. At the sound of the gunboat fire, the Union infantry attacked across an open field toward the Rebel breastworks that protected the rear of the fort. Burbridge heard the cheering and musketry on his right, and ordered his front line to advance, which was done under a "murderous fire of musketry, shell, round shot, and grape and canister." Observing that his line was waver-

Union gunboats bombard Fort Hindman, Arkansas Post, Arkansas, during the attack of January 11, 1863.

ing under such a destructive fire, especially on his right and left, the right having received a heavy fire from one of his own regiments on his right, he marched up his three regiments to their relief. The three front regiments refused to be relieved, and, supported by the three relieving regiments, the whole six regiments went forward and drove the Confederates from their houses in front of their works and the six Union regiments took the Confederate position.

Finding an open space on his right, between his troops and those of General Sherman, Burbridge filled the space with the 23rd Wisconsin, which held their position. On his left, he extended the length of his line by throwing into that position the 67th Indiana, under Colonel Emerson, who was slightly wounded while leading and urging his men.

Lieutenant Colonel John Orr, commanding the 16th Indiana, was severely wounded in the head by a piece of shell while leading on his men, when they were within 30 yards of the outer works. After Lieutenant Colonel Orr was wounded, Colonel Lucas came out and was in command of the regiment when the fort surrendered. Lieutenant Colonel Templeton, of the 60th Indiana was also wounded during the battle.

Finding his right was being pressed, Burbridge ordered Colonel Landram, commanding the 2nd Brigade, First Division, asking for reinforcements. Colonel Landram sent the 19th Kentucky and the 97th Illinois. Burbridge ordered the 19th Kentucky to relieve the 23rd Wisconsin. The 23rd Wisconsin almost silenced the Confederate rifle fire from their pits directly in front of the regiment. The 97th Illinois was held in reserve, but fought "most gallantly" in front, while under the protection of a clump of woods which was located close to the right of the fort.

Burbridge reported that his whole command was under heavy fire for three and a half hours, and had to make the greater part of his assault through an open, marshy field, where the Confederates had a full and fair range with grape shot and musketry.

The 16th Indiana was the first regiment in the fort, followed by the 83rd Ohio, who were the first to plant their regimental colors on the Confederate works, with the balance of his command soon within the works. As he approached the entrance of the fort, the guard presented bayonets and stated that they had not surrendered. Burbridge told him that they had fought gallantly, but were whipped, and he demanded the Confederates to surrender. The Confederates dropped their arms and allowed Burbridge to enter, which he did, and hoisted the first national United States flag. Confederate General Thomas Churchill, commanding the fort, surrendered the fort to Burbridge in person. In his after battle report, Burbridge stated that the battle was "hard fought and a complete success. All I have to regret is the loss of the brave and wounded who fell gallantly fighting for our glorious old Union."[97] According to General Smith, the brigade lost 47 killed, 381 wounded, and six missing for a total of 434. In his after action report, General Smith gave great praise to General Burbridge. The brigade captured three flags: the Confederate garrison flag, taken at the headquarters in the fort, McCulloch Avengers' flag, taken on the right breastwork, and the 10th Texas, Company A. Nelson's regiment, taken at the hospital.[98]

The Union victory was complete. Union casualties were 140 men killed and 923 wounded. Rebel casualties amounted to 109 killed and wounded, but the Confederates lost 4,791 captured, including a reinforcement regiment that marched up during the surrender.

On January 13, Sherman's troops boarded their transports and rendezvoused in the Mississippi at Napoleon, at the mouth of the Arkansas. The War Department ordered Sherman's troops to Milliken's Bend to await General Grant's arrival. On January 21, Sherman reached Milliken's Bend. General Grant ordered Sherman and McClernand to Vicksburg, to land on the west bank, and to resume work on his canal across the peninsula, which General Thomas Williams had already started earlier that summer. The object of the canal was to make passage for the Union gunboats and transports across the peninsula, opposite Vicksburg. General Grant returned to Memphis and ordered McClernand to Lake Providence. Sherman's men worked on the canals at Young's Plantation, Lake Providence, and Yazoo Pass.

February 14-26, 1863
Expedition to Greenville, Mississippi, and Cypress Bend, Arkansas

While Sherman's men worked on the canals, Burbridge's command had other plans. On February 13, 1863, Burbridge's brigade left on another expedition into Louisiana. He and his men left on transports and sailed towards Greenville. The next day his brigade reached Greenville and moved out on the Vicksburg road to the plantation of Smith and Hood, on Deer Creek, seven and half miles from Greenville. At that point, he learned that the rebel force, consisting of six pieces of artillery and a force of cavalry and infantry, amounting to around 300 to 1,000 men, had passed Greenville and were heading for

97 O.R. Series I, Vol. XVII/1 Jan. 4-17, 1863-Expedition against Arkansas Post, or Fort Hindman, Arkansas and operations in the vicinity. No. 8 Report of Brigadier General Stephen G. Burbridge, U. S. Army, commanding First Brigade.

98 O.R. Series I, Vol. XVII/1 Jan. 4-17, 1863-Expedition against Arkansas Post, or Fort Hindman, Arkansas and operations in the vicinity. No 5. Report of Brigadier General Andrew Smith, U.S. Army, commanding First Division.

Bolivar, 20 miles away. Rain made the roads impassable, so Burbridge turned his command around and headed back for the transports.[99]

On February 18, 1863, Burbridge moved the fleet to Cypress Bend and the next day he sent a detachment of the 6th Missouri Cavalry, under Major Bacon Montgomery and Captain Chambers, and about 50 infantry, mounted on mules. About four miles from the river they encountered a small picket force and drove the picket force to their camp, killing one and capturing the lieutenant in command. Six miles farther on they encountered a battery, which opened upon them from the opposite bank of Boggy Bayou, which ran parallel with the river and connects with Cypress Bayou eight miles from where Burbridge's transports were located.[100]

Major Montgomery retired to the banks of Cypress Bayou and was engaging a small Confederate force from the opposite bank of the stream when the advance of the infantry came up. Burbridge ordered the 23rd Wisconsin to open fire upon the Confederates, but the Rebels were not dislodged until a few rounds of canister had been fired into their ranks. Burbridge moved his command to the point where the artillery had been in the morning. He had some difficulty in crossing at this point, as the Rebels had taken the skiff and ferry boat up the other bayou. He sent men over after them on temporary rafts. After shelling the Confederates from the bank with two pieces of the 17th Ohio Battery, a private of the 6th Missouri Cavalry attempted to swim it, and reached the opposite bank, but was compelled to return after the Confederates fired at him. Night came on, and Burbridge was compelled to halt the command because he had no knowledge of the land.[101]

On February 20, 1863, the Confederates abandoned one cannon, which they concealed in a canebreak, which was taken by Burbridge's cavalry. The 12-pound howitzer had been stamped U.S in 1828. Three deserters told Burbridge that the Confederates were beyond his reach. Burbridge returned to his transports and remained there, hoping to sail down to Perkin's Landing, four miles from Cypress Bend. He learned that a road leading into the Bolivar and Vicksburg road, cut off the retreat of Colonel S. W. Ferguson's force and compelled him to surrender or fight. However the rainy weather prevented Burbridge from leaving Cypress Bend, while Captain Sutherland, of the steam ram Monarch went up to Bolivar to find the location of the Confederates. Sutherland reported that the Confederate force had left

99 O.R. Series I, Vol. XXIV/1 Feb. 14-26, 1863, Expedition to Greenville, Miss., and Cypress Bend, Arkansas, with skirmishes (19th) at Cypress Bend and (23rd) at Deer Creek and Fish Lake Bridge, near Greenville. No 1-Report of Brig. Gen. Stephen Gano Burbridge, U. S. Army.

100 Ibid.

101 Ibid.

Bolivar and returned to Greenville.[102]

The rain continued to fall and on February 22, 1863, Burbridge landed at Perkin's Landing and sent his cavalry out to ascertain where the Confederates were located and their retreat toward Greenville was accurate. He moved down to Greenville and remained that night on the transports.[103]

On February 23, 1863, Burbridge ordered one regiment, the 83rd Ohio, Major L'Hommedieu commanding, to move out on the road previously marched over, in order to flush out the enemy, while he moved the remainder of his command by another route, but the streams were narrow.[104]

On the former road was a bridge about 150 feet in length, crossing Fish Lake, six miles from Greenville. The brigade had already been burned by Burbridge. On the road he marched his command, there was one stream, which was very narrow, to be crossed; the bridges over both had been burned. He took the staging of the steamboat with him for the purpose of making a bridge. He did not use them, as they had left a bridge near the one they had burned. Burbridge took the timber from this bridge, and reconstructed the bridge which had been burned.[105]

His force of cavalry had been increased by a small detachment of the 2nd Illinois Cavalry, under Major John J. Mudd, who were on their way to Young's Point. He gave Colonel Wright, of the 6th Missouri Cavalry, command of all the cavalry. His force had almost completed the bridge, when the Confederates opened fire with three cannons on the 83rd Ohio from the opposite side of Fish Lake, and he immediately ordered the cavalry forward, hoping he might be able to cut off the Confederate retreat before they discovered his movements, but the Rebel pickets gave them the word, and they had the advance of Burbridge's cavalry for two miles. A short distance beyond Smith and Hood farm is a bend in Deer Creek, where a plantation was located. They had taken the road, and Burbridge ordered the cavalry forward across the field. As they crossed this field the Rebels opened the battery on them. They encountered the Confederate cavalry, and drove them, separating them from their artillery.[106]

Burbridge heard of a bridge in another bend of the creek and directed the cavalry to take the bridge, which they did and drove the Rebel guard from the bridge. In the skirmish, Burbridge lost one killed, of the 6th Missouri Cavalry, and two prisoners, of the 2nd Illinois. The Confederate loss was reported by the inhabitants at 30 killed and about the same in wounded. The Confederates

102 Ibid.

103 Ibid.

104 Ibid.

105 Ibid.

106 Ibid.

escaped. About 50 prisoners who were left with a small guard escaped into the woods, and Burbridge was left with only nine prisoners. Two wounded men were paroled by Major Mudd and left at the house of Judge Dickenson.[107]

The infantry halted at this place, which was located 15 miles from his transports. They had marched through a swamp three miles wide and forded a stream which was about three feet deep. Burbridge pushed his cavalry forward four miles farther, but the Confederates had crossed the stream and burned the bridge after them. At one time Burbridge had three caissons and 20 men, which had been captured by seven men under Adjutant Conover, of the 16th Indiana. When he was in advance of the command with his small force, he saw these wagons retreating in advance of the guns, and made a dash upon them, capturing the whole number, and held them until the Rebels came up and drove him away with his cannon. The prisoners escaped into the woods.

On February 24, Burbridge returned to his transports, bringing with him all the cattle, mules, and horses that he could collect – 200 mules, 100 head of cattle, and 25 horses – and returned to Young's Point, Louisiana. He found the citizens more than willing to give up their slaves than their stock, especially mules and horses. He found the country abundant in corn, and where cotton had been burned it was where they were afraid of the cotton falling into Union hands. In Greenville, Burbridge saw 2,000 bales of cotton. [108]

Burbridge reported that infantry could not act against cavalry in a part of the country that had no road improvements. The Confederate information was always better than his own, since the citizens all sympathized with the Rebels. The only force which could capture any of the Rebel forces that fired into his transports was cavalry or mounted infantry, and light mountain howitzers. He believed that there was hardly 20 miles between Young's Point and Greenville where the Rebels did not have spies or pickets and since they would not fight, they could only be captured by a chase.[109]

On March 16, 1863, General Grant ordered Sherman to Deer Creek, and, with the gunboats, proceeded into the Yazoo River to determine whether the army could take a route that would place them on the east bank of the river in order to attack Vicksburg. Sherman moved out with the gunboat Sterling Price into the Black Bayou. The gunboats forced their way through the cypress and cotton-wood trees. The fleet entered into Deer Creek. On March 19, Sherman heard the gunboat's cannons firing and a message arrived informing him that Admiral Porter encountered infantry and artillery and asked for help. Sherman

107 Ibid.
108 Ibid.
109 Ibid.

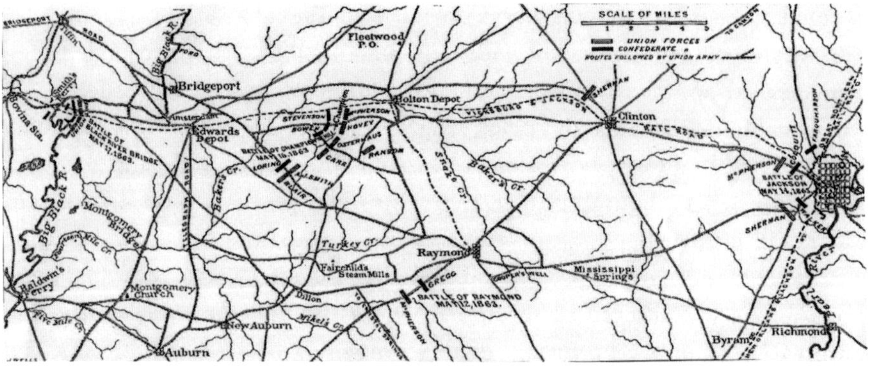

ordered General Giles A. Smith with 800 men to Deer Creek.

On March 21, Sherman arrived at Deer Creek and discovered that Admiral Porter could not advance his boats through the obstructions and had turned back. A rebel infantry force with six-pounders fired at the Union gunboats. Sherman ordered the gunboats to return to Black Bayou, which took three days. General Grant ordered the gunboat fleet to Young's Point. By March 27, 1863, the gunboats returned to Young's Point.[110]

By early April Sherman realized that he could not divert the main river Mississippi or get practicable access to the east bank of the Yazoo River, in the rear of Vicksburg, by any passes. General Grant set up his headquarters at Milliken's Bend and his army stretched all along the river from Young's Point to Lake Providence. General Grant realized that the only approach left to take Vicksburg was to move his army farther down the west bank of the Mississippi, below Vicksburg, then cross over and attack from the south. He personally took control of three Federal corps.[111]

On April 13, 1863, Burbridge's brigade left Milliken's Bend and headed for Oak Grove Plantation. On April 15, he proceeded as far as Holmes's plantation and set up camp. The next day on April 16, 1863, when night fell, Union Admiral Porter sent 12 vessels downstream to run the batteries at Vicksburg. As the convoy approached Vicksburg, the alarm went out, and the Confederate batteries from atop the bluffs at Vicksburg opened up. After two and a half hours, a steamer and a few barges caught fire, but for the most part all of Grant's vessels made their way to New Carthage. Grant's plan had succeeded.[112]

On April 24, Burbridge left his camp and moved to Smith's plantation. The brigade remained there until Sunday, April, 26, when they boarded trans-

110 Sherman, 336.

111 Sherman, 343.

112 Jerry Korn, *War on the Mississippi: Grant's Vicksburg Campaign* (Alexandria: Time Life Books, 1985), 85.

ports in Roundaway Bayou. The transports headed for the Mississippi River opposite Carthage, proceeded down the river to Perkin's plantation and unloaded his troops.[113]

Grant decided to keep Confederate General John Pemberton confused as to where General Grant's men would land. He would send a force to Grand Gulf. On April 28, Burbridge received orders to load four of his regiments and the 17th Ohio Battery on transports and barges, to proceed to a point near Grand Gulf and participate with Brigadier General Peter Osterhaus, commanding the 9th Division, 13th Army Corps, and act as a reserve to his division. Burbridge took with him the 16th and 67th Indiana, 83rd Ohio, and 23rd Wisconsin and boarded upon barges and transports, leaving behind his transportation, including his horses, and headed for Hard Times Landing, opposite and above Grand Gulf, and remained during the unsuccessful attempt by the gunboats to reduce Grand Gulf on April 29, 1863.[114]

Burbridge was on the gunboat General Price which had in tow a transport containing two of his regiments. The attempt to reduce the principal batteries at Grand Gulf proved a failure, so his men left the gunboats and marched across the Bend, to a point below Grand Gulf, where his men camped for the night.

On April 30, Burbridge and his men got back onto the transports and gunboats and proceeded to run the blockade during the night and proceeded to Bruinsburg, where his men drew six days rations. At 11:00 p.m., Burbridge and his men marched for Port Gibson, Mississippi. They marched all night and about sunrise heavy and rapid cannonading was heard in front and shortly afterward the advance became engaged with the Confederates.[115]

Burbridge and his men pressed on, until they reached the scene of the engagement, when he formed his men behind General Alvin Hovey's division, with his division acting as a reserve. Burbridge continued to support Hovey's line, until he was ordered with his brigade farther to the left, to relieve the Second Brigade under Colonel William Landram, who had fought desperately through the day. He advanced farther to the front than any other troops, driving the Confederates from the hill. Night put an end to the fighting. Completely exhausted, Burbridge's men fell to the ground. They had marched all night and fought all day under a burning sun, without having a bite to eat since the previous

---

113 O.R. Series I, Vol. XXIV/2 May 16, 1863. Battle of Champion's Hill, or Baker's Creek, Miss. No. 8 Report of Brig. Gen. Stephen G. Burbridge, U. S Army, commanding First Brigade, 10th Division, including operations April 13-May 24.

114 O.R. Series I, Vol. XXIV/2 May 16, 1863. Battle of Champion's Hill, or Baker's Creek, Miss. No. 8 Report of Brig. Gen. Stephen G. Burbridge, U. S Army, commanding First Brigade, 10th Division, including operations April 13-May 24.

115 Ibid.

evening. By late in the day the Confederate forces under Confederate General John Bowen retreated in good order. Grant's forces were within two miles of Port Gibson.[116]

On May 2, General McClernand ordered Burbridge to advance with his brigade, and proceed into Port Gibson, where Burbridge raised the Stars and Stripes. The Confederate rear guard retreated out of town, having fired the bridge over the South Fork of the Little Bayou Pierre. Burbridge had the 17th Ohio Battery to fire on the fleeing Confederates, but they succeeded in retreating out of sight.[117]

Burbridge remained at Port Gibson until May 3, when he was ordered to take his brigade to the hills in back of the town, since the Confederates attempted to take the Union rear. Remaining in position until he was satisfied that there were no enemy in his rear, he marched toward Willow Springs. Late in the afternoon, Burbridge crossed Big Bayou Pierre and went into camp. By May 7, General Bowen gave up Grand Gulf. Grant ordered General McClernand to pursue the retreating Confederates and instructed Sherman to move up. On that same day, May 7, 1863, Burbridge marched to a point half a mile beyond Cayuga, where he remained until May 12, when he countermarched to Cayuga. He camped for the night near Fourteen Mile Creek, six miles from Edwards Station.[118]

Confederate General Pemberton's troops dug trenches west of the Big Black River. Pemberton could not decide as to whether stay in Vicksburg or leave the city and fight Grant's men. He tried to do both. He concentrated his men near Edwards Depot and awaited Grant's attack. He ordered General John Gregg's troops to Raymond. He hoped Gregg would attack Grant's rear and flank. He did not know that Grant did not head for Big Black but for Jackson. McPherson's XVII Corps head straight for Gregg's men. On May 12 the armies collided. By 2:00 p.m., Gregg's men fell back to Raymond, pursued by the Union troops. Gregg abandoned Raymond and head for Jackson. On May 13, Confederate General Joseph Johnston arrived in Jackson. Pemberton was at Edwards Depot cut off from Johnston.[119]

On May 13, 1863, Burbridge's brigade marched back to the Jackson Road and remained until May 15, 1863, when, following General Francis Blair's division, they marched to Raymond and camped for the night. Confederate General Johnston withdrew his troops north, leaving Confederate General Gregg

116 Ibid.

117 Ibid.

118 Ibid.

119 Jerry Korn, *War on the Mississippi: Grant's Vicksburg Campaign*, (Alexandria, Virginia, Time Life Books) 1985), 110-113.

to cover his retreat. Confederate General W.H.T. Walker and Colonel Peyton Colquitt came across McPherson's soldiers. The Confederates built entrenchments on the outskirts of Jackson. The Federals charged and drove the Confederates from their entrenchments. That night, General Grant slept in the same hotel that General Johnston had used the previous night. Mississippi's capital had fallen to Federal troops.[120]

Union General Grant ordered Union General McClernand to move north and place his army between the two Confederate armies. McPherson marched out of Jackson to support McClernand. Pemberton ordered his army to stop moving south and turn toward the north to support Johnston at Clinton. Pemberton's 23,000 men at Champion's Hill faced 32,000 men under McClernand and McPherson.[121]

On May 16, 1863, Burbridge marched out on the Vicksburg road toward Edwards Station, with his brigade in the advance. About six miles outside Raymond, Burbridge's brigade came across the Confederate pickets. His men formed into a line of battle, with heavy skirmishing parties in front. He ordered his batteries into position and shelled the Confederate forces "very successfully." His brigade skirmished with the Confederates, driving them back, while the main force followed along the road until they reached a water course, across which the Confederates destroyed the bridge. Finding the Rebels in retreat only a short distance ahead, and fearing they might take some of the prominent hills, from which they could sweep the plain Burbridge's men were in, he pushed his brigade ahead until the skirmishers began to find the battle heating up, and as his brigade rose to the crest of the hill, the Confederates rallied and planted their battery on the second hill, since the Rebels did not have time to form their lines on the first hill. The Confederates poured a "terrific fire of shot, shell, grape, and canister," but Burbridge's men were well protected by the crest of the hill, and his sharpshooters forced the Confederates to abandon some of their guns. After repeated pleas for help from General Smith for reinforcements, both of infantry and artillery, Burbridge succeeded in obtaining the 19th Kentucky and 77th Illinois, of Colonel Landram's brigade, who were "ready and impatiently awaiting orders to move forward." He also obtained four guns of the 17th Ohio Battery, which was preceded by part of the Chicago Mercantile Battery.[122]

120 Korn, 114-115; O.R. Series I, Vol. XXIV/2 May 16, 1863. Battle of Champion's Hill, or Baker's Creek, Miss. No. 8 Report of Brig. Gen. Stephen G. Burbridge, U. S Army, commanding First Brigade, 10th Division, including operations April 13-May 24.

121 Korn, 116.

122 O.R. Series I, Vol. XXIV/2 May 16, 1863. Battle of Champion's Hill, or Baker's Creek, Miss. No. 8 Report of Brig. Gen. Stephen G. Burbridge, U. S Army, commanding First Brigade, 10th Division, including operations April 13-May 24.

Union General Smith ordered Burbridge to halt, holding his position. Burbridge felt the order to halt was a mistake, stating that if supported properly by General Blair's division he could have captured the whole Rebel force and reached Edwards Station by nightfall.

Burbridge learned from prisoners that he had captured that Confederate General Lloyd Tilghman had been killed by a shot from the Union batteries. They had attempted to run off with their artillery, but failing to do so, abandoned them, since which time, the Union forces had obtained 12 artillery pieces. According to Burbridge, the Rebel forces retreated in great disorder. Pemberton issued a general retreat.[123] The Confederates crossed the Raymond road bridge, but Confederate General William Loring's 6,500 men were cut off from the main army. Three days later he joined Johnston's army at Jackson. At the battle of Champion's Hill, Grant lost 2,441 men and Pemberton lost 3,389 men.[124]

The night after the battle, the men slept on their guns, expecting an attack at any moment. The night passed quietly, and when daylight broke, Burbridge moved on, but soon gathered intelligence that the Confederates "skedaddled most hurriedly", leaving arms, ammunition, etc., all over the road. Burbridge moved towards Edwards Station without any problems.[125]

As he approached Big Black River, Burbridge heard heavy firing and received orders from General Smith to move rapidly and take position on the left of General Osterhaus's division. Burbridge formed his men into the line of battle. Burbridge marched to the edge of a forest through which he advanced. His men could not advance across an open field without being exposed to Confederate fire. He changed his front, so that his left could cover the Rebel's works on the left of a cotton gin. Burbridge ordered a charge across the field. When his skirmishers arrived to within 200 yards of the Confederates, a white handkerchief appeared on the Rebel entrenchments. Burbridge sent his acting assistant adjutant general, Lieutenant Conover, and Captain Keigwin, acting aide, to ride forward and receive the Confederate surrender and the colors of the 60th Tennessee Regiment, under Lt. Colonel N. Gregg. About the same time as the surrender, the Union forces took possession of the entire Rebel line of works. The Confederates retreated across the Big Black River and set fire to the bridge.[126]

---

123 Ibid.

124 Korn, 122.

125 O.R. Series I, Vol. XXIV/2 May 16, 1863. Battle of Champion's Hill, or Baker's Creek, Miss. No. 8 Report of Brig. Gen. Stephen G. Burbridge, U. S Army, commanding First Brigade, 10th Division, including operations April 13-May 24.

126 Ibid.

Since the Confederates burned the Big Black River Bridge, Burbridge ordered his men to build a bridge in order for his men to cross. Pemberton ordered his men to fall back to Vicksburg. Grant ordered four bridges built across the Big Black and moved his men west, while Sherman arrived in Jackson.

On May 18, 1863, Burbridge advanced and proceeded cautiously, expecting an attack at any moment, never dreaming that the Confederates could have abandoned the advantageous position and fortifications afforded by the natural layout of the land.

Burbridge learned from the local slaves that there were no Confederates between him and Mount Alban, a small place half way between Black River and Vicksburg. About half a mile beyond Mount Alban, he found the bridge burned. He decided to take a detour route to the left, taking a route through the country which struck the Baldwin's Ferry Road. Proceeding slowly and cautiously, he camped two and a half miles from the Confederate earthworks in the rear of Vicksburg.[127]

When Confederate General John Pemberton arrived in Vicksburg, he still had a powerful army of 30,000 men, and Confederate General Joseph Johnston had an army at Jackson containing 20,000 men. Pemberton also left 10,000 men in Vicksburg to defend the city. On May 19, 1863, Grant decided to attack Vicksburg. McClernand attacked from the east, McPherson and Sherman from the north. During the battle, Burbridge moved toward the fortifications, when, within one and half miles from the fortifications, the Confederate skirmishers appeared. He immediately formed his regiments on the Vicksburg Road, with the 16th Indiana and 83rd Ohio in front, supported by the 67th Indiana and 23rd Wisconsin, covered by the 17th Ohio Battery. Burbridge sent out a heavy force of skirmishers under the command of Major Redfield, 16th Indiana, who drove the Confederate skirmishers back. He advanced his brigade to a ravine running at right angles with the railroad, and in the rear of the hill, where a cotton gin was located. As the Confederates were driven farther in, Burbridge advanced until his brigade was about 400 yards from the forts.[128] During the assault, Grant lost 942 men, Pemberton lost 250 men.

The next day, on May 20, Burbridge received orders to be ready to charge the Confederate works. At the given signal the brigade, with "tremendous cheering," his men rushed over the crest of the hill in front of them, taking a moment's breathing time, and continued the ascent of the hill. Finding it unadvisable to advance in line of battle, on account of a greater exposure to gun

127 Ibid.
128 Ibid.

fire, Burbridge ordered the regiment forward by companies as skirmishers. He managed to drive the greater part of the Confederate's sharpshooters within the entrenchments, with his men lying immediately under the works, and silencing the Confederate's artillery. He maintained his position, keeping up a constant fire, until 10:00 p.m., when General Benton's brigade relieved his brigade. By 2:00 a.m., on May 21, 1863, all of Burbridge's men finally left their position.[129]

On May 22, 1863, Grant ordered another assault. Burbridge received orders to prepare for an assault on the Confederate works to support General William Benton's brigade. Burbridge had four of his regiments arranged to where the 67th Indiana occupied the road passing down the hill to the right of the burnt chimneys, the 23rd Wisconsin to their rear, the 16th Indiana on the hillside of the ravine to the right, and in front of the road, supported by the 83rd Ohio. Burbridge advanced his regiments. His men gave a yell and rushed up over the hill into the last ravine, and advanced up the hill to the fort they were attacking.[130]

By 10:30 a.m., Burbridge's brigade silenced the Confederate batteries and the regiments had their colors flying against the walls of the fort. The Confederate tried to turn Burbridge's flank, but Burbridge sent four companies of the 23rd Wisconsin to support the 67th Indiana on the right, and the remaining companies to the left in support of the 16th Indiana.[131]

While the attack continued on the Confederate forts, Burbridge received orders from General Andrew Smith to send two of his regiments to support General Benton's left, but this move would have reduced Burbridge's force by half and left his front exposed. He sent a message to General Smith informing him of the facts. His answer was: "It is an order from General Carr, and must be obeyed." He again sent an aide to state his case and received permission from General Smith to keep his position, but he received an inquiry from General Eugene Carr why the regiments were not coming to his support. Burbridge personally rode to General McClernand and told him that not only would his regiments face destruction, but the entire front if he followed General Carr's order. General McClernand, while agreeing to Burbridge's representations, referred him to General Carr, who commanded the advance. General Carr renewed his order concerning the regiments. Burbridge followed General Carr's order, but under protest. He returned to his command and with a "heavy and foreboding heart" gave the orders for the 23rd Wisconsin and 67th Indiana to withdraw from the ground which had been gained "with so much labor and

129 Ibid.
130 Ibid.
131 Ibid.

maintained so much valor," leaving only two regiments, the 16th Indiana and 83rd Ohio, unsupported.[132]

The Rebels found the Union fire slackened and the line weakened in their front, and opened a "most destructive fire." Burbridge consulted with General Benton and determined to take the responsibility to replace his regiments, but the work was difficult, since the Confederates had the advantage. Just as Burbridge had ordered his regiments back, a message came from General Carr telling him to use his discretion in withdrawing his regiments. He pointed out in his report that if the message had arrived ten minutes before, or such consent given when he had early pleaded for it, would have saved hundreds of lives.[133]

After repeated messages for help, Burbridge succeeded in getting permission to carry a piece of artillery to his front line. A gun from the Chicago Mercantile Battery was taken by a squad of the 23rd Wisconsin close to the point held by the 16th Indiana and supported by the latter regiment no more than 25 to 30 feet from the fort. By that time the muskets of his command had become so fouled by the constant firing, he had no choice to switch his rounds from .58 caliber to .54 caliber. Union General Quinby's division sent a brigade, but because of their reckless manner of approaching, drew from the Confederates a galling fire of musketry and artillery, followed by an attempt by the Confederates to charge, with the hopes of capturing one of Burbridge's guns. The brigade reinforcing Burbridge broke and ran in disorder to the rear. Burbridge's brigade, reduced in strength, held their ground and the 16th Indiana prepared with fixed bayonets to receive the threatened charge, which did not come. Nightfall put an end to the hostilities. He drew off his men, after having maintained the ground for nearly ten hours of continuous fighting.[134]

Burbridge stated in his after-action report that had he been reinforced or the battle kept up along the line to his right, preventing the Confederates from massing directly in his front, he could have gained a lodgment in the Confederate works.[135]

During the battle, Grant's attack came to a halt all along his line. McClernand send him a message stating that he had secured two forts and asked for more troops. Grant sent him additional men, but McClernand could not hold onto the two forts. Grant lost 3,199 men. The Confederates lost only 500 men.[136]

In June Grant received more reinforcements strengthening his force to 70,000 men. Grant gave up his plans of directly attacking the fort and decided

132 Ibid.
133 Ibid.
134 Ibid.
135 Ibid.
136 Korn, *War on the Mississippi: Grant's Vicksburg Campaign*, 132.

to lay siege to Vicksburg. He shelled the city of Vicksburg every hour, and the Union infantry pushed their lines closer to the town. Union soldiers dug trenches. By mid-June 200 cannons fired on Vicksburg from the land and river.[137]

On June 23, Grant asked for soldiers with coal mining experience to dig a tunnel toward the Confederate entrenchments northeast of town. Three days later, the men managed to dig a tunnel 45 feet long and the men stuffed the tunnel with 2,200 pounds of black powder. The Confederates heard the digging and built a countermine. On June 25, the Federals set off the charge creating a massive crater in the Confederate redan. General Mortimer Leggett's Union soldiers rushed into the crater, but the Confederate troops pulled back to a new line and waited for the Federal soldiers. On June 28, the Federals could not hold the crater and fell back to their own trenches. On July 1, Grant dug another tunnel and set off another charge beneath the same redan, but the Federal soldiers did not attack the redan.[138]

By July, the Confederate soldiers and the citizens of Vicksburg were starving and exhausted. The livestock ran out and the people of Vicksburg turned to eating horses. Water became scarce. On July 3, Pemberton sent Grant a message for an armistice and the eventual surrender of Vicksburg. On midnight, July 3, Pemberton agreed to Grant's surrender terms. On July 4, 1863, Grant took control of Vicksburg after a 48-day siege. July 4, 1863 marked a turning point in the Civil War. Union General George Meade defeated Confederate General Robert E. Lee at Gettysburg and General Grant took Vicksburg. On July 9, the Confederate commander at Port Hudson, Major General Franklin Gardner, learned of the surrender at Vicksburg and decided to surrender. Union forces controlled the entire Mississippi River.[139]

During the Vicksburg Campaign, General Burbridge gained valuable experience in fighting and made a favorable impression upon General Sherman. Once Union forces took control of Vicksburg, the War Department sent Burbridge home to Kentucky, but his stay in his native state would be short lived. In late 1863, he finally got what he had wanted since 1862: a command of a division. Because of Burbridge's service during the Vicksburg Campaign, the War Department assigned him a division and sent him to Louisiana to fight in the Bayou Teche Campaign. Although the Bayou Teche Campaign did not fare well for Burbridge, he continued to build his battlefield experience. He continued to wait until he received his final assignment: commander of Kentucky.

137 Ibid., 134.
138 Korn, 148-149.
139 Korn, 149-156.

Chapter 4

The Bayou Teche Campaign

By the end of July, Burbridge found himself back in Kentucky. He had fought well during the Vicksburg Campaign and made a favorable impression upon General William T. Sherman. Once Burbridge arrived in Kentucky, he had to deal with the numerous Confederate raids. On July 29, 1863, Burbridge found the Rebel forces under Colonel John S. Scott's cavalry in camp on the Winchester Pike. Burbridge would attempt to surround the Confederates, but feared an attack by the other Rebel force on the bridge. The Rebels drove in Burbridge's pickets, but he drove the Confederates back for two miles. The Confederates divided their force, half crossing the Stoner Creek, with the intention of attacking the bridge on the railroad below Paris, Kentucky. The Rebels remained on the Winchester Pike. Burbridge feared that the Rebels under Colonel Scott could cut the road between Paris and Lexington, Kentucky. If attacked, Burbridge would defend the town as long as possible, and then fall back to the bridge and fort, where he could hold them in check with 2,000 men until Union reinforcements arrived.[140]

The next day, the 45th Ohio arrived from Winchester. They reported the main rebel force at 2,000 men, with eight pieces of artillery. They also reported that Colonel Scott and his men retreated on the Irvine Road. Colonel Scott held the town of Irvine for only a few hours. Union Colonel William P. Sanders led the pursuit after Colonel Scott's forces. The Confederates retreated after being driven back by the Union forces, finding the place too strong for them. Colonel Ross captured one captain and 15 men near Paris and waited for the force that crossed Stoner Creek. Burbridge ordered his men to pursue the fleeing Confederate force.[141]

By August 17, 1863, Burbridge commanded the First Brigade, 4th Division, 13th Army Corps, Department of the Gulf, but by September 20, 1863,

140 O.R. Series I, Vol. XXIII/1 July 25-August 6, 1863-Scott's raid in Eastern Kentucky. No. 8-Reports of Brig. Gen. Stephen G. Burbridge, U. S. Army, of skirmish at Paris.

141 Ibid.

he commanded a division. By mid-September the War Department ordered General Burbridge to Louisiana to participate in the Bayou Teche Campaign. On September 24, Major General Edward Ord ordered Burbridge to proceed up the Mississippi River with 1,500 infantry, one battery of light artillery and the 16th Indiana Infantry, mounted, to a point near Donaldsonville and land on the left bank of the river, destroy, capture, or break up the Confederates, as well as force the evacuation of all the space between the Mississippi River and Lakes Maurepas and Pontchartrain.[142]

Burbridge ordered Colonel Owen, commanding the First Brigade, 4th Division, to prepare his command for the expedition. The boats arrived and Burbridge, along with the 83rd Ohio, pushed forward to make sure all the arrangements had been made to prepare for the arrival of the rest of his forces at Donaldsonville.[143]

Burbridge arrived at Donaldsonville at 7:00 a.m. on September 25, and delivered orders to Captain Carnahan for additional cavalry. The captain arrived with 120 men. Burbridge's remaining forces arrived at 4:00 p.m. on September 25, and he landed the infantry and artillery at a point four miles below Donaldsonville, at a town called Manning's, and proceeded into the interior for about 10 miles to New River, and camped for the night at a point called Lannaries.[144]

Colonel Lucas, 16th Indiana, was put in charge of the cavalry and mounted infantry and ordered to land nine miles above Donaldsonville, to proceed by the way of Dutch Store, cross Bayou Manchac at Hampton's Ferry, and then to Amite, cross at Bennett's Ferry, and join Burbridge at Galveston, by approaching from the rear. On September 26, Burbridge sent forward his mounted forces to meet Colonel Lucas at Galveston and ordered him to march to Civique's, five miles below, on the Amite, destroy the bridge and rejoin Burbridge at his camp on New River.[145]

Colonel Lucas met the mounted force sent forward to Galveston. He was not able to cross the Amite and was compelled to proceed to Civique's, on the east side of the river. At 10:00 p.m., Burbridge received a dispatch from Colonel Lucas reporting that there were no Confederates in that area of the country and that the bridge had been destroyed; that he could not cross there; and that he would return by the way of Bennett's Ferry and rejoin Burbridge.[146]

After receiving the dispatch, Burbridge ordered the infantry and artillery

142 O.R. Series I, Vol. XXVI/1 September 24-29, 1863. Expeditions from Carrollton and Baton Rouge to New River and to the Amite River, La. No. 1 Report of Brig. Gen. Stephen G. Burbridge, U.S. Army, commanding 4th Division, 13th Army Corps.

143 Ibid.

144 Ibid.

145 Ibid.

146 Ibid.

to return to the Mississippi at Manning's and sent forward couriers ordering the transports to meet him there. On September 27, all the infantry and artillery had arrived safely back on the Mississippi. He sent a dispatch to General Charles Stone, chief of staff, asking for instructions. General Stone ordered Burbridge to return. He arrived at his headquarters at Carrollton.[147]

In the fall of 1863, Union General Nathaniel Banks, commander of the Army of the Gulf, tried to invade Texas, but he was repulsed at the Battle of Sabine Pass, on September 8, 1863, and forced to return to Louisiana. He decided to invade Texas by an overland route. He chose the Bayou Teche, a long river that extended north through central Louisiana from the Gulf of Mexico, as the route for his invasion. On October 3, 1863, Banks ordered Union General William B. Franklin to Texas. Franklin led two divisions of his own XIV Corps out of Fort Bisland, on the lower Teche, toward Opelousas, while Major General Cadwallader Washburn, with the XIII Corps divisions of Major Generals Michael Lawler and George McGinnis and General Burbridge, left Berwick, Louisiana, southeast of Bisland, and marched north. Along the march Confederate General Richard Taylor, commander of the District of Western Louisiana, harassed the Union column. Fighting broke out at Nelson's Bridge, Carrion Crow Bayou, and Grand Coteau. By October 14, 1863, the Union forces united at Bayou Carrion Crow and continued their march. Franklin commanded 20,000 troops. Their plan was to move north until they cleared Louisiana's swamps and march west into Texas. General Franklin's superior numbers pushed aside Taylor's men and by October 21, 1863, the Union army reached and occupied Opelousas. The Union army had difficulty in foraging in the swamp infested area. Heavy rains swelled the bayous and the roads became muddy quagmires. Discouraged by his slow progress and lack of supplies, General Franklin did not want to continue north or turn his column west toward the Sabine River and Texas. Instead, Franklin gave up the expedition and marched his men south toward New Iberia. On October 27, 1863, the First Division of 13th Corps, under Brigadier General Lawler, moved from Opelousas back to New Iberia. General Franklin left at Opelousas, the Third Division, under General McGinnis, and one brigade of the 4th Division, under General Burbridge, at Barre's Landing, eight miles east of Opelousas and east of the Bayou Teche. Franklin left his guard down and allowed his divisions to march and camp eight miles from each other. Taylor found his opportunity to attack the spread out Union forces.[148]

On November 1, 1863, Major General Franklin ordered the troops of the 3rd Division to march and camp at Carrion Crow Bayou, while General Franklin

147 Ibid.

148 Foster, Stephen, *Bayou Teche Campaign*, Atlas Editions, MCMXCV.

ordered General Burbridge to march down the Teche and cross it, and move via Grand Coteau, where the road from Vermillion to Opelousas crosses the Muddy Bayou, about three miles from Carrion Crow Bayou and camp on the north side of the bayou. General Franklin also ordered Colonel Fonda, with 500 mounted infantry, to camp with Burbridge. On November 3, General Burbridge, with one brigade of the 4th Division, 1,200 strong, with one six gun battery of 10-pound Parrot rifles, and Colonel Fonda's 500 mounted men and a section of Nim's battery, was located on the north side of the Muddy Bayou. The 3rd Division, under General McGinnis, with 3,000 men, with one battery, was located at Carrion Crow Bayou, three miles in the rear of Burbridge. To the right of General Burbridge was an extensive and dense area of woods, while his left consisted of open prairie. His camp was located three miles from Bayou Carrion Crow, near the head of a small bayou which ran in the direction of Opelousas through a ravine one mile wide, with a prairie on each side.

On that day, Confederate General Thomas Green's Rebel cavalry division and three regiments of infantry, numbering around six to seven thousand men, caught up with Franklin's rear guard, under the command of General Burbridge. After skirmishing with Confederate General Thomas Green's 2,500 men all day, Burbridge knew that the men under Green's men would continue to harass his forces. Burbridge's outposts at Grand Coteau on the Bayou Bourbeau were driven in, and a heavy Confederate force was seen on his front and left. He sent a dispatch to General Cadwallader Washburn, commanding the detachment of the 13th Army Corps, informing him of the Confederate presence. Burbridge formed his lines, the artillery was placed, and a few well directed rounds from the artillery and some maneuvering forced the Rebels to retire. By 10:00 a.m., most of the Rebels left the battlefield. Burbridge ordered the troops to retire to camp. He sent a dispatch to Major General Washburn that the Confederates had retired and he had returned to his headquarters.[149]

At 12:30 p.m., Burbridge received a message from Colonel Fonda, 118th Illinois Mounted Infantry, stating that the Rebels were approaching, with infantry, cavalry, and artillery. He sent a dispatch to General Washburn and ordered his artillery and infantry to prepare for action. The Rebel infantry approached through a ravine from the direction of Opelousas. On the left, across the prairie, a heavy column of cavalry could be seen moving on Burbridge. He ordered one of his largest regiments, the 67th Indiana, about 260 strong, one section of Nims's battery, and one section of the 17th Ohio Battery, to take position on

149 O.R. Series I, Vol. XXVI/1 No. 6-Reports of Brig. Gen. Stephen G. Burbridge, U.S. Army, commanding 4th Division, of engagement at Bayou Bourbeau, and operations (Nov. 12) about Saint Martinsville.

his left. He then posted about 150 cavalry on the battery's left and ordered the whole to guard against any attack on his rear and left. Burbridge's remaining regiments, the 83rd Ohio and four pieces of artillery from the 17th Ohio Battery, were placed to meet the Rebel infantry in the ravine. He ordered Colonel Fonda's cavalry, 118th Illinois, to protect his right.[150]

The Confederates under General Green pressed on Burbridge's men in overwhelming numbers, and he feared that he could not hold his position until reinforcements could be brought up. He directed his wagons to be moved to the rear. After engaging the Confederates for a short time, Burbridge discovered the Rebels attempted to flank him on the right. The Confederate line was three times the size of Burbridge's and the Confederate cavalry bore down upon his left. Burbridge had no choice but to extend his lines to the right, so he would not be completely surrounded. Burbridge ordered the 67th Indiana, under Lt. Col. Theodore Buehler, to guard his left, while he advanced his right. From a misunderstanding of the orders, Colonel Buehler failed to move his regiment until Burbridge dispatched him a note for the third time. Colonel Buehler was almost completely surrounded by ten times his number of Confederate cavalry and Buehler had no choice but to surrender. The artillery fired at the oncoming Confederates until they were almost surrounded, but managed to withdraw, except one piece of the 17th Ohio battery and a caisson which fell into Confederate hands.[151]

Burbridge's left collapsed and the Confederate's cavalry pressed down on General Burbridge, forcing him to fall back through the ravine. General Washburn heard the cannonade from the battle and sent two members of his staff to the rear to bring up the 3rd Division. Washburn rode back to the front, crossed the bayou, and passed through the timber to the open ground. He discovered the Confederates in overwhelming numbers assailing Burbridge on his front and both flanks. Washburn wrote: "Many of the troops had broken and were scattered over the field, and the utter destruction or capture of the whole force seemed imminent."[152] Washburn ordered the 3rd Division at the double-quick to Burbridge's support.[153]

Seeing Union reinforcements from the Third Division, arriving to secure his left, Burbridge formed the 83rd Ohio upon the plain, upon which his

150 O.R. Series I, Vol. XXVI/1 No. 6-Reports of Brig. Gen. Stephen G. Burbridge, U.S. Army, commanding 4th Division, of engagement at Bayou Bourbeau, and operations (Nov. 12) about Saint Martinsville.

151 Ibid.

152 O.R. Series I, Vol. XXVI/1 Oct. 3-Nov. 30, 1863. Operations in the Teche Country, La. No. 5-Reports of Maj. Gen. Cadwallader C. Washburn, U.S. Army, commanding detachment 13th Army Corps, of operations Oct 23-Nov. 3, including engagement at Bayou Bourbeau.

153 Ibid.

shattered forces rallied. His artillery was placed upon the left and the cavalry on the right. He stopped the Rebels until his support had come up. The Confederates retired. As soon as Burbridge managed to distribute ammunition to his men, he advanced toward the Confederates in the woods. Union General Robert Cameron, on his left, charged the Confederates through the ravine and 100 Rebel prisoners fell into Cameron's hands. After pursuing the Confederates for a short distance beyond the ravine, Burbridge returned, picked up his wounded and dead, and fell back to Carrion Crow Bayou. General Green could make no further headway and withdrew his troops.[154]

During the engagement, Burbridge had 1,625 men against 3,500 Rebel infantry and 2,500 cavalry and a battery on his left. After the battle, he counted 42 Rebel dead. He lost 26 killed, 124 wounded, and 566 missing. He also lost 36 horses, one 10-pound Parrot rifle, and one caisson. In his after-action report, General Washburn stated that the "action of General Burbridge was gallant and judicious from the time I first saw him until the close of the engagement."[155] In contrast, during the engagement, Confederate General Thomas Green only suffered 125 casualties.

On November 4, the Confederates sent a flag of truce, proposing to give up the Union wounded since they did not have any means of caring for them. General Washburn received 47 men. The Confederates refused to give up the wounded Union officers, among them Colonel Guppey of the 23rd Wisconsin. After the battle, General Franklin's men, including General Burbridge's men, withdrew south and reached New Iberia, Louisiana.[156]

On November 12, Burbridge reported to General Franklin that Confederate forces fired upon a Union boat. He sent out his cavalry and infantry over the bayou after them. His forces closed in on the Confederates. Burbridge's scouts reported 500 Confederates at Saint Martinsville, who were attacking the Union boats below the area. The party who attacked the boat escaped in the direction of Saint Martinsville. All his scouts confirmed that Major Dupeire and 500 French guerillas converged near Saint Martinsville. Burbridge's cavalry chased the Confederate party below New Iberia and left them near Saint Martinsville. Lt. Colonel V. A. Fournet, who resigned from the Confederate

154 O.R. Series I, Vol. XXVI/1 No. 6-Reports of Brig. Gen. Stephen G. Burbridge, U.S. Army, commanding 4th Division, of engagement at Bayou Bourbeau, and operations (Nov. 12) about Saint Martinsville.

155 O.R. Series I, Vol. XXVI/1 Oct. 3-Nov. 30, 1863. Operations in the Teche Country, La. No. 5-Reports of Maj. Gen. Cadwallader C. Washburn, U.S. Army, commanding detachment 13th Army Corps, of operations Oct 23-Nov. 3, including engagement at Bayou Bourbeau.

156 O.R. Series I, Vol. XXVI/1 No. 6-Reports of Brig. Gen. Stephen G. Burbridge, U.S. Army, commanding 4th Division, of engagement at Bayou Bourbeau, and operations (Nov. 12) about Saint Martinsville.

service, was arrested by Burbridge's scouts at Saint Martinsville.

On November 14, 1863, Burbridge reported that Confederate General Sterling Price and John Magruder were on their way to reinforce the Rebels in front of General W. B. Franklin. Contrabands reported that the Rebels knew that reinforcements had been sent to Texas. Burbridge feared that the Rebels could pass down in the rear of Saint Martinsville and get below his forces. He reported that he did not have enough cavalry to watch both points. The Treasury Department sent an agent to New Iberia and told Burbridge that all cotton and sugar should be shipped to New Orleans. All abandoned property was claimed by the speculators. Union Major Cowan, 1st Louisiana Cavalry, shipped 76 bales of cotton and 82 hogshead of sugar to New Orleans.[157]

General Franklin sent a message to Burbridge to send any information about Price and Magruder reinforcing the Rebels in his front. Franklin reported that he maintained a good position. He wrote to Burbridge that if the rebels got below him on the other side of the Teche, they could never get above his forces. Franklin told Burbridge to see Major Cowan's papers as to whether he had the authority to ship sugar.

On November 15, Burbridge's scouts reported that the Confederates were in Saint Martinsville. They saw several small squads of guerillas on the other side of the bayou and exchanged shots with some of them. They brought in two prisoners and reported a camp of several hundred all across the bayou. Slaves reported that Rebel citizens were jubilant over the arrival of General Price and Magruder's reinforcements. Burbridge's scouts from Saint Martinsville heard cannonading. He used soldiers, citizens, slaves, and spectators to finish his earthworks. He reported that he could send all his mounted force to Saint Martinsville and attack the camp.

While Burbridge fought in the Bayou Teche Campaign, his powerful friends in Kentucky worked on securing him a command in Kentucky. Burbridge's friends in Congress and the state of Kentucky laid out to General Grant, Governor Thomas Bramlette, and the War Department, his experience as a leader of men in a brigade, and later a division, and his participation in the Vicksburg Campaign and the Bayou Teche Campaign. By February 14, 1864, General Grant ordered Burbridge to take military command of Kentucky. Burbridge had waited since 1862 to take command in Kentucky; he finally had his chance. Only time would tell if Burbridge would live up to his superiors and his radical friends' expectations.

---

157 O.R. Series I, Vol. XXVI/1 No. 6-Reports of Brig. Gen. Stephen G. Burbridge, U.S. Army, commanding 4th Division, of engagement at Bayou Bourbeau, and operations (Nov. 12) about Saint Martinsville.

Chapter 5

Taking Command In Kentucky

The year 1864 was the most violent year of the war in Kentucky. Civil and military authorities cooperated in establishing a reign of terror not unlike that of the French Revolution of 1789 and the Russian Revolution of 1918. Brutality, tyranny, rankest injustice, prevailed. And the people submitted to the oppression that war had created, helpless to combat it.[158]

While Burbridge fought in the Bayou Teche Campaign, his powerful friends in the radical Unionists in Kentucky worked behind the scenes to secure him a command in Kentucky. On January 21, 1864, J. R. Bailey wrote to General Burbridge from Frankfort, Kentucky, informing that he received General Burbridge's letter. Bailey wrote to Burbridge that he wrote to Colonel Bristow and Dr. Gano, in which he had laid out the facts to Kentucky Governor Thomas Bramlette urging him to keep General Burbridge in Kentucky. He wrote that the Governor was in favor of Burbridge holding a command in Kentucky and that Union General Ulysses S. Grant telegraphed the Governor that he would be in Frankfort, Kentucky, that week. Bailey wrote that he hoped Burbridge would be kept in Kentucky and thought that he would.[159]

While Burbridge's political friends worked on bringing him to Kentucky, Governor Thomas Bramlette issued a proclamation directing the arrest of Confederate sympathizers. He requested that the various military commanders in Kentucky arrest at least five of the most prominent and active rebel sympathizers for every loyal citizen that was taken away by guerrillas. Governor Bramlette stated that the sympathizers would be held as hostages until the loyal citizens were returned by the guerillas. Governor Bramlette had no legal power to issue such a proclamation, but by early 1864, Kentucky was overrun by guerillas. The guerrillas attacked both loyal citizens and Confederate sympathizers

158 Butler, Lorine, *John Morgan and His Men* (Philadelphia: Dorrance & Company, 1960), 284.

159 Letter from J. R. Bailey to Stephen G. Burbridge, January 21, 1864, Frankfort, Kentucky, Stephen Gano Burbridge letters, 1 reel of microfilm, University of Kentucky Special Collections and Digital Programs, Lexington, Kentucky.

and he felt he had to do something against the guerillas. Unfortunately, Governor Bramlette's proclamation did more than any other act to treat detached Confederate commands as guerrilla bands.[160] Governor Bramlette also let his feelings be known about black Union soldier recruitment. On January 13, 1864, Governor Bramlette wrote to Union General J. T. Boyle, military district commander of Kentucky, that recruiting for the 1st Michigan Colored Regiment would not be tolerated in Kentucky. He stated that "Summary justice will be inflicted upon any who attempt such unlawful purpose." He earlier wrote to Captain Cahill that he would only furnish white men to fill the state's quota for troops. He would not enlist black soldiers.[161] Although Burbridge would later support Governor Bramlette on his treatment of guerrillas, he would have a falling out with the Governor over black Union soldiers.

On February 14, 1864, Major General Ulysses Grant ordered Brigadier General Burbridge to Camp Nelson, located in southern Jessamine County, Kentucky, to command the District of Kentucky until relieved by General Jacob Ammen, who was on court-martial duty. When relieved by General Ammen, Burbridge would report to Grant for an assignment. By Order Number 41, Burbridge was assigned to command the District of Kentucky. [162]

On February 22, the Kentucky legislature passed a resolution that protested the enlistment of blacks for army service and added a request, directed at President Abraham Lincoln, to remove camps for United States black troops beyond the state lines. The legislature also prohibited any recruiting other than that of the United States and each recruit could be fined $500 and imprisonment from two to six months if violated. Union authorities ignored the Kentucky legislature and ordered Union General James B. Fry, United States Provost Marshall, to enroll all male blacks in Kentucky between 18 and 45.[163]

On February 25, 1864, Burbridge issued his first order as commander of Kentucky. He ordered Colonel C. J. True, commanding the 40th Kentucky Mounted Infantry, to send two companies of his command, under an experienced and discreet officer, to protect the loyal citizens of Owen County, Kentucky, and break up all the bands of guerillas in the area. He ordered Colonel True to prevent his men from committing crimes on the citizens of Kentucky, including their property, and give proper vouchers for forage and subsistence

---

160 The Military Department of Kentucky, *Military History of Kentucky*, (The American Guide Series, Works Projects Administration, 1939), 203.

161 Ibid., 204.

162 O.R. Series I, vol. XXXII/2 Union Correspondence, Orders, and Returns Relating to Operations in Kentucky, Southwest Va, Tennessee, Mississippi, Alabama, and North Georgia, from January 1, 1864 to February 29, 1864.

163 *Military History of Kentucky*, 205.

taken by his men, indorsing the loyalty or disloyalty of the citizens from whom the forage or subsistence was taken.[164]

The next day, Burbridge issued Order Number 25, in which he stated that the early completion of military roads in Kentucky was necessary and ordered the enrollment of slaves to complete the work. He referred to General Order Number 41 of August 10, 1863, that provided for the impressments of black slaves in the counties of Harrison, Bourbon, Scott, Clark, Fayette, Woodford, Jessamine, Mercer, Boyle, Garrard, Lincoln, Marion, Washington, and Nelson, Kentucky. He extended the impressments to Taylor, Adair, Green, Casey, Russell, Pulaski, Rockcastle, Laurel, Jackson, and Madison counties. All black males from the ages of 16 to 45 were subject to impressments, but Burbridge did not want to interfere with the cultivation of crops, so he stipulated that if a citizen had only one male slave, he would be exempted from impressments. If a citizen has more than four slaves, one-third of them would be impressed into working on the roads. Burbridge authorized the Louisville and Nashville Railroad Company to hire the slaves belonging to owners who were subject to impressments. The slaves hired were to be employed as laborers on the extension of the railroad from Lebanon, Kentucky. to Stanford and to the state line and all slaves hired would be exempt from impressments for works on other roads. All slaves hired to the railroad company would be fed, clothed, and their services paid for by the L & N railroad. The slaves employed by the railroad company were to be used only on the work of the railroad extension.[165]

On February 29, General Ulysses S. Grant wrote to Burbridge that all work by the government on the railroads in Kentucky should cease. He ordered Burbridge to revoke his impressment's orders if the slaves being employed were at a public expense.[166] General Burbridge complied with General Grant's request and released all impressed blacks from their work and sent them home to their owners, so he could comply with General Speed Fry's request to enroll blacks into the army.[167]

Several days later, on March 8, 1864, Governor Thomas Bramlette wrote to General Grant that General Ammen did not desire the command of Kentucky, and he asked if General Burbridge be retained as commander in Kentucky. Governor Bramlette telegraphed Union General John Schofield and hoped he ordered for Burbridge to stay in Kentucky.[168] Bramlette was good friends with

164 Ibid.
165 Ibid.
166 Ibid.
167 *Military History of Kentucky*, 205.
168 O.R. Series I, Vol. XXXII/3 Union Correspondence, Orders, and Returns Relating to Operations in Kentucky, Southwest Virginia, Tennessee, Mississippi, Alabama, and North Georgia, from March 1, 1864 to April 30, 1864.

Burbridge. Before the war, Bramlette practiced law, served in the Kentucky legislature and became a commonwealth attorney before becoming a judge in 1856. In October of 1861, Bramlette raised the 3rd Kentucky Union Infantry Regiment and was assigned the rank of colonel. He resigned his commission over a dispute over the regiment he should command and became a district attorney. On May 2, 1862, the Union Democratic Party nominated Bramlette as governor, and, in November 1863 he won the election. The Union Democratic ticket also took control of both branches in the legislature. When Bramlette took office he showed considerable zeal in supporting the war and the Federal administration. In his first message to the legislature in December 1863, he stated that: "We have no cause of complaint against the Federal government."[169]

On March 8, 1864, General Burbridge laid the groundwork on how to deal with guerrilla warfare and who he claimed were disloyal citizens. To show that he did not invent his orders against guerrillas, he published the Acts of the Kentucky Legislature. Burbridge used the acts in almost every one of his controversial orders during his military command in Kentucky. What Kentucky citizens failed to realize was that he only carried out Kentucky's acts passed by the Legislature. Unfortunately, Burbridge carried out the Kentucky acts to the letter of the law with no restraint. He stated that all acts passed by the Kentucky Legislature concerning civil law would be relied on in military cases.

In Act 548 of the Kentucky Legislature, the act stated that if any person should counsel, advise, aid, assist, encourage, or induce any officer or soldier of the Confederate States, or either of them, or any guerilla, robber, bandit, or armed band, or persons or person engaged, or professing to be engaged in making or levying war upon the government of the United States or State of Kentucky, or upon any citizen or resident of Kentucky, to destroy or injure any property of Kentucky, or shall counsel, encourage, aid, advise, or assist any such person or persons to injure, arrest, kidnap, or otherwise maltreat any citizen or resident of Kentucky, or shall harbor or conceal or shall voluntarily receive or aid any such persons, knowing them to be such, shall be guilty of a high misdemeanor, and upon conviction shall be fined not less than $100 and not more than $10,000, or confined in the county jail not less than six months and not any more than 12 months, and may be both fined and jailed at the discretion of the jury.[170]

If any person spoke or wrote against the government of the United States

169 E. Merton Coulter, *The Civil War and Readjustment in Kentucky*, (Chapel Hill: The University of North Carolina Press, 1966, original printing 1926), 173, 178-179.

170 O.R. Series I, Vol. XXXII/3 Union Correspondence, Orders, and Returns Relating to Operations in Kentucky, Southwest Va, Tennessee, Mississippi, Alabama, and North Georgia, from March 1, 1864 to April 30, 1864. Order No. 29.

or of Kentucky, or in favor of the Confederate States shall willfully endeavor to excite the people of Kentucky or any of them to insurrection or rebellion against the authority or laws of Kentucky or of the United States, or who shall willfully attempt to terrify or prevent by threats or otherwise the people of Kentucky or any of them from supporting and maintaining the legal and constitutional authority of the Federal Government or of Kentucky, or endeavor to prevent or shall oppose the suppression of the existing rebellion against the authority of the Federal government, every such person being legally convicted would be fined $100 to $5,000, or confined in the county jail between six months to a year, or both. The act stated that the constitutional right of speaking or writing in reference to the manner of administering the government, state or national, or against the conduct of any officer of either, when done in good faith with the intent of defending and preserving either of the said governments or of exposing and correcting the maladministration of either government or the misconduct of any officer, civil or military, would not be interred with.[171]

The act also stated that any person who did not give information to the nearest military authorities or civil officer of the presence in, or raid, or approach of any guerilla or guerillas in the vicinity would be guilty of a misdemeanor and if convicted would be fined between $100 to $1,000 or confined in a county jail between three months and six months, or both.[172]

In any trial, the jury would hear whether the character and reputation of the accused were loyal or disloyal to the government of the United States. The test of loyalty of the defendant or defendants would be whether they adhered to and supported the Constitution of the United States and Kentucky and complied with all their laws. Any Kentucky attorney who violated any of the provisions of the act would be debarred from practicing law.[173]

The act also stated that if any Confederate soldier or body of soldiers, or armed bands belonging to the Confederacy, or the Confederate Provisional government of Kentucky, or any armed band not acting under the authority of the U.S. or Kentucky, or any guerilla or guerillas, should injure or destroy or take or carry away any property of any person, county, city, corporate body, association, or congregation of Kentucky, or shall arrest, kidnap, imprison, or wound shall be entitled to recover damages as a jury may find and if dead, his wife or personal representative or heir of law, should be entitled to recover damages to the same extent that the person himself might for any of said injuries if death

171 Ibid.
172 Ibid.
173 Ibid.

had not ensued and for the property injured, destroyed, taken or carried away, the person, city, corporation, body, association, or congregation so injured should be entitled to recover double the value of damages and the damages of any of said injuries may be recovered of any persons doing any of said wrongful acts, and of any person or persons who shall aid, advise, abet, encourage or counsel such acts, would harbor conceal, aid, or encourage such wrongdoing or would permit, when it was in his power to prevent it, any member of his family living with him under his control so to aid, abet, advise, encourage, or counsel such acts, or harbor, conceal, aid or encourage such wrongdoers may be sued jointly with or without such wrongdoers, or some or any or all may be sued until the damages sustained as above provided may have been recovered by the party or parties aggrieved. Any disloyal person who has knowledge of the presence within the county of his residence of such guerilla or guerillas or predatory band, and fails to give immediate notice to either civil or military authorities would be guilty of aiding, harboring, and abetting the wrongdoer and be held jointly and severally reliable with such wrongdoers for all illegal acts done by such guerillas or predatory band.[174]

On March 10, 1864, the citizens of Lexington, Kentucky presented Union Colonel Frank Wolford, commander of the 1st Kentucky Cavalry, a set of cavalry officer accoutrements. After the presentation, Colonel Wolford gave a speech to the crowd accepting their gift, but his speech turned political and he denounced the enrollment of Kentucky blacks by the United States Army, calling the enrollment "unconstitutional, unjust, and another of a series of startling usurpations." He stated that the people of Kentucky should "resist it as a violation of their guaranteed right." He also urged the Governor to resist the enrollment with all "the constitutional power of the Commonwealth."[175] The speech would soon reach the ears of Union officials and General Burbridge.

On March 14, 1864, General Grant wrote to Major General John Schofield that General Burbridge "seems to be doing so well in Kentucky that I think he had better be retained permanently in the command of the district."[176] On that same day, Governor Bramlette wrote to Burbridge that he was not able to meet with Burbridge in his headquarters at Louisville because he had an appointment with Doctor Robert Breckinridge. He was going to send Doctor Breckinridge on a mission to Washington, D.C. to save them from a collision over the question of recruiting slaves into the Union army. Bramlette was determined to carry out his laws and punish anyone if they violated the laws. Bramlette stated that

174 Ibid.
175 *Military History of Kentucky*, 205.
176 Ibid.

the forcible abduction of slaves, the enlistment of slaves without the consent of their owners, enticing slaves to run away, were against the laws of Kentucky. Bramlette stated that the duty of every Union officer was to arrest the violators and hand them over to the civil magistrates for trial. He wrote that the President did not have the right to violate any of Kentucky's laws. If the President would not submit to the judgment of the courts on the question as to whether to recruit black soldiers for the Union army, then Bramlette would perform his duty as an elected official and uphold Kentucky's laws. Bramlette also felt his duty was to maintain and enforce the laws against those accused of breaking the law, but he wrote to Burbridge that he wished to avoid if possible any hint of a collision with the President and therefore would use every means to resolve the problem.[177] Bramlette sent Dr. Robert Breckinridge to Washington, because Breckinridge was a prominent member of Kentucky and an abolitionist.

Robert Breckinridge was born in March 8, 1800, near Lexington, Kentucky. Called the father of the public school system in Kentucky, he attended Yale and Princeton, graduating from Union College in Schenectady, New York, in 1819. He served on the Kentucky legislature from 1825-1830. In 1832, he became a member of the Presbyterian Church. In 1841 he became embroiled in religious controversy and split the church over his anti-Catholicism. Between 1845 to 1847, he served as president of Jefferson College in Pennsylvania, but returned to Kentucky to become superintendent of public instruction. In 1853, he was professor of the Danville Theological Seminary. Although a slave owner, he gradually supported emancipation and colonization. In 1849, he ran as an emancipation candidate and became an abolitionist. When the war broke out, he became a radical Republican and supported the Unconditional Union Party. He also opposed Confederate sympathizers.[178]

On March 16, 1864, Burbridge sent a telegram to President Lincoln stating that he spent the night with Governor Bramlette and heard his proclamation concerning the recruitment of black soldiers. He reported that the speech had a national ring to it and stated Kentucky would do her duty to the Nation. He wrote to the President that there was no need for fear about the enrollment of black soldiers in Kentucky. He stated that the law would be obeyed.[179]

On March 23, 1864, Governor Bramlette met with Dr. Robert Breckinridge, accompanied by Archibald Dixon and A. G. Hodges. Dixon and Hodges

---

177 Letter from Governor Bramette to General Stephen G. Burbridge, March 14, 1864, Frankfort, Kentucky. Stephen Gano Burbridge letters, 1 reel of microfilm, University of Kentucky Special Collections and Digital Programs, Lexington, Kentucky.

178 James Clotter, *The Breckinridges of Kentucky*, (Lexington, Kentucky, 1986), *The Kentucky Encyclopedia*, (University of Kentucky Press, 1992), 120.

179 O.R. Series III, Vol. IV, [#125] March 16, 1864, Dispatch from Burbridge to Lincoln.

met with President Lincoln. The conference ended with a compromise where the Governor agreed to black enrollment on the condition that no enlistment of blacks would take place so long as Kentucky continued to furnish their quota of white men.[180]

In order to improve relations with the citizens of Kentucky, Burbridge ordered all churches, courthouses, jails, fair grounds, and all other public buildings occupied by military authorities to be vacated and delivered to the proper authorities. No public or private buildings would be taken for military use except in cases of great emergency and only with the consent and approval of the sub-district commanders.[181]

During the first week of March 1864, Burbridge dealt with his first Confederate invasion of the state. The Confederate high command gave Confederate Major General Nathan Bedford Forrest permission to raid the state. Born in Bedford City, Tennessee, Nathan Bedford Forrest became known during the Civil War as the "Wizard in the Saddle." His father was a blacksmith, who barely made a living for his family. At the age of 16, Forrest took care of his family. He became a successful slave trader and planter by 1861. He enlisted in the Confederate army in 1861 as a private, but promoted to brigadier general on July 21, 1862, and major general by December 4, 1863. Despite a lack of military training, he displayed extraordinary ability as a tactician and strategist. He once made the statement that "War means fightin' and fightin' means killin'." He became one of the most feared cavalry leaders in the Western Theater.

For Forrest's raid the Confederate high command gave him three Kentucky infantry regiments for his invasion, which Forrest turned into cavalrymen. Confederate Brigadier General Absalom Buford became commander of the Second Division, which consisted of the 3rd Kentucky, commanded by A. P. Thompson and the 4th Kentucky commanded by Colonel T. H. Bell.[182]

While in his headquarters in Columbus, Tennessee, Forrest set about collecting absentees and putting an end to the marauders in Alabama. He was also determined to make another raid along the line of the Memphis and Charleston Railroad into west Tennessee, and possibly into western Kentucky. His troops were in desperate need of clothes, equipment, and horses. Forrest hoped to pick up recruits and capture and destroy Union supplies in west Tennessee. On March 15, Forrest took only 2,800 men – the 2nd Division under General Buford, the

---

180 *Military History of Kentucky*, 207.

181 O.R. Series I, Vol. XXXII/3 Union Correspondence, Orders, and Returns Relating to Operations in Kentucky, Southwest Virginia, Tennessee, Mississippi, Alabama, and North Georgia, from March 1, 1864 to April 30, 1864. [#58] General Order No. 30.

182 Bryan Bush, "Battle of Paducah," in Jerlene Rose, ed., *Kentucky's Civil War Back Home in Kentucky, Inc.*, (2002-2003 edition), 24-25.

7th Tennessee Cavalry, and McDonald's Battalion – and headed out on his raid. On March 23, Confederate Colonel W. L. Duckworth, with McDonald's battalion and Faulkner's regiment, numbering 500 men, seized Union City, captured 475 men and 300 horses along with all their equipment, arms, and ammunition.

Meanwhile, Forrest and Buford headed for Paducah, Kentucky. On March 25, Forrest arrived in Paducah, having ridden over 100 miles in 50 hours. The Union troops in Paducah amounted to 665 men under the command of Colonel Stephen Hicks, 127th Illinois Infantry, 16th Kentucky Cavalry, and the 1st Kentucky Heavy Artillery (Colored). There were also two gunboats, the Peosta, under the command of Captain Smith, and the Paw Paw, under the command of Captain O'Neil.[183]

Colonel Hicks prepared for the oncoming attack. He sent scouts out on the old Mayfield road where they encountered Forrest's advance guard on Eden's Hill. Forrest pushed back the scouts. He captured several squads of infantry on Broadway. Colonel A. P. Thompson reached 15th and Broadway at 3:00 p.m. and could see the Federals rushing into Fort Anderson, which was located 100 yards from the river bank west of town and wanted to pursue them, but Forrest told Thompson that their main objective was ammunition and medical supplies, not prisoners.[184]

Shells from the gunboats began to fall into the city. General Buford raided the stores, warehouses, and stables, taking clothing, supplies, and horses. He also sent separate parties of men to destroy public property and war material. Colonel Thompson decided to attack Fort Anderson and made three attempts to take the parapets, but failed. Colonel Thompson was seated on his horse and surrounded by his staff officers near the alley of Trimble between Fifth and Sixth streets, directing movements.[185]

General Buford sent an order for Colonel Thompson to fall back under the cover of a line of horses, but before the order could reach Colonel Thompson, a cannon ball from one of the gunboats came directly up Trimble Street and hit the pommel of Thompson's saddle, killing him instantly. The Federals in the fort saw the Confederates falling back and changed their sights on their cannons to fire on the horses. The Confederates left Paducah at 11:00 p.m.

During the battle of Paducah, Forrest destroyed 60 bales of cotton, a steamer in dry dock, took 50 prisoners, and 400 horses and mules, and a considerable amount of supplies. Colonel Hicks reported 14 killed and 46 wounded. Forrest

183 Bryan Bush, "Battle of Paducah: A raid for clothes, equipment, arms, ammunition and horses." *Kentucky's Civil War 1860-1865, Back Home in Kentucky, Inc.*, 2002-2003 edition.

184 Ibid.

185 Ibid.

Union gunboats fire on Forrest's men, who were located in the city of Paducah, Kentucky, March 25, 1864.

reported 25 lost, with General Buford reporting 10 killed and 40 wounded.[186]

On March 28, Burbridge received word of Forrest capturing Paducah and his command was between the Tennessee and Cumberland Rivers. He thought that Forrest was going to cut the Nashville Railroad. Burbridge reported to Union General Schofield that he had enough men to protect the railroad. He ordered four mounted regiments in supporting distance of General Sturgis's force at Mount Sterling, Kentucky.[187]

The next day, Union Assistant Adjutant General R. M. Sawyer reported to General William T. Sherman that a small party of guerillas captured a train in Lebanon, Kentucky. Burbridge sent a force to pursue the guerrilla party. Burbridge reported to Sawyer that the Rebel squad that captured the train at Lebanon was small and thought that the force was only returned rebel soldiers organized in the state. They were being pursued by several detachments. One of Forrest's soldiers who surrendered to Burbridge at Eddyville told Burbridge that Forrest started from Demopolis on February 28 with 15,000 men; part went toward Memphis, part into middle Tennessee, and the remaining 4,000 went with Forrest to Paducah. Those who crossed the Cumberland were furloughed for six days, with orders to report to Mayfield. Burbridge's men

186 Ibid.

187 O.R. Series I, Vol. XXXII/3 Union Correspondence, Orders, and Returns Relating to Operations in Kentucky, Southwest Virginia, Tennessee, Mississippi, Alabama, and North Georgia, from March 1, 1864 to April 30, 1864. [#58]

were on the hunt for the Confederate soldiers at Mayfield.[188]

On March 31, 1864, Burbridge furnished General Samuel Sturgis with a battery and ordered four regiments of cavalry and infantry to report to him. He reported Forrest crossed 100 men at Eddyville. He captured a portion of them and thought that he could capture the rest. Gunboats guarded the crossings. The next day, Burbridge reported that Forrest was near Mayfield. About 100 of his men crossed the Cumberland and were captured. General Sturgis dispatched a message to Burbridge that 300 Confederate cavalry appeared in his front.

On April 2, 1864, General Sherman wrote to Burbridge that Union General John Schofield reported the Confederates were leaving east Tennessee for Virginia. General Schofield occupied Bull Gap with his infantry and his cavalry. Sherman asked Burbridge to stop the *Louisville Journal* from alarming the people about an invasion of Kentucky. In his opinion, "such articles are calculated to produce raids – the very thing Kentucky does not want."[189] He reported that there was no real army to threaten Kentucky except Confederate General Joseph Johnston's, but he could not advance. The mountains of east Kentucky were a barrier against any Confederate invasion and Burbridge could collect enough men to stop any attempt the Confederates made to enter the state. The only force in southwest Virginia left was used to guard the Confederate salt works against a raid by Union forces from the Kanawha or up from Knoxville, Tennessee.[190]

He recommended Burbridge to push a light cavalry force toward Pound Gap. Sherman was never a fan of the press and told Burbridge that he noticed that the newspapers were "falling into the bad habit of publishing rumors and nonsense. Check this as much as possible and I will stop them at the front, even if I have to banish all the tribe."[191]

Sherman wrote to Burbridge that all railroads in front of Nashville were to be used for military freight, so citizens were not to come to Nashville with the expectation of going beyond Nashville. No private freight or citizens should use the military railroad until the army supplies were complete. He told Burbridge not publish any of this information.[192]

On April 2, 1864, Burbridge reported that Confederate General George B. Hodge's brigade passed through Pound Gap and Union Lieutenant Colonel Ferguson drove his advance to Prestonburg, but the Confederates forced him

188 O.R. Series I, Vol. XXXII/3 Union Correspondence, Orders, and Returns Relating to Operations in Kentucky, Southwest Va, Tennessee, Mississippi, Alabama, and North Georgia, from March 1, 1864 to April 30, 1864. [#59].

189 Ibid.

190 Ibid.

191 Ibid.

192 Ibid.

to fall back. Citizen scouts reported that Confederate General John Hunt Morgan was at Abingdon with a large force and moved toward Kentucky.

Confederate General John Hunt Morgan was no stranger to Kentucky. Born in Huntsville, Alabama, on June 1, 1825, he became a member of a prominent Kentucky family. He attended Transylvania College in Lexington, Kentucky, but left the school after the college suspended him for an altercation with another student. Between 1846 to 1847, he served in the Mexican War as a first lieutenant with the 1st Kentucky. After the war, he bought a hemp factory and woolen mill and became a prominent member of society in Lexington. In 1857, he formed the Lexington Rifles, a local militia unit. When the war broke out, Morgan joined the Confederate army. He became a colonel of the 2nd Kentucky Cavalry and fought at the battle of Shiloh in April 1862. On December 11, 1862, the Confederate government promoted Morgan to brigadier general. Morgan served under Confederate General Joseph Wheeler. He conducted a series of raids into Kentucky and Tennessee. Morgan became known for his daring newspaper headline raids. He became the epitome of the cavalry leader. He always dressed impeccably and mounted only the finest Kentucky thoroughbreds. He earned the reputation as a shrewd and fearless winner. His Second Raid on Kentucky, which started in October 17, 1862 and ended on November 1, 1862, disrupted railroads and Union supply routes. He captured Lexington, Kentucky, on October 18, 1862 and rode throughout many Kentucky counties. Union forces were unable to keep up with his cavalry. He suffered very few casualties. In his Christmas Raid which started on December 12, 1862 and ended on January 2, 1863, Confederate General Braxton Bragg ordered Morgan to slow down Union General William S. Rosecrans' army and sever his supply lines. Morgan's main goal was to destroy the Louisville and Nashville Railroad. He captured Elizabethtown on December 27, and the next day he cut Rosecrans' supply line by destroying the large trestle near Elizabethtown. Morgan also destroyed $2 million worth of Union supplies and captured 1,800 prisoners and pulled 20,000 Union troops away from Rosecrans. His Great Raid of 1863, which started on July 2 and ended July 26, 1863, became the longest raid of the Civil War. Morgan held businesses for ransom, destroyed commercial buildings, and looted local banks. The raid brought panic to the North and made Morgan public enemy number one in Kentucky and Indiana. During Morgan's raid he managed to capture 6,000 Union troops, caused 120,000 militia to be mustered into service, destroyed 34 bridges, demolished railroads, and damaged thousands of dollars worth of Union property. But on July 19, Union forces under the command of Union General Edward Hobson defeated Morgan's forces at Buffington Island. On

July 26, Hobson captured Morgan at New Lisbon, Ohio. The War Department sent Morgan and 30 of his men to the Ohio State Penitentiary, but on November 27, 1863, Morgan and six of his officers escaped the Ohio Penitentiary. On December 23, 1863, Morgan made his way back to Franklin, Tennessee.[193] By April 1864, Morgan commanded in east Tennessee and southwestern Virginia.

On April 2, 1864, Sherman ordered Burbridge to concentrate all his forces at Lexington, Kentucky. General Grant wanted to move into southwest Virginia which would stop any move through Pound Gap and by the way of east Tennessee. Confederate General James Longstreet headed back into Virginia, and sent a small force through the Cumberland Gap to cover his movements. Union scouts reported General Forrest at Jackson, Tennessee. Sherman had an infantry force at Purdy and stated that if General Stephen Hurlbut acted with energy, Forrest would not be able to leave the state.

On April 4, Colonel Frank Wolford and Lieutenant Governor Richard T. Jacob spoke at Paris, Kentucky. Immense crowds gathered during court day in Bourbon County. Men came to town to horse trade and buy cattle. Auctions were held for land and blacks slaves. On the April court day in central Kentucky counties held their horse shows and in the square around the court house, livestock and thoroughbreds went up for auction. With a massive audience already present, Colonel Wolford and Lieutenant Governor Jacob gave their speeches. Both men spoke out against black recruitment.[194]

On April 6, Burbridge reported Confederate General Hodge's brigade at Pound Gap, General John Breckinridge at Tazwell, and General John Hunt Morgan at Abington. Burbridge rode to Paris, Kentucky to look for General Hodge's force.

While Burbridge rode to Paris, Kentucky, he received an order from the War Department to not only command the District of Kentucky, but by an order from Congress he was also charged with raising troops in Kentucky by voluntary enlistment and by drafting.[195] Burbridge issued an order on April 8, 1864, stating that the Acting Assistant Provost Marshal General was authorized to receive recruits into the United States service black males offered by their owners. The camp of instruction was to be established in Kentucky, but the black recruits as soon as they were enlisted and mustered into service, were to

---

193 Patricia Faust, *Historical Times Illustrated Encyclopedia of the Civil War* (New York: Harper and Row, 1991), 510-511, 543; Sifakis, Stewart, *Who Was Who in the Confederacy, Volume II*, (New York & Oxford: Facts on File, 1988), 203-204.

194 Loraine Butler, *John Morgan and His Men* (Philadelphia: Dorrance & Company, 1960), 293.

195 O.R. Series III, Vol. IV [#125] Correspondence, Orders, Reports, and Returns of the Union Authorities from Jan. 1, 1864 to April 20, 1865.

be sent to Gallatin, Nashville, and Clarksville, Tennessee.[196] Governor Bramlette appointed J. P. Flint commissioner and agent to visit black Union camps and obtain for their legal owners proper vouchers. Bramlette also appointed Flint to obtain evidence for enlistments of Kentucky black troops in Tennessee and other states to allow Kentucky to obtain proper credits against the state's quota for troops.[197]

On April 13, Burbridge reported to Union Gen. John Schofield that the Confederates appeared at Proctor and Gen. John Hunt Morgan passed through Pound Gap with 3,000 cavalry, supported by infantry. The next day, 1,000 Rebels attacked Colonel Gallop at Paintsville. Burbridge ordered General Hobson to send the Union troops at West Liberty to Saylersville road toward Pound Gap and unite with Colonel Gallop. Burbridge also ordered the 11th Michigan to support the force moving from West Liberty. He ordered General Hobson to hold the balance of his command in preparation to move in any direction.

While Burbridge readied the state for Confederate invasion into Kentucky, Union Secretary of War Edwin Stanton wrote to General Grant stating that Governor Bramlette wanted the western counties of Kentucky included in the same command as the remainder of the state, so that the whole state could be under the command of General Burbridge. Grant wrote to Stanton that the only objection to west Kentucky being placed under General Burbridge was that west Kentucky belonged to a different department from the rest of the state. He pointed out to Stanton that one officer cannot make returns and reports to two departments, and he did not think it was advisable to add west Kentucky to the Department of the Ohio. The weakness exhibited by the command of west Kentucky forced Grant to send another general to that region of the state. He wrote to Stanton that Burbridge already had enough to attend to in his region of the state.[198]

Two days later, Secretary of War Stanton ordered Burbridge to recruit able-bodied slaves and free blacks in Kentucky. In the case of slaves, their owners could request the enlistment and no one would be permitted to recruit or enlist slaves or free blacks except provost marshals and authorized Union agents.

As soon as the slave enlisted, the new recruit would be sent to the provost marshal of the district for muster into service and as soon as he mustered into the service and squads of recruits were collected, they would be forwarded to the general rendezvous camp at Louisville and then by the commandant of the

196 Richard Sears, *Camp Nelson*, (Lexington: University of Kentucky Press, 2003), 54.

197 *Military History of Kentucky*, 208.

198 O.R. Series I, Vol. XXXII/3 Union Correspondence, Orders, and Returns Relating to Operations in Kentucky, Southwest Va, Tennessee, Mississippi, Alabama, and North Georgia, from March 1, 1864 to April 30, 1864. [#59]

rendezvous to the nearest rendezvous or camp of instruction outside the state, for the purpose of being equipped and assigned to companies and regiments. When the provost marshal accepted and mustered into service a slave belonging to a Kentucky citizen, he gave the citizen a certificate which would enable the slave owner to receive government compensation for the recruits.[199]

On April 19, 1864, General Sherman reported to Union Gen. A. Rawlins, Chief of General Grant's Staff in Washington, D.C., that Union General George Thomas moved his command to Chattanooga, Tennessee. Union General John Schofield had his infantry force at Bull's Gap and a small cavalry force beyond, but prepared to have 12,000 infantry near Hiwassee by May 1, 1864, with his cavalry and Gen. George Stoneman's, remounted and refitted as quickly as possible, near Lexington, Kentucky. Union General James McPherson had Decatur well fortified and planned to cross the river at Guntersville or Whitesburg.

Sherman planned to attack Confederate General Joseph Johnston in Georgia. Union General Benjamin Grierson had 7,000 horses and General Smith had captured 4,000 animals, but he could not attack Confederate General Nathan B. Forrest, because he could only mount only 2,400 men. According to Sherman, General Grierson should have attacked Forrest at Somerville. Forrest was in Paducah with a considerable force and what was at Somersville was only a part of Forrest's command and should have been fought at all odds. General Ralph Buckland's full brigade of 2,000 men was at Memphis. Three other white regiments and one black artillery regiment was at Fort Pickering. Four thousand infantry and 2,500 mounted cavalry could have attacked Forrest. Sherman sent General Sturgis to take command of all the cavalry and whip Forrest, and if necessary, mount enough men to seize any and all the horses in Memphis, Tennessee.

The force at Fort Pillow, Tennessee, had a regiment of Tennessee troops, and four black regiments. Sherman sent for Governor Bramlette. Bramlette assured Sherman that all the steps taken and undertaken by his militia, and the troops under Burbridge, they could catch the wandering guerillas and keep peace in the state.[200]

On April 23, Sherman wrote to General Burbridge that he had a series of papers from Union General Henry Halleck which showed a conspiracy on the part of mischievous men in Kentucky, Indiana, Ohio, and Canada for the purpose of destroying steamboats and even cities. Sherman wrote to Burbridge

---

199 O.R. Series III, Vol. IV [#125] Correspondence, Orders, Reports, and Returns of the Union Authorities from Jan. 1, 1864 to April 20, 1865.

200 O.R. Series I, Vol. XXXII/3 Union Correspondence, Orders, and Returns Relating to Operations in Kentucky, Southwest Va, Tennessee, Mississippi, Alabama, and North Georgia, from March 1, 1864 to April 30, 1864. [#59]

that they could not operate by military force against such "devils," but they could shelter and protect the steamboat captains who resorted to extraordinary measure to guard the property and lives in their charge against such 'villains." He wrote to Burbridge that he could notify them that if they detected among their passengers or crew one or more whom they knew to be engaged in such a scheme that they should be disposed of by drowning or killing them on the spot. The only question was of proof, which should be as clear as possible. He wrote to Burbridge that: "It is not war for individuals to burn steamboats or supply them with coal or wood charged with gunpowder, and the laws of war do not apply to such people; therefore, I don't care to have our military prisons or courts encumbered with such cases."[201]

The provost marshal of Louisville and Union Lieutenant Colonel J. R. Smith informed Sherman of the plot. Two of the principal men engaged in the plot were men named McRay and Jones, residing in Windsor, Canada. Sherman wrote to Burbridge that he thought if the captains of the steamboats were notified, they could more effectually counteract the plot, than could any military interference.[202]

On May 1, 1864, Aleck Webster, reputed to be a member of the notorious Confederate guerrilla band of Mose Webster, returned to Grant County, Kentucky to work on his father's farm near Crittenden. Union Captain Thomas W. Hardiman's 55th Kentucky Infantry arrested Aleck Webster under Burbridge's orders. Hardiman had orders to "lose him on the way." Hardiman tried to get Webster to escape. Whether Webster tried to escape is not clear, but Haridman carried out his order and shot Webster and buried him along the roadside.[203]

As April came to a close, Burbridge dealt with Confederate raids under Confederate General Nathan Bedford Forrest, Confederate General Hodge, and Confederate guerrilla attacks. He also had to deal with recruiting black soldiers for the Union army, which was never popular with Kentucky citizens and Governor Bramlette. Burbridge also had to contend with secret plots. As the month of May progressed, Burbridge would have to deal with one of Kentucky's most notorious raiders: Confederate General John Hunt Morgan. Morgan entered the state of Kentucky on another raid. By the end of the raid, Morgan would find his army in shambles and Burbridge earning himself a brevet of major general.

---

201 O.R. Series I, Vol. XXXII/3 [59] Union Correspondence, Orders, and Returns relating to operations in Kentucky, Southwest, Va., Tennessee, Mississippi, Alabama, and North Georgia, March 1, 1864, to April 20, 1864. Letter from Union General William Sherman to General Burbridge, April 23, 1864.

202 Ibid.

203 Jim Reis, "The Ugly Side of War," *The Kentucky Post*, June 1, 1998.

Chapter 6

Morgan's Last Raid and the Battle of Cynthiana

By the middle of May, Burbridge prepared to attack the salt works in Virginia, but Confederate General John Hunt Morgan put an end to his plans. Morgan planned one of his famous raids into Kentucky. By the end of the raid, Morgan's command would be in shambles and Burbridge would earn himself a brevet of major general.

Burbridge received word from General Henry Halleck and General John Schofield that he should watch General Schofield's left flank and if possible to make a diversion in his favor by attacking the Confederates in Virginia. Having had Union General Edward Hobson, commanding the Eastern Division, to concentrate all the force he had in central Kentucky at Mount Sterling, Burbridge ordered him to move on May 23, 1864, for the mouth of Beaver Creek and await Burbridge's arrival with the remainder of his forces. On May 24, 1864, Burbridge left Cincinnati for Catlettsburg and arrived the next day. On May 26, he left for Louisa and remained all day looking into the condition of the troops and making preparations for the expedition. On May 27, he left Louisa, taking with him the 37th Kentucky Mounted Infantry and the 11th Michigan Cavalry, along with two twelve-pound howitzers, under the command of Colonel D. A. Mims, 39th Kentucky.

On May 28, 1864, Burbridge arrived at the mouth of Beaver Creek, where he found General Hobson encamped. Burbridge determined to rest the whole command for one day in order to supply them with rations and forage. He hoped to find a ten days supply of food and forage, but to his "surprise, disappointment, and intense chagrin," he found only a two days supply of rations. On May 30, Burbridge ordered every horse available under the command of Colonel Mires, of the 39th Kentucky back to Louisa, with orders to get the needed supplies and forward them to Burbridge as soon as possible.

On May 31, 1864, General John Hunt Morgan started on his expedition. Confederate General Simon B. Buckner, commander in east Tennessee, gave orders for Morgan to strike a blow at the Yankees in Kentucky. While Morgan planned to move out, the Union forces rode into the Kanawha valley in the direction of the Tennessee railroad. Morgan felt he should remain with his command and cooperate with the other forces in the area to protect the public interests. Since the repulse of the Union forces, Morgan obtained permission from General William Jones to carry out the original plan to ride into Kentucky.

Morgan learned that Union General Hobson left Mount Sterling on May 23, 1864, with six regiments of cavalry for Louisa. At Louisa, there was another force of about 2,500 cavalry, under the 11th Michigan Regiment. He learned that General Hobson planned to unite with the 11th Michigan Regiment and cooperate with Union General William Averell and George Crook in another movement upon the salt works and lead mines of southwestern Virginia. Generals Averell and Crook established themselves in Mercer County, Virginia, and awaited the arrival of General Hobson for a combined movement upon the works indicated by three different lines of approach. Morgan decided to move at once into Kentucky and divert the plans of the Federal forces by initiating a movement within their own lines. He had 2,200 men. Morgan planned to move through Pound Gap, detach a portion of his command to move toward the Yankees at Louisa, with instructions to join him in the interior of the state, while he moved with his main force to strike for Lexington and Frankfort. He would destroy as much of the Covington and Lexington Railroad and push toward the Louisville and Frankfort and Louisville and Nashville Railroads and damage them. Morgan would try to avoid contact with the Union force at Louisa and make his way back into the department south of the Kentucky River, and through some of the passes in the Cumberland Mountains between Pound and Cumberland Gaps. If pursued too strongly, he would change his course and turn south toward some passes between Tennessee and Kentucky and make his way back through east Tennessee. He planned to destroy the road between Knoxville and Chattanooga.[204]

Not everyone agreed with Morgan's raid into Kentucky. Confederate General Braxton Bragg wrote that the raid was "a most unfortunate withdrawal of forces from an important position at a very critical moment." Confederate Secretary of War J. A. Seddon wrote that he saw "no remedy for this movement now."

On June 4, 1864, Union Colonel Mires returned with the badly needed supplies for Burbridge's entire command. In the meantime, Burbridge sent Colonel John Mason Brown, of the 45th Kentucky, to Pound Gap to watch-Morgan's movements, with instructions to keep him advised. Colonel Brown

204 O.R. Series I, Vol. XXXIX/1 [#77] May 31-June 20, 1864-Morgan's Raid into Kentucky. No. 14-Reports of Brig. Gen. John H. Morgan, C.S. Army.

reported that Morgan was in force on the Virginia side of the mountain. Morgan flanked Brown's 500 Federals on the Stony Gap Road and forced Brown to withdraw. Colonel Brown left a small scouting party to watch Morgan's movements. Morgan rode toward Mount Sterling. Mount Sterling was an important depot for Federal supplies. On June 5, Burbridge started with his command to Pound Gap, but a courier from Colonel Brown informed him that Morgan rode through the gap. Burbridge called together for consultation with General Hobson and his brigade commanders, and they decided that General Hobson should return to prepare for Morgan's force. Burbridge sent Colonel John Brown, with his regiment and a detachment of the 39th Kentucky, with instructions to watch Morgan's men and, if possible, slow their progress until Burbridge could attack him in the rear, but with discretionary power as to when and where he should reveal himself to Morgan, thereby letting him know his movements were observed. With the rest of the command, Burbridge moved on toward Pound Gap, intending to throw General Morgan off his guard and also give him time that would allow Burbridge to overtake Morgan in a country where he could not follow his favorite course of tactics, which included breaking up his command into small squads, following secret paths and the fastness of the country.

On June 5, 1864, Burbridge arrived about 20 miles from Pound Gap and learned from one of his scouts that Morgan camped on the Rockhouse fork of the Kentucky River. The next day Burbridge sent Colonel Grider, 52nd Kentucky, with a part of his regiment and a detachment of the 37th Kentucky, toward Pound Gap, with instructions to obstruct the gaps and roads so that if Morgan should attempt to return before Burbridge reached him, Colonel Grider could easily hold his position until he could come up with his command. With the remainder of the command, Burbridge marched back to the mouth of Beaver Creek, where he selected all the men and horses who could rapidly march. Burbridge left the rest of his command, along with his artillery, except the two mountain howitzers, under the command of Colonel C. J. True, 40th Kentucky, to ride to Louisa as soon as possible. Burbridge retraced his steps as far as Prestonburg.

Four days later, on June 8, 1864, Burbridge took the direct line of pursuit. When he arrived at Salyersville, he received a courier from Colonel John Brown informing him he was on the tail of Morgan's main force. Burbridge ordered Colonel Brown to continue scouting in advance, and pushed forward the command, traveling without resting.

On that same day, June 8, 1864, Morgan completely surprised the Union force at Mount Sterling, who fought Morgan stubbornly for some time, but

Confederate General John Hunt Morgan (Courtesy of the Civil War Battles of the Western Theater Museum, Bardstown, Kentucky.)

were driven from the field, with Morgan capturing all their camp equipage, transportation, etc, with supplies, and about 380 prisoners. Morgan's men also robbed the bank at Mount Sterling of $80,000. Morgan remained in Mount Sterling for one day and moved on to Lexington. Morgan left Colonel Giltner's 4th Kentucky and Lt. Colonel Robert Martin's dismounted regiments behind to complete the destruction of the Federals' stores and search for horses to remount Martin's regiment. He also sent Captain Peter Everett to Maysville with 100 men to capture the town and return to Mount Sterling within three days. Morgan sent Captain Jenkins and a small company to wreck the bridges on the railroad between Frankfort and Louisville and Major Chenoweth to destroy the bridges on the Kentucky Central between Cincinnati and Lexington.[205]

Meanwhile, Burbridge rode to within ten miles of Mount Sterling, when Colonel Brown reported to him in person that he had followed until he found Morgan, who had already taken Mount Sterling and the small Union garrison. Morgan's cavalry and his infantry arrived and had gone into camp without any suspicion that Colonel Brown had also arrived near Mount Sterling.

On June 9 at 4:00 a.m., Burbridge ordered Colonel John Brown, with the 45th Kentucky and the 11th Michigan Cavalry to advance and ordered them to charge and attack one camp. Colonel Ratliff, of the 12th Ohio Cavalry, with the 37th and 39th Kentucky and one battalion of the 12th Ohio Cavalry was to take the center and attack the other camp. Union Colonel Charles Hanson, of the 37th Kentucky, with the 40th Kentucky, two battalions, 12th Ohio Cavalry and the two twelve-pound howitzers was to comprise the reserve. Unfortunately Burbridge's plans did not go as planned; one of the howitzers was sent to the front, blocking the road, cutting off a portion of the 11th Michigan from Colonel Brown's brigade, and prevented them and the entire center brigade from reaching their assigned position in time to join effectively in the charge. At that point, the horses being all killed by their sharpshooters, the howitzer was captured by Morgan's men. Burbridge called for volunteers to retake the gun, and Captain Hicks, 12th Ohio Cavalry, sprang forward with his company and charged, recapturing the gun. The attack was a "thorough surprise," and after a battle lasting two hours, the Confederates ran in every direction. From the prisoners taken during the engagement, Burbridge learned that General Morgan had left, with a considerable part of his cavalry, toward Lexington. Burbridge was apprehensive that Morgan would collect and reinforce his defeated men and attack him again before his men had any chance of rest. Burbridge decided to stay at Mount Sterling, giving his men a rest. According to Union Captain J. Bates Dickson, Assistant Adjutant General, his men buried 200 Confederates, and Union losses amounted to 25 killed. Union forces captured nearly 200 Confederates.[206]

On June 10, 1864, Morgan rode into Lexington at 2:00 a.m. and captured Captain Hawes' Union battery, seized a number of outposts, and took the city. Morgan seized 2,000 U.S. horses found in the stables and about 5,000 horses that had been sent to Lexington for protection. Morgan's entire command was "elegantly mounted" and the greater portion of his command were clothed

---

205 Lorine Butler, *John Morgan and His Men*, (Philadelphia: Dorrance & Company, 1960), 299.

206 O.R. Series I, Vol. XXXIX/1 [#77] May 31-June 20, 1864, Morgan's Raid in Kentucky. No. 2 Report of Capt. J. Bates Dickson, Assistant Adjutant General, U. S. Army.

and shod. After burning the government stables, depot, etc., and securing 200 prisoners, Morgan moved to Georgetown. Morgan sent Captain Cooper with a detachment to Frankfort to make a reconnaissance and to take Fort Clay. Union Colonel George W. Monroe, 22nd Kentucky Infantry, and his 150 men defended Fort Clay against Captain Cooper's men. During one of the assaults against Fort Clay, Captain Cooper's men managed to take Frankfort's four pound gun, but Monroe's men managed to recapture the gun. Captain Cooper made several assaults on Fort Clay, but Colonel Monroe held his ground. Captain Cooper burned the barracks at the edge of town, but Captain Cooper never took Fort Clay.[207]

On June 10, 1864, Union General William T. Sherman sent Burbridge a message stating that he should not assume a defensive stance toward Morgan, but should follow him and "cut him off from every direction with infantry and cavalry. Morgan would have to scatter for food, and infantry could pick up his detachments. He should never be permitted to leave Kentucky, and I will be disappointed if he succeeded to escape."[208] Meanwhile, Burbridge marched for Lexington, taking all his prisoners captured at Mount Sterling, except the wounded. When Burbridge started his expedition, he had left his assistant adjutant general, Captain J. Bates Dickson, in charge, who upon Morgan's approach to the city, put Colonel Wickliffe Cooper, 4th Kentucky Cavalry, at home on leave, in command of the place and the troops in the vicinity. Under the direction of these two officers, all the Government property, except a few horses, were moved to Fort Clay, and Colonel Cooper, after skirmishing with Morgan's advance, with the few men at his command, withdrew to the fort, from which he presented such a formidable front that Morgan did not venture to attack him. According to Burbridge, all the damage done by Morgan at Lexington consisted of the loss of the horses, except that he robbed the bank and citizens of their money, watches, and goods of various descriptions. Union Colonel Israel Garrard, of the 1st Brigade, Union General George Stoneman's cavalry, reported to Burbridge at Lexington, and Burbridge spent the rest of the day in obtaining fresh horses, rations, and ammunition. Burbridge thought that Morgan headed for Paris and planned to attack and destroy the railroad bridge at Paris. Burbridge moved with his command on the road to Paris.

On June 10, 1864 at 2:00 p.m., General Morgan heard General Edward Hobson advancing and, although Morgan was almost out of ammunition, he

207 Lorine Butler, *John Morgan and His Men*, (Philadelphia: Dorrance & Company, 1960), 301.

208 O.R. Series I, vol. XXXIX/2 [78] Confederate Correspondence, Orders, and Returns Relating to Operations in Kentucky, Southwest Va., Tennessee, Mississippi, Alabama, and North Ga., from May 1, 1864 to September 30, 1864.

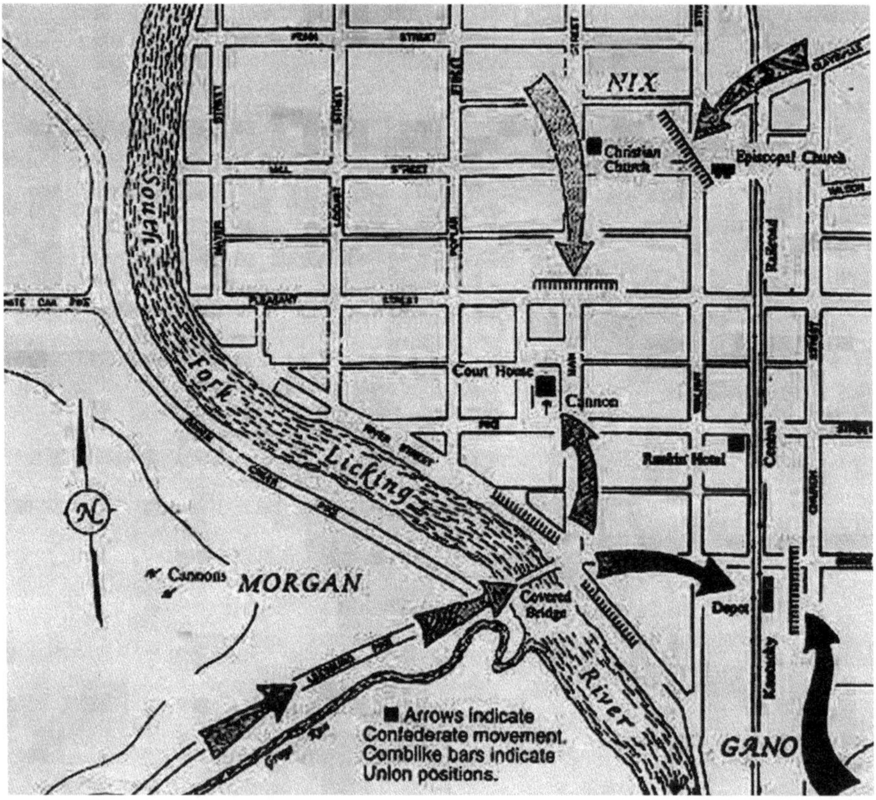

The Battle of Cynthiana (Map courtesy of the Cynthiana Historical Society Museum.)

decided to meet him in battle. General Hobson, with 600 men and the 171st Ohio National Guard, arrived on a train at Keller's Bridge, about one mile north of Cynthiana. Union Colonel Joel F. Asper, of the 171st Ohio, got his men off the train cars and was in the process of distributing rations and extra ammunition to his men, when firing was heard in the direction of Cynthiana. A man from the town reported that a detachment from the 168th Ohio needed help. Colonel Asper sent two companies to reconnoiter from a small hill, and determine how close the Rebels were to General Hobson's position. The two Union companies reached the top of the hill, when a small Confederate squad of cavalry rushed towards the train. The two Union companies fired into them and they turned and ran. A few seconds later, a Rebel cavalry force moved to Hobson's right, as if to intercept the train, which had been ordered back with the horses. Hobson observed a line of Rebel skirmishers advancing through a field. Captain J. S. Butler, Assistant Adjutant General of Hobson's staff, mounted one of his horses and one company from the 171st Ohio National Guard and some convalescent men of the 52nd Kentucky, threw out a line of skirmishers and attacked the Rebels in the field and drove them until they were reinforced and sheltered themselves in the woods. Hobson's line reinforced and skirmishing kept up for an hour, when the town was seen to be on fire and the firing ceased in Cynthiana. The shouts from the rebels led Hobson to believe that the detachment from the 168th Ohio had been captured. Hobson observed the Rebel cavalry to the right and a large dismounted force advanced upon Hobson's front. Hobson's line of skirmishers were pushed back on the main force, and the detachment of the 47th Kentucky, about 30 men under Captain Wilson, was driven back from the protection of a fence. The 171st Ohio National Guard had never been under fire and Hobson moved them to the rear and formed on a small hill in the woods, to prevent from being flanked by a Rebel force still moving to Hobson's right. Hobson defended the small hill for five hours.[209]

Colonel Giltner's First Brigade, of Morgan's force arrived at Keller's Bridge with 1,500 men. Morgan arrived on the field. General Hobson reported that he drove the Rebel force back, but Hobson's men had been reduced in force to only 400 men, who were exhausted from the lack of sleep and hard fighting. Morgan's men rallied and attacked Hobson's rear and flanks. Taking command of Major Cassell's battalion in person, Morgan maneuvered his command to get in the rear of General Hobson, surrounding him. By this time, Morgan reduced Hobson's force to only 300 men. General Morgan sent in two flags of truce and demanded Hobson surrender. Colonel Asper met the flags and reported Morgan's terms of surrender as prisoners of war. Hobson called his staff and the field officers of the 171st Ohio National Guard. Hobson realized that his force had been reduced, and knowing there was no chance of being reinforced, and the troops in town surrendering, the train being captured, and nothing more could be accomplished from fighting, and 2,500 Confederates surrounded him, General Hobson's decided to surrender his entire command. Morgan rode up to General Hobson and modified the terms of surrender allowing Hobson's officers to retain their side arms and private property, and the men to keep their haversacks, private property, and blankets. After Hobson surrendered, Morgan captured three railroad trains, with baggage and horses, and destroyed 1,500 muskets. General Hobson and his staff were sent under a flag of truce to Falmouth, Kentucky, and arranged with Gen. Samuel Heintzelman for an exchange. If an exchange could not be obtained, Hobson was to report to Morgan in Virginia. In the meantime, Confederate Major Chenoweth had destroyed the railroad between Lexington and Boyd's Station on the Kentucky Central Railroad; Captain Jenkins had destroyed

209 O.R. Series I, Vol. XXXIX/1 [#77] May 31-June 20, 1864. Morgan's Raid in Kentucky. No. 5 Reports of Brig. General Edward H. Hobson, U.S. Army.

the railroad between Louisville and Frankfort; Captain Cooper took the fortifications around Frankfort, and Captain Everett took Maysville.

Morgan rode onto Cynthiana, where he arrived on June 11, 1864, and met a force of 400 Union soldiers under Colonel Berry. A severe engagement broke out between Morgan's men and the Union force. The Federal soldiers took shelter in the houses in town and fired on Morgan's men. Morgan's men set the houses on fire that contained the Union soldiers. Unfortunately, the fire spread from the Union soldier's refuge to the entire town. Twenty-seven buildings caught fire in Cynthiana. During the engagement Colonel G. W. Berry was killed.[210]

When Burbridge arrived at Paris, he found the town had been threatened by Morgan with a small force, but a couple of shells from the guns of Fort Robinson sent the small force off in another direction. During the day, Burbridge heard heavy cannonading from Frankfort and the Confederates were reported in the area of Georgetown, but the telegraph lines had been cut. Burbridge had to wait until his couriers and scouts returned with information. General Hobson sent a dispatch to Burbridge informing him that he was surrounded and could not hold his position much longer. Burbridge received word that Morgan was in Cynthiana and had taken the town and destroyed nearly all the businesses and that General Hobson had surrendered with his command. Burbridge moved out with his command, with Colonel Garrard's brigade, with 2,400 men, in the direction of Cynthiana, sending Colonel Brown on a reconnaissance toward Cynthiana, Millersburg, and Carlisle.

On June 12, Morgan's command consisted of only 1,200 men. Most of his command guarded prisoners and protected the wagon trains, but they also destroyed two lines of the railroad. On that same day at 2:30 a.m., Burbridge's advance, under Major Tyler, 52nd Kentucky approached Morgan's pickets two miles and a half from the town of Cynthiana, drove them back upon their skirmish line, and held them there until the column closed up. Burbridge formed his line of battle across the turnpike leading to Millersburg, and on either side of the road, three dismounted regiments formed the center, with a cavalry regiment on each flank, and the cavalry brigade of Colonel Garrard served as a reserve. At the word "Forward" the line advanced, driving Morgan's men back from their first line. The command "Charge" was given. The Confederates were driven in, except upon their flanks, where they took refuge behind stone walls and high rail fences. Burbridge had to send in an additional force. He ordered Colonel Garrard to send one cavalry regiment to the right and one to the left to attack the extreme Rebel flanks, leaving one cavalry regiment as a reserve. Finding

210 Butler, *John Morgan and His Men*, 306-307.

Morgan's men repulsing his attack on the left, Burbridge sent the 7th Ohio Cavalry to the left to assist in the charge. Burbridge's entire cavalry force, aided by the dismounted men, succeeded in completely routing Morgan's force in the area from which the most desperate resistance occurred. Meanwhile, in the center and right the Union force took the town and pushed Morgan's men back from their positions. Morgan's men fled in the "wildest confusion." Many of Morgan's men drowned in their attempt to cross the Licking River, which was the only other avenue of escape, since Burbridge blocked the escape on the right. Only 250 men from Morgan's command managed to escape from Cynthiana.[211] Having learned from the citizens and prisoners that General Morgan, when he learned the tide of battle had turned against him, had fled with his best troops in the direction of Claysville, Burbridge ordered Colonel Garrard, with his brigade, to pursue Morgan. Morgan had no choice but to release General Hobson's prisoners. According to Union Captain J. Bates Dickson, Union forces captured 500 of Morgan's men and killed 300 men At Flemingsburg, Morgan abandoned the greater part of his transportation, together with his sick and wounded. Colonel Garrard continued to pursue Morgan until he reached the mountains, when he turned back, determining any further pursuit useless. After several hours of rest at Cynthiana, Burbridge ordered Colonel Hanson to move with his brigade through Carlisle and Mount Sterling and to dispose of Morgan's forces and to scatter and capture as many of Morgan's retreating men as possible.

Burbridge ordered the remainder of his forces to Lexington by the way of Georgetown, determining that Morgan's men were so completely demoralized, they would not make any further stand in Kentucky. He placed his prisoners for safe conduct under Colonel John Mason Brown. On June 13, Burbridge reached his headquarters at Lexington. Burbridge lost 53 killed, 156 wounded, and 205 missing.

On June 20, 1864, Morgan made his way back to Abington, Virginia. According to Morgan, he lost 80 killed, 125 wounded, and 150 captured. He stated that recruits who enlisted in Kentucky made up for his losses and his command would be as strong as when he entered Kentucky. He stated that during his raid, he defeated the Union plans to capture the salt works and lead mines of southwest Virginia. He also remounted 900 men with horses and equipment. He captured a sufficient amount of clothing and shoes to equip his command. He claimed that he destroyed $2 million worth of U.S. property. He claimed that he managed to break up Union black recruiting operations in middle and eastern Kentucky and the discovery on the part of the people of an almost "unanimous sentiment of sympathy with our cause, and which

211 Dee Brown, *Morgan's Raiders*, 263.

promises much support to any advance of our troops in the state."[212]

Although Morgan tried to put a successful spin on his raid, the Confederate government began to investigate the bank robbery at Mount Sterling that occurred on June 7, 1864. Confederate Colonel R. A. Alston wrote to Confederate Kentucky Governor Richard Hawes, in Abington, Virginia, asking him to investigate Morgan's raid in Kentucky. He regretted to state that plundering prevailed on the whole raid. Alston stated that property was forcibly taken from citizens for private purposes; houses were plundered of silver-plate, and even the clothing and jewelry were taken from women, and violence was threatened against them if they did not give up their jewelry. He stated that a staff officer drew his pistol on Miss Todd of Cynthiana and ordered the ladies to deliver their money and jewelry to him. Mrs. Hamilton was riding to Mount Sterling with delicacies for the Confederate wounded when she was halted, made to give up her watch and other jewelry and her horse to the Confederates. Banks were robbed. He stated that the conduct of Morgan's command of the raid "was such as to disgrace the country and cause a man to blush at the name of Confederate soldier."[213] "The conduct of our command in Kentucky is to be deeply regretted, not only for the discredit which it brought to our arms, but I feel that in the disaster which was brought on us by converting the expedition into one of plunder and robbery we lost the greatest political opportunity which has yet been offered in Kentucky. . . . Men who six months ago would have offered rewards for our capture were out to greet us and say 'God speed.' Recruits were flocking to us every hour, and but for the reckless mismanagement of the whole expedition, which was directly the result of our unlicensed and thieving course, we would this day have been in Kentucky with an army of 20,000 men, and Sherman would have been fleeing before our army in Georgia. The State would have stood self-redeemed before the world."[214]

Colonel Giltner asked that Seddon investigate the forcible entry of the bank at Mount Sterling, Kentucky, and the seizure and carrying away of the funds by a portion of Morgan's command. Money amounting to $80,000 in gold, silver, bank notes, and Federal currency was taken from the bank. A large portion of the money belonged to depositors who were friendly to the Confederate cause and the whole sum to private individuals. Giltner asked General Morgan to take action. A few hours after the robbery, Colonel D. Howard Smith urged Morgan to investigate, but according to Colonel Giltner,

212 O.R. Series I, Vol. XXXIX/1 [#77] May 31-June 20, 1864-Morgan's Raid into Kentucky. No. 14-Reports of Brig. Gen. John Hunt Morgan, C.S. Army.

213 O.R. Series I, Vol. XXXIX/1 [#77] May 31-June 20, 1864-Morgan's Raid into Kentucky. No. 14-Reports of Brig. Gen. John Hunt Morgan, C.S. Army.

214 Ibid.

Union General Stephen Gano Burbridge

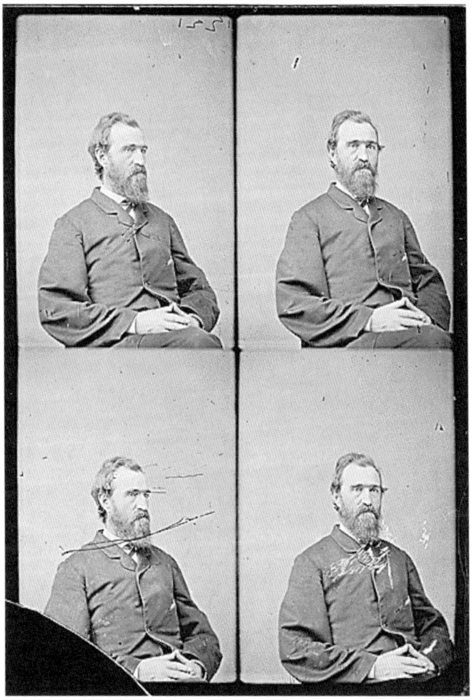

Above: Portrait of Governor Thomas Bramlette (Photo courtesy of the Library of Congress). Left: Front view of Bramlette's hat (Photo courtesy of the Civil War Battles of the Western Theater Museum). Below: Inside of Bramlette's hat (Photo courtesy of the Civil War Battles of the Western Theater Museum).

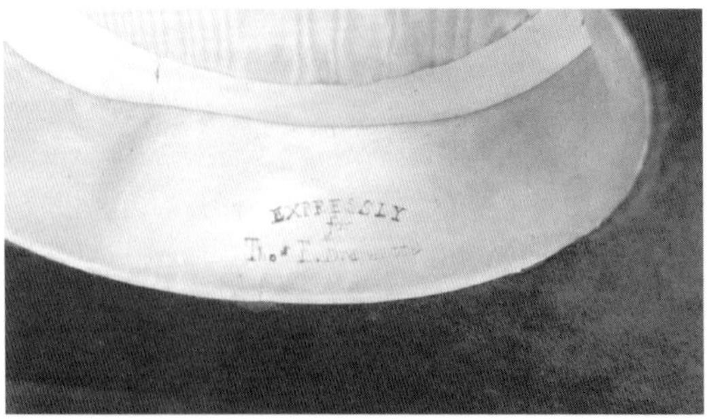

Left: Union General William T. Sherman became a personal friend of General Burbridge. Right: Union President Abraham Lincoln appointed General Burbridge commander of the Kentucky district, but lost confidence in him, removing him from the position. (Courtesy of the Library of Congress)

Burbridge's foes on the battlefield. Above left: Confederate General John Hunt Morgan faced General Burbridge in the Battle of Cynthiana, Kentucky. Above right: Confederate General Nathan Bedford Forrest invaded Kentucky and took on Burbridge forces. Right: Confederate General Thomas Green fought General Burbridge at the Battle of Bayou Bourbeau.

Left: Union Secretary of War Edwin Stanton. Right: Judge Advocate General Joseph Holt.

Union General Stephen Gano Burbridge in Harper's Weekly, January 1865.

Top: A tombstone marks the resting place of two Confederate guerillas ordered executed by General Burbridge. These executions were one controversial aspect of Burbridge's reign in Kentucky:

A court-martialed soldier hangs from the gallow. (Courtesy of the U.S. Military History Institute)

A photograph of General Stephen Burbridge taken after the war. (Courtesy of the Library of Congress)

Union General Stephen Burbridge's gravesite at Arlington National Cemetery.

Morgan moved with a portion of his command to Lexington. Since the return of the command to Abington, Virginia, appeals had been made to Morgan by Colonels R. A. Alston and R. M. Martin and others to investigate the matter, but Morgan failed to do so, except to appoint Captain B. H. Allen inspector-general. Colonel Giltner wrote to Seddon that Captain Allen went on 30-day leave and did not take any steps to investigate the incident. Colonel Giltner considered this outrage as "most high handed and disgraceful, and having been associated with General Morgan during his Kentucky expedition, neither myself nor my officers are willing to be identified with it."[215] Giltner asked for a full investigation into Morgan's raid.

Morgan wrote to Confederate Secretary of War James Seddon that some of his soldiers of his command robbed the bank at Mount Sterling. Colonel Smith informed Morgan of the robbery, but Morgan stated that the enemy was rapidly moving on his flank and rear, hoping to get between him and Lexington, and if he had remained in Mount Sterling to investigate the bank robbery would have destroyed the object of the expedition and compromised the safety of his command. Once Morgan arrived at Abington, Virginia, Morgan reported that the incident was being thoroughly being investigated by Morgan's acting assistant inspector general. Morgan assured Seddon that parties were written to in Kentucky to furnish statements in regard to the affair. The cashier of the bank at Mount Sterling was requested to furnish a list of depositors, with the amounts. Morgan stated that if any of the property of the citizens of Mount Sterling bank were found in the possession of any soldier under his command, the property would be returned to the citizens. As for his inspector general, Morgan did grant Captain Allen a leave of absence for 30 days, but a surgeon's certificate of disability was given to Captain Allen. Morgan assured Seddon that Allen was doing all he could to ascertain a true understanding of the affair. According to Morgan, Allen's investigation had been delayed because of the distance and difficulty involved in acquiring testimony and by fact that some of the principal witnesses among the soldiers of his command were either absent in Kentucky or were captured on the expedition and currently resided in a Federal prison. Morgan wrote to Seddon that Colonel Giltner made the complaint because of a "pique toward me more than indignation of my delay."[216] Morgan later determined that his surgeon R. R. Goode robbed the bank and disappeared after the robbery.[217]

---

215 O.R. Series I, Vol. XXXIX/1 [#77] May 31-June 20, 1864-Morgan's Raid into Kentucky. No. 14-Reports of Brig. Gen. John Hunt Morgan, C.S. Army.

216 Ibid.

217 Dee Brown, *Morgan's Raiders*, 258.

The damage had already been done. Some of Morgan's most staunch civilian supporters and loyal citizens to the Confederacy in Kentucky turned against Morgan and changed their sympathy when they discovered that Morgan's men had robbed a civilian bank in Mount Sterling and looted his home town of Lexington. Confederate General Braxton Bragg, chief of staff, wrote to President Jefferson Davis that Morgan's raid did not produce satisfactory results. He stated that if Morgan returned to the Confederacy, his command would be disorganized and unfit for service until again armed, equipped, and disciplined. He wrote to President Davis that Morgan's loss of a large number of men on the raids, because many of them became prisoners, had been the source of "great evil, placing us, in that respect, at the mercy of a cruel foe. Had this force been with us in the valley of Virginia we should probably not have to regret a defeat there and mourn the loss of one of our most gallant leaders, who fell in striving to save that invaluable region from devastation."[218]

In September 1864, the Secretary of War and President Davis set up a court of inquiry into the "robberies, depredations, or unwarrantable injuries to the people or corporations" during Morgan's raid. On March 20, 1865, as the Confederacy collapsed, charges were brought against Private Humphrey Castelman, 1st Kentucky Cavalry, who was accused of removing from the bank about $10,000 and used the money for his own use. Captain E. P. Byrne was also accused by the court of inquiry of robbing the bank in Lexington. Surgeon R. R. Goode was also accused of taking $72,000 from the Farmer's Bank in Mount Sterling.

The Union army, the Secretary of War Edwin Stanton, and President Lincoln were delighted with General Burbridge's successful campaign against Morgan. President Lincoln wrote to Burbridge: "Have just received your dispatch of action at Cynthiana. Please accept my congratulations and thanks for yourself and command."[219] Secretary of War Edwin Stanton wrote to Burbridge: "Please accept for your gallant command the thanks of this Department for the brave and successful operations of the last six days in Kentucky, achievements of valor, energy, and success that will be regarded with admiration by all loyal people of the United States."[220] Major General John Schofield, commander of the Army of the Ohio, wrote to Burbridge: "Your dispatch of yesterday announcing your rapid pursuit and complete victory over Morgan is

218 O.R. Series I, Vol. XXXIX/1 [#77] May 31-June 20, 1864-Morgan's Raid into Kentucky. No. 14-Reports of Brig. Gen. John Hunt Morgan, C.S. Army.

219 O.R. Series I, Vol. XXXIX/1 [#77] May 31-June 20, 1864.-Morgan's Raid into Kentucky. No. 1 Reports of Brig. Gen. Stephen g. Burbridge, U.S. Army, commanding District of Kentucky.

220 Ibid.

received. Most heartily I congratulate you and your command, and thank you for your efficient service."[221] General Sherman sent a message to Burbridge stating: "Your dispatch received and is very satisfactory. Go on, raise the hue and cry, and don't mind the cost of money or horseflesh to hunt down every robber and guerilla in your state. Make a clean job of it, and Morgan and all other such men will let Kentucky alone in all time to come. Seize fresh horses wherever they can be had, and leave the tired ones, giving a certificate for after settlement."[222] For his successful campaign against Morgan, President Lincoln brevetted Burbridge a Major General.

After the successful defeat of Morgan's raid and his brevet to major general, Burbridge felt a sense of pride and thought that everyone from the President to General Sherman supported his efforts in Kentucky. When the elation of victory wore off, Burbridge had to deal with the same problems as before the raid: guerilla warfare, secret conspiracies, and disloyal citizens. As June came to an end, Burbridge stepped up his dealings with guerillas and disloyal citizens. He also stepped up his recruitment of free black soldiers, which led to the citizens of Kentucky hating him.

---

221 Ibid.

222 O.R. Series I, vol. XXXIX/2 [78] Confederate Correspondence, Orders, and Returns Relating to Operations in Kentucky, Southwest Va., Tennessee, Mississippi, Alabama, and North Ga., from May 1, 1864 to September 30, 1864.

Chapter 7

His Controversial Reign Begins

While General Burbridge began his campaign against Morgan's raid into Kentucky, he had to deal with two issues: guerillas in the state and the recruitment of blacks into the Union army. Both issues led to Burbridge becoming one of the most hated figures in Kentucky's history.

On May 12, Burbridge issued Order Number 41, which stated that the practice of giving employment and contracts in the military service to rebels and rebel sympathizers in Kentucky became so frequent as to become a monopoly. He ordered all such employments and contracts to be terminated. Only citizens of unquestionable loyalty to the U. S. government would be given employment or contracts in the military service. All violations or evasions of the order would be dealt with. Contractors would not be allowed to have rebel partners or agents in the performance of their contracts. All contractors would have to give a description of all persons hired or contracted to do work for them.[223]

In effort to stem desertions, President Abraham Lincoln issued amnesty oaths. If all soldiers who were "improperly absent" returned to their regiments by April 1, 1863, they would not be punished; failure to return to their respective units would result in their loss of citizenship and court martial for desertion. Lincoln's amnesty oath led to 12,000 to 15,000 soldiers returning to their regiments. Lincoln passed the Confiscation Act of 1862 which authorized the President to pardon at his discretion anyone involved in the rebellion and his December 8, 1863, Amnesty Proclamation extended limited pardon contingent on swearing an oath of allegiance, excluding all Confederates who had held civil office and anyone guilty of mistreating prisoners. On May 26, 1864, Lincoln issued another restrictive amnesty aimed at civilians.[224]

On May 13, 1864, D.P.H., Burbridge's brother in law, wrote from Washington, D. C., to Burbridge that Union Secretary of War Stanton told him that he authorized Burbridge to try every man he took, who violated the Amnesty

223 O.R. Series I, Vol. XXXIX/2 [#78].

224 Patricia Faust, Historical Times Illustrated Encyclopedia of the Civil War, (New York: Harper & Row Publsihers, 1986), 12.

Oath, and execute the guilty. Stanton told D. P. H. that "no other General stood higher with the President and Grant himself than you did, and the friends of the government need have no fear that you would be ordered from command of Kentucky, as you were specially chosen for your skill, courage and ability for that command. You may be assured that this was most gratifying to my feelings. What little I could say to strengthen his feeling I said, and said it without stint. He told me to give you his kindest regards. He says he never saw you but has the highest opinion of you."[225]

He wrote that Burbridge must be "merciful and be just. Punish the wicked, protect the innocent, and redeem our loved state from savage rule and cruelty. . . . Your position is responsible. Never mind croackers and fault finders, but keep your eye steadily on truth and right and God will bless you."[226]

D.P.H. stated that he had great confidence in Burbridge and hoped that he would do good and honor to his Nation and state. "Do not forget my brother that you are a Christian. Be humble, be prayerful, be pious."[227] He hoped that Burbridge would write the President and get the amnesty oath suspended.

On May 14, 1864, General Burbridge issued General Order Number 39, which ordered the circulation of the book *The Life of Stonewall Jackson* and similar books to stop, and he threatened the seller with arrest and confiscation of his entire stock of books.[228]

On that same day, Burbridge issued Order Number 42 which stated that all persons discouraging volunteer enlistments into the Union army, resisting militia drafts, or guilty of any disloyal practice, affording aid and comfort to the Rebels against the authority of the United States, would be subject to martial law and liable to trial and punishment by court martial or military commission. Provost marshals and deputy provost marshals would arrest and press charges against any person violating the law and send all those arrested under the law to Burbridge's headquarters and be tried by a court martial.

On May 16, 1864, T. S. Bell[229] wrote to Burbridge from the headquarters of the Provost Marshal, 5th Kentucky Congressional District. He stated that he had written a letter to President Abraham Lincoln and laid the letter before him in the presence of Postmaster General and former Wisconsin Governor Alexander Randall, Senator John Brooks Henderson (Democrat) of Missouri, Honorable

225 Letter from D.P.H. to Stephen Gano Burbridge, May 12, 1864, Washington, D.C., Stephen Gano Burbridge Papers, 1862-1865, 1 reel of microfilm, University of Kentucky Special Collections and Digital Programs, Lexington, Kentucky.

226 Ibid.

227 Ibid.

228 Collins, Lewis & Collins, Richard, *History of Kentucky, Vol. 1* , 1874, 133.

229 T. S. Bell was a Kentucky physician and Unionist who served as President of the Kentucky branch of the U.S. Sanitary Commission.

Joseph Holt,[230] Professor Mullins, Dr. Pannley, J. Torbitt of Louisville, and D. P. Henderson. The President sent Mr. Bell word that "General Burbridge stands very high with the government." The President told Bell that no effort had been made yet for Burbridge's removal from command in Kentucky. He wrote to General Burbridge that he felt at ease about Burbridge's position at Washington. Bell could not understand President Lincoln's course, but he thought it was very curious that the President never yet refused him a request, and many of his most important moments toward Kentucky were made upon his application. He asked the President a personal favor, but Mr. Lincoln needed more important information. He hoped Burbridge would see Bell before leaving Lexington. Bell stated that the President wanted Burbridge to send him a recommendation for the suspension of the Amnesty Proclamation in Kentucky and that the President would grant the request. Bell wrote that Burbridge's recommendation for the suspension of the Amnesty Proclamation "cannot be done too soon. Orders will be issued to bring to speedy trial all the villains who have violated the Amnesty oath. So you see that the labors of Captain Jones were not in vain. The President has at last awakened from his dream of leniency toward the demons of rebellion, and he intends now to do what he should have done three years ago—run a red hot ploughshare through them and all their works."

Bell went to the Union press and made some remarks for Burbridge on his Order Number 41. He wrote that Burbridge must "push it without fear or affliction. Spare not the rod if the State is to be saved." He wrote to Burbridge that Captain J. Bates Dickson, his adjutant, was "a noble adjutant. He will do his duty. I wrote something about him for the Press." He informed Burbridge to send to Captain Dickson all his special dispatches to the Union press. Bell wrote the dispatches "will help the paper greatly, and whatever does that will help the Union cause in Kentucky."[231]

On a personal note, T. S. Bell wrote that he was sorry to hear about "Mrs. Burbridge's suffering. I regret that I cannot be near her to alleviate her pains. Give her and the children my affectionate regards."[232]

On May 25, 1864, the Union Democratic ticket state convention was held in Louisville, Kentucky. During the convention, Colonel Wolford, Lieutenant Governor Richard T. Jacob, Richard H. Hanson, and John Houston gave

---

230 Joseph Holt was a former secretary of war under President James Buchanan, judge advocate general, Democratic politician from Kentucky and chief of military justice.

231 Letter from T. S. Bell to Stephen Gano Burbridge, May 16, 1864, Headquarters Provost Marshal , 5th Congressional District, Louisville, Kentucky., Stephen Gano Burbridge Papers, 1862-1865, 1 reel of microfilm, University of Kentucky Special Collections and Digital Programs, Lexington, Kentucky.

232 Ibid.

impassioned speeches against the Administration and especially against emancipation and black enlistment into the Union army. During the "Union Democratic" state convention, Union authorities arrested Wolford after he made a fiery outburst in which he denounced the order for enrollment of blacks in Kentucky as "unconstitutional, unjust and another of a series of startling usurpations."[233] The committee instructed the delegates that when they arrived at the Chicago national convention, they were to vote for Union General George B. McClellan and Governor Thomas Bramlette for president and vice president. At the same time, the Unconditional Union Party state convention was held in Louisville. Speeches were made by Rev. Robert Breckinridge, Judge Rufus K. Williams, Colonel Benjamin H. Bristow, Curtis F. Burnam and Lucius Anderson.[234]

On June 1, 1864, Governor Bramlette continued to resist the effort of Union authorities to recruit black soldiers by authorizing Colonel Frank Wolford to raise a regiment of six months men, allowing him to fill his quota for white troops for the Union army. Under his agreement with President Lincoln, as long as he filled his quota for white troops, he did not have to recruit for black troops.

On June 2, 1864, Captain J. Bates Dickson, Burbridge's assistant adjutant general, wrote to Burbridge that guerrillas were very troublesome in General Hugh Ewing's division. Dickson authorized Ewing to mount the 48th Kentucky. Two Indiana regiments were turned over to General Ewing, but Sherman ordered all of them to be sent to Nashville. Dickson stated that he could not rely on the promises of the Kentucky militia. He asked General John Schofield to send him 5,000 troops. Governor Thomas Bramlette protested against recruiting blacks, claiming that there is no authority for it and that it is in violation of promises made by him by the President and the Secretary of War.

In a follow up to Burbridge's Order Number 42, he issued Order Number 45, which stated that his headquarters had received complaints that slaves who had presented themselves for enlistment and were, on examination, rejected were subjected to harsh treatment in punishment for the attempt. Burbridge declared that any person discouraging enlistments would be subject to Order Number 42 and that return passes would be given to all blacks who were rejected and Burbridge would secure their immunity from harsh treatment or punishment on account of their attempt to enlist.

On June 6, Adjutant General D. W. Lindsey issued an order on the behalf of Governor Bramlette, which postponed the Union draft so that the

233 Robert McDowell, *City of Conflict: Louisville in the Civil War. 1861-1865*, (Louisville Civil War Roundtable Publishers, 1962), 163.

234 Collins, *History of Kentucky*, 133.

six months enlistments could be filled. On that same day, Captain Dickson wrote to Burbridge informing him that the one hundred days Indiana troops were sent to Nashville, by Sherman's orders. He stated that any dependence on Governor Bramlette for militia, or six months Kentucky troops, was worthless. He also stated that most of the blacks throughout the district knew they did not need their master's permission to enlist. They were flocking by the hundreds to enlist. The enlistment of blacks created "considerable excitement" in many districts, but Dickson reported there were no incidents of violence. He wrote that the enlistment of slaves into the Union army would unite masters in resisting the enlistment.

On June 7, Colonel Cunningham, in charge of black troops in Paducah, made a raid into Union County and impressed a steamboat load of blacks into the United States service. The boat consisted of 158 slaves who were being taken by their owners to a point where the Union army could not enroll the black slaves into Union service.[235] Lieutenant Commander Le Roy Fitch wrote to Rear-Admiral David D. Porter, Commander of the Mississippi Squadron, that some gross outrages had been committed in the area of the Cumberland River by Colonel Cunningham, from Paducah. Fitch learned from reports that Colonel Cunningham went up into the Cumberland River area with a number of black soldiers and sent them on shore to conscript every black man they could find. The black soldiers were sent on shore armed and without an officer, entered private houses, broke open the doors, and entered ladies' bedrooms before they woke up, insulted women, and plundered and searched generally. Fitch reported to Admiral Porter that the actions of Colonel Cunningham and his men were a "gross outrage and disgrace to our cause." Fitch reported that Colonel Cunningham had a gun-boat convoy them up the river. Fitch reported that none of his gun-boats convoyed them.[236]

On June 11, Union General Henry Halleck, Chief of Staff, reported to Burbridge that Colonel Frank Wolford, commander of the 1st Kentucky Union Cavalry, made to soldiers and others, speeches of an "insurrectionary and treasonable" character. If the allegations were true, Halleck ordered Burbridge to arrest Colonel Wolford and send him to Washington under guard.

On June 16, 1864, Burbridge wrote to Governor Bramlette that the Acts of Congress on July 17, 1862 and the act of February 1864, furnish ample author-

---

235 The Military Department of Kentucky, *Military History of Kentucky*, (The American Guide Series, Works Projects Administration, 1939), 209.

236 O.R.--Series I--Volume XXXIX/2 [S# 78] Union Correspondence, Orders, and Returns Relating to Operations in Kentucky, Southwest Virginia, Tennessee, Mississippi, Alabama, and North Georgia (The Atlanta Campaign Excepted), from May 1, 1864, to September 30, 1864.(*)--#5.

ity for him in relation to the enlistment of slaves in the Union army. Burbridge told Governor Bramlette that he could not determine to what extent if any he had violated the agreement between the President, the Secretary of War, and the Governor.[237]

His orders charged him with the execution of the laws of July 17, 1862, and February 1864, and he hoped he had the full cooperation of the governor. The draft which had recently taken place only yielded fewer than one third of the soldiers called for and as far as Burbridge was advised, voluntary enlistments had not yet made up the deficiency.[238]

Burbridge wrote to Adjutant General that great numbers of black men desired to enlist and the system of having black men enlisted by Deputy Provost Marshals, who then sent the black men in squads to be mustered by district Provost Marshals and then sent from Louisville to Tennessee for organization was inadequate. He suggested that Major William H. Sidell, Acting Assistant Provost Marshal General be authorized to appoint recruiting agents, and that a rendezvous camp to be established at Jeffersonville, Indiana, where regiments could be organized. He also asked to use a few black regiments for garrison duty at remote points in his district, such as Louisville and Camp Burnside.[239]

On June 20, 1864, Governor Bramlette wrote to Secretary of War Edwin Stanton. In the letter Bramlette stated that on March 1, in Washington, D.C., he met with Stanton and the President and understood that when the quota for volunteers was filled in Kentucky, recruiting of slaves for the army would cease. Bramlette understood that the offensive recruiting carried on by Colonel Cunningham and others was without authority or approval from the War Department, and to prevent such offensive courses, and confine the recruiting of slaves within the purview of the law, General Burbridge was appointed supervisor of enlistment and draft in Kentucky, with powers to see that only regularly appointed officers prescribed by law should enlist or draft slaves. Being satisfied that the offensive course of Colonel Cunningham and others would stop, Governor Bramlette returned home gratified at the result of his visit. Believing that Cunningham acted on his own authority and without the authority of the War Department, Governor Bramlette forwarded to General Burbridge documents setting forth his acts, and encouraged Burbridge to stop Cunningham's

237 Letter from General Burbridge to Governor Thomas Bramlette, June 16, 1864, Lexington, Kentucky, Stephen Gano Burbridge Papers, 1862-1865, 1 reel of microfilm, University of Kentucky Special Collections and Digital Programs, Lexington, Kentucky.

238 Letter from General Burbridge to Governor Thomas Bramlette, June 16, 1864, Lexington, Kentucky, Stephen Gano Burbridge Papers, 1862-1865, 1 reel of microfilm, University of Kentucky Special Collections and Digital Programs, Lexington, Kentucky.

239 Richard Sears, *Camp Nelson*, (Lexington: University of Kentucky Press, 2003), 69.

actions. Burbridge returned the documents stating that he did not have control of the Tennessee River counties.[240]

Governor Bramlette stated that Cunningham's conduct violated the laws of Kentucky and authorized to have him arrested for unlawful recruiting, but he feared that Cunningham's arrest might lead to accusations that the Governor was hostile to the government and might encourage rebels and their sympathizers. Bramlette stated that his rule of action was not to obstruct or resist where competent authority was given, no matter how rigidly his judgment may condemn the policy or justice of the course authorized. He hoped that Stanton would remove Cunningham's offense, which would result in a greater Union sentiment in that section of the state and stop further bloodshed.[241]

On June 21, 1864, General Sherman wrote to General Burbridge a letter advising him on how to deal with guerilla warfare in Kentucky. He wrote that General Morgan's recent raid and the acts of men who called themselves Confederate partisans or guerillas called for action on his part. Even on the southern states rights theory, Kentucky had not seceded. Sherman stated to Burbridge that the people of Kentucky by their vote and by their actions adhered to their allegiance to the National government and the South would try to coerce Kentucky out of the Union and into the Confederacy. The very dogma of coercion upon which so much stress had been laid at the outset of the war carried into rebellion the middle and border slave states. Sherman stated that the acts of partisans and guerillas "were nothing more than murder, horse stealing, arson, and other well defined crimes, which do not sound as well under their true names as the more agreeable ones such as warfare." Sherman knew that the Confederate campaign would cause problems and asked Governor Bramlette to organize at once in each county a small trustworthy band under the sheriff and arrest every man who was dangerous to the community, and also every man who was hanging around the towns, villages, and cross roads, who had no honest calling, which Sherman thought made the material out of which guerillas are made up, but the Governor thought that this sweeping exhibition of power was arbitrary. Sherman felt that the citizen's personal liberties were so secure that public safety was lost in the country's laws and constitutions, and the Union army was thrown back a "hundred years in civilization, law and everything else, and will go straight to anarchy and the devil if somebody don't arrest our downward progress." Sherman stated that

240 O.R.--Series III--Volume IV [S# 125] Correspondence, Orders, Reports, and Returns of the Union Authorities from January 1, 1864, to April 30, 1865.(*)--#18, Governor Thomas Bramlette to Secretary of War Edwin Stanton, Frankfort, Kentucky, June 20, 1864, 436.

241 Ibid.

the military must do it and had the right and law on their side. He wrote to Burbridge that all governments and communities had the right to guard against real or even supposed danger. He also wrote that the people of Kentucky must not be kept in a state of suspense and real danger unless a few innocent men should be wrongfully accused.[242]

Sherman ordered Burbridge to tell all his post and district commanders that guerillas are not soldiers but "wild beasts unknown to the usages of war."[243] He wrote to Burbridge that to be recognized as soldiers, they must be enlisted, enrolled, officered, uniformed, armed, and equipped by the Confederate government and must be of sufficient strength with written orders from an army commander, to do some military thing. Sherman stated that the Union army denied the Confederacy their right to the Union's lands, territories, rivers, coasts, and nationality. He also stated that the Union army did not admit the right for the Confederacy to rebell. He suggested that the Confederates move to some other country where laws and customs are more in accordance with their own ideas and prejudices.[244]

Sherman wrote to Burbridge that since the civil power was insufficient to protect life and property, to prevent anarchy the military should step in and was constitutionally lawfully right to do so. Under this law everybody can be made to "stay at home and mind his or her own business,"[245] and if they will not do it, they can be sent away where they will not keep their honest neighbors in fear of danger, robbery, and insult.[246]

Sherman ordered Burbridge to tell his military command, provost marshals, and other agents they could arrest all males and females who had encouraged or harbored guerillas and robbers, and have them collected in Louisville, and when he had enough citizens, around three or four hundred, Sherman would send them down the Mississippi through the guerilla gauntlet and by sailing ship send them to a land where they would take their slaves and make a colony with laws and a future of their own. If they would not live in peace in Kentucky, the Union army would send them to another better land.[247]

Sherman wrote that Burbridge should be careful that no personalities were mixed up in the campaign, nor did a full and generous love of country, of the South, their state or county form a cause of banishment, but the "devilish spirit which will not be satisfied and that makes war the pretext" for murder,

242 O.R. Series I, Vol. XXXIX/2, Union Correspondence, 135-136.
243 Ibid.
244 Ibid.
245 Ibid.
246 Ibid.
247 Ibid.

arson, theft, perjury, and all the crimes "of human nature."[248] He advised Burbridge that the civil authorities in Kentucky should enforce the arrests, but if they were not able to, then the military would step in and perform their duties. Sherman stated that there must be an end to the civil strife and the honest, industrious people of Kentucky, and the whole world, would benefit and rejoice at the conclusion. Sherman did not object to women and men having Southern feelings, if confined to love of country and peace, honor, and security, and even family pride, but these become a crime when enlarged to mean love of murder, of war, desolation, famine, and anarchy.[249]

Sherman sent his letter written to General Burbridge on to General Henry Halleck along with a letter on the subject of guerilla warfare. He wrote to Halleck that he doubted if President Lincoln would support his orders to Burbridge, but hoped Lincoln would not interfere. He stated that he could get the malcontents on board ships at sea without traveling outside of his authority, but then the jurisdiction was doubtful. He stated that he would never have peace as long as the Union army tolerated in their midst a class of men that the Union government knew were conspiring against Kentucky's peace, and yet who if tried by jury could not be convicted. He wrote that the Union army's civil power in the South was "ridiculously impotent."[250] He stated that as the Union army traveled the land, disaffection, sedition, and crime followed the army closely. Sherman wanted to send the malcontents to Honduras, British or French Guiana, or San Domingo, but the countries might object to the "restless democrats." He also suggested Madagascar or Lower California as places to send the malcontents. He wrote to Halleck that there was a class of people, men, women, and children, "who must be killed or banished before you can hope for peace and order, even as far as Tennessee." He wanted Halleck to name the place to send a few cargoes of people.[251]

Several weeks later the *Richmond Daily Dispatch* published General Sherman's letter to General Burbridge from June 21, 1864. Sherman decided that his instructions on how to handle guerrillas in Kentucky would be carried out in Georgia and Tennessee. His letter to Burbridge was published while he was in front of Kennesaw Mountain, Georgia, as a warning to the people of Georgia and Tennessee in his rear that guerillas would be treated as "wild beasts,"

---

248 Ibid.

249 Ibid.

250 O.R. Series I, Vol. XXXIX/2 [#78] Union Correspondence, Orders, and Returns Relating to Operations in Kentucky, Southwest Virginia, Tennessee, Mississippi, Alabama, and North Georgia (The Atlanta Campaign Excepted), from May 1, 1864, to September 30, 1864.(*)--#6, General William T. Sherman to Secretary of War Edwin Stanton, June 21, 1864, 131-132.

251 Ibid.

that the Confederate government was a "belligerent power," that the civil authorities were insufficient to protect life and property, and military commanders and provost marshals could arrest all males and females who encouraged or harbored guerillas and robbers and send them to a land where they could make their own colony.[252]

On June 23, 1864, Union General Halleck ordered Burbridge to arrest and punish all disloyal citizens in Kentucky. The order arose from reports from Cynthiana that disloyal citizens assisted Morgan's raid and, after the battle, buried Morgan's dead with honors, while the Union dead was treated with insult.

On that same day, Burbridge reported to Secretary of War Stanton that he could raise five black regiments for service if he had officers. He needed black troops for garrison duty and asked permission to use them. Stanton replied that his telegram was "very gratifying." He would promote officers immediately for Burbridge's black regiments. He gave Burbridge the power to promote anyone he saw fit and designate whatever rank he chose. He wrote to Burbridge that he could use black troops for infantry or artillery or wherever they were needed, whether in garrison service or the field.[253]

On June 25, 1864, General Halleck ordered Burbridge to declare martial law in Kentucky. He was to arrest all disloyal citizens in Kentucky that gave aid and assistance to armed rebels and sought to incite insurrection and rebellion in the state. He also stated that among the aiders and abettors of rebellion and treason were distinguished officers of state government and members of Congress. Secretary of War Stanton directed Burbridge, under the authority of the President, to arrest and send all persons inciting insurrection or aiding and abetting the enemy to Washington. The President gave Burbridge authority to use the military, and if necessary to call upon Major General Samuel Heintzelman and the commanding officer in Tennessee for assistance. Halleck instructed him to use discretion, but at the same time promptly and energetically arrest the people guilty of insurrection and aiding or abetting the enemy. He wrote to Burbridge that any attempt at rebellion in Kentucky "must be put down with a strong hand, and traitors must be punished without regard to their rank or sex."

On June 25, 1864, Thomas Sawyers, Deputy Provost Marshall for Pulaski County, wrote to General Burbridge requesting a squad of 25 men to Somerset, Kentucky. He stated that citizens and deserters were banding together for the purpose of murdering Union men, stealing, and resisting the enlistment of

252 *The Daily Dispatch*, Richmond, Virginia, July 22, 1864, "General Sherman's instructions to General Burbridge—the same to be carried out in Georgia and Tennessee".

253 O.R. Series III, Vol. IV [#125] Correspondence, Orders, Reports, and Returns of the Union Authorities from January 1, 1864, to April 30, 1865.

blacks and several Union men had already been killed in his sector and many more had been threatened.[254]

Burbridge acted on Halleck's orders. According to the *Cincinnati Commercial*, General Burbridge arrested Perry Wherritt, the mayor of Cynthiana and suspected Confederate sympathizer. Federal officials accused Wherritt of ordering the burial of Union soldiers killed in the battle of Cynthiana in the black section of the Cynthiana cemetery. The *Cincinnati Commercial* was the main northern Kentucky newspaper and provided most of the local news, since Burbridge had shut down the *Covington Journal*.[255]

General Sherman wrote to Burbridge on June 30, 1864, that Union General Robert Allen had written to him stating that he controlled his employees and contractors. Sherman assured Burbridge that anything he did to eradicate the mischievous class who were afraid to fight and wanted to keep alive the feelings of mistrust and enmity was appropriate, but he reminded him that he could only control the acts of staff officers who properly belong to his command. Quartermasters and commissaries detailed by the War Department or who belonged to General William Sherman and General John Schofield's staff were not subject to Burbridge's supervision or interference. He told Burbridge to clear out guerillas, root and branch, and banish the "vagabonds that, under the pretense of being Confederates, commit murder and highway robbery, and don't bother too much with the fellows who make money, as they are not a dangerous set. Their self interest and fear of danger will keep them quiet enough."[256]

On July 1, the War Department stepped up their efforts to help Burbridge in his recruitment and equipping of black soldiers at Camp Nelson, in Kentucky. Secretary of War Stanton informed Burbridge that he had sent 1,200 horses in order to mount his black regiments. He informed Burbridge that his department would do everything in its power to render the command Burbridge had so "bravely exercised efficient in every respect."

Two days later, on July 3, Adjutant General L. Thomas reported to Secretary of War Stanton that 3,000 blacks were at Camp Nelson, Kentucky. General Burbridge expected to give Thomas officers for three regiments. He needed officers for six more regiments. General Schofield ordered several white

254 O.R.--Series I--Volume XXXIX/2 [S# 78] Union Correspondence, Orders, and Returns Relating to Operations in Kentucky, Southwest Virginia, Tennessee, Mississippi, Alabama, and North Georgia (The Atlanta Campaign Excepted), from May 1, 1864, to September 30, 1864.(*)--#6, Letter from Thomas Sawyers to General Stephen Burbridge, June 25, 1864, 145.

255 Jim Reis, "The Ugly Side of War," *The Kentucky Post*, June 1, 1998.

256 O.R.--Series I--Volume XXXIX/2 [S# 78] Union Correspondence, Orders, and Returns Relating to Operations in Kentucky, Southwest Virginia, Tennessee, Mississippi, Alabama, and North Georgia (The Atlanta Campaign Excepted), from May 1, 1864, to September 30, 1864.(*)--#6, Letter from General William T. Sherman to General Stephen Burbridge, June 30, 1864, 153.

regiments to the front and the employment of black troops in Kentucky became a necessity. Burbridge wanted to use the black regiments. As soon as Thomas received officers, recruiting would increase at a rapid rate. In Thomas's naïve opinion, the people of Kentucky realized the fact that slavery had ceased to exist and the true Union men were satisfied that able bodied men should be enlisted, and Southern sympathizers could see the same fact, and know they could not prevent their enlistment. Taking the slaves from their owners would interfere with saving the crops, but Thomas stated that the women and children should be required to remain at home and be cared for by their owners. They could be useful in securing the grain. In Thomas' opinion, women and children should not be allowed in the Union army, because they would only be a Government expense. The railroad terminal at Nicholasville, Kentucky, was only six miles from Camp Nelson. Camp Nelson was comprised of 4,000 acres and was a good central point, and an important base of supplies for Tennessee. General Burbridge told Thomas that he wanted to arm the blacks, a controversial move on Burbridge's part. Most plantation owners feared armed blacks would either take revenge on them or destroy their property. The slave owner's wildest dreams could become a reality. As Thomas concluded his letter to Stanton, he wrote that Burbridge was a good commander and hoped he continued in his present position.[257]

Provost Marshal General J. B. Fry wrote to Adjutant General L. Thomas that General Burbridge had chief control of recruiting for black and white troops in Kentucky. General Burbridge enlisted blacks in Kentucky for Union service for several weeks and Stanton did not want Thomas to supersede or disturb the arrangements made by General Burbridge. Stanton wanted Thomas to give any aid in his power to carry out the plans General Burbridge acted on and to put under General Burbridge's control all the officers whom Thomas deemed best to connect with recruitment and organization.[258]

On that same day, Burbridge wrote to General L. Thomas that in addition to his duties as District Commander of Kentucky, he was also charged with the "general superintendence of the execution of the acts of Congress for raising troops in Kentucky by volunteer enlistment and draft." He immediately adopted measures to organize black troops. In view of the hostility toward the recruiting of black troops in Kentucky by a considerable part of the population, including all rebels and Unionists, and to bring the Union party up to the standard of loyalty, he thought that the plan to recruit black soldiers be carried out with some

257 O.R. Series III, Vol. IV [#125] Correspondence, Orders, Reports, and Returns of the Union Authorities from January 1, 1864, to April 30, 1865

258 Ibid.

caution. He wrote to Thomas that several days before he had been instructed to organize black troops in the state and was assured by the War Department that he should be supplied with Kentucky officers. His next goal was to garrison all fortifications with his black troops and use his white troops for other more active duties. But in the midst of his arrangements, he found Thomas's orders to General Augustus Chetlain, which conflicted with his intentions by taking the enlistment and organization of black troops out of his hands. Burbridge wrote to Thomas that he was charged with the military conduct of the State and had no control over a part of the forces quartered in his district and a part of the forces to which he relied on to assist in conducting the defenses.[259]

Burbridge thought that the perplexities arising out of the conflict in raising troops, such as the irregularities of enlistment, marauding by the recruits, abuse of authority of those placed in charge of the troops, and the organization of black troops, would be left in his hands. Any grievances would be submitted to Burbridge since he was the military commander and told Thomas that being a Kentuckian and a large slaveholder, the people of Kentucky would feel less hostility to the organization of black troops in the state if conducted under his supervision than if controlled by any authority outside of the state.[260]

On July 4, 1864, Secretary of War Stanton informed Burbridge that the President brevetted him a major-general for his "meritorious and distinguished service," and the Senate unanimously confirmed his nomination.

The next day, on July 5, Lincoln renewed the suspension of the writ of habeas corpus in Kentucky and declared martial law. Burbridge wrote to Stanton that he would spare no effort to protect loyal citizens and carry into effect the enlistment of troops, black or white, and suppress treasonable and disloyal practices within his command.

On July 10, 1864, Colonel Frank Wolford returned to Louisville from Washington, D. C., under parole. Thirteen charges pended against him as a result of his campaign speeches. The Federal government allowed Wolford to return to Kentucky to stand trial on the various charges before a military court. The next day, Governor Bramlette wrote to Colonel R. T. Jacob in reference to Colonel Wolford's arrest, stating that:

> the loyal people of Kentucky cannot be provoked or driven into rebellion against the government, but in self defense might justly retaliate political arrests-upon those who, among our own citizens,

259 O.R.--Series III--Volume IV [S# 125] Correspondence, Orders, Reports, and Returns of the Union Authorities from January 1, 1864, to April 30, 1865.(*)--#19, Letter from Union General Stephen Burbridge to General L. Thomas, July 3, 1864, 469.

260 Ibid.

> urge or provoke political arrests, and seek to inaugurate political terrorism. By this time, Dr. Robert Breckinridge no longer held esteem with Governor Bramlette, because Breckinridge protested against the raising of troops in Kentucky for home defense and placing them under the command of Governor Bramlette and Colonel Wolford. Colonel Wolford was a Union Democrat who supported Union General George B. McClellan as President. Breckinridge was a Unconditional Union Party man who nominated the re-election of Lincoln for President.[261]

On July 12, 1864, Union Assistant Adjutant General E. D. Townsend wrote to Adjutant General Joseph Holt at the War Department's Adjutant General's office that Secretary of War Stanton had directed him to proceed to Kentucky and meet with Governor Bramlette and Burbridge in relation to military and political affairs in the state and the administration of military justice. The particular object of Holt's mission was to acquaint himself with the facts in regard to secret and open organizations against the Government which intended to give aid and comfort to the Confederates and to ascertain the operations of disaffected and disloyal people in Kentucky acting in conjunction with people of similar disposition in other States. Townsend was referring to the organizations such as the Knights of the Golden Circle, the Sons of Liberty, and Copperheads which existed in Ohio, Indiana, Illinois, Kentucky, and Missouri. Many of those organizations supported Confederate General John Hunt Morgan's 1863 Great Raid in Kentucky and Indiana. These organizations were an embarrassment to the Union government and according to Townsend could lead to armed opposition and rebellion.

Townsend also informed Holt that he turned his attention to the carrying out of the laws in regard to the enlistment of black troops in Kentucky and to any secret or open hostility manifested by disloyal citizens against the enlistments. He would ascertain the extent of the opposition and the manner of its operation and then consider in his conference with the Governor or Burbridge what measure, if any, should be adopted by the government upon black enlistments in order to enforce the acts of Congress and the regulations of the department and to bring to trial and punishment those who were guilty of opposition to the laws relating to them. Holt was to make reports to the department and make detailed reports on the whole subject when his investigations came to a close.[262]

261 *Military History of Kentucky*, 207.

262 O.R. Series III, Vol. IV [#125] Correspondence, Orders, Reports, and Returns of the Union Authorities from January 1, 1864, to April 30, 1865.

Guerilla warfare increased and word of the atrocities reached Richmond, Virginia. The *Richmond Daily Dispatch* reported that passengers on the Tarascon, who resided in Union County, Kentucky, told the newspaper that guerillas overran the country and the lives and property of Union men were no longer safe in the state. Guerillas robbed Union and Southern supporters. They stated that at Caseyville and Uniontown, guerillas raised the "black flag" and killed every citizen and Union soldier. Union citizens fought back and decided to take no prisoners, which resulted in daily murders. According to the *New Albany Daily Ledger*, in New Albany, Indiana, Henderson County, Kentucky, swarmed with hordes of rebel guerillas. Union Lieutenant Colonel Fitch of the gunboat fleet stated that no one could conduct business safely and property could no longer be protected from the guerillas. According to Fitch the guerillas operated from the Green River to the end of Union County. Fitch demanded immediate attention from military authorities to take necessary steps to rid the country of "pestilent robbers and cut throat highwaymen."[263]

As a result of the guerilla raids in Kentucky, on July 16, Burbridge issued Order Number 59, which stated that a rapid increase in his district of lawless bands of armed men engaged in interrupting railroad and telegraphic communications, plundering and murdering peaceful Union citizens, destroying the mails, etc., called for the adoption of stringent measures by the military for their suppression. In his order, he stated that all guerillas, armed prowlers, or by whatever name they were known, and Rebel sympathizers, were warned and that in future stern retaliatory measures would be adopted and strictly enforced, whenever the lives or property of peaceful citizens were jeopardized by the lawless acts of such men. He wrote that any Rebel sympathizers living within five miles of any scene of outrage committed by armed men, not recognized as public enemies by the rules and usages of war, would be arrested and sent beyond the limited of the United States. The property of Rebel sympathizers would be used to repay the government or loyal citizens for losses incurred by the acts of lawless men would be seized and appropriated to those who had lost property. Burbridge stated that whenever an unarmed Union citizen was murdered, four guerillas would be selected from the prisoners in the hands of the military authorities and publicly shot to death in the most convenient place near the scene of outrage.[264] The *Louisville Daily Journal* published his Order Number 59 on July 20, 1864, and

263 *The Daily Dispatch*, July 13, 1864, Richmond, Virginia. "News From Kentucky."

264 O.R.--Series I--Volume XXXIX/2 [S# 78] Union Correspondence, Orders, and Returns Relating to Operations in Kentucky, Southwest Virginia, Tennessee, Mississippi, Alabama, and North Georgia (The Atlanta Campaign Excepted), from May 1, 1864, to September 30, 1864.(*)--#7, General Order Number 59, General Stephen Gano Burbridge, Hdqrs. District of Kentucky, and 5th Division, 23rd Army Corps, Lexington, Ky., July 16, 1864, 174.

added that murder of Union men would be avenged. The paper asked that the guerilla bands lay down their arms and quietly return to the "peaceable pursuits of life." The paper also stated that the guerilla bands have "trampled all laws under their feet and erased all forms that might grant to them a show of trial." According to the paper, General Burbridge's order "falls like a stream of golden sunshine upon the dark storm clouds of an angry sky."[265]

Unfortunately, General Burbridge's Order Number 59 caused Confederate prisoners to be mistaken for outlaws and many innocent men paid with their lives. The evidence against many of the Rebels or guerillas was very often flimsy. With a few choice words of criticism against a Federal officer, or the report that a son or brother in the Confederate army had returned home, or the personal grudge of some Unionist against one of his enemies was enough for Burbridge to arrest, imprison, and confiscate property.[266] The reign of terror had begun and Burbridge did not take long to implement his Order Number 59.

The next day, on July 17, General Burbridge informed General Henry Halleck that he had information that another Rebel invasion was imminent. In addition, the Rebel invasion was to coincide with a general insurrection in Kentucky of Rebel sympathizers who were to assist the raiding forces and act in concert with them. Burbridge called upon Governor Oliver Morton of Indiana and General Heintzelman for troops. General Burbridge wrote to General Schofield that August 3, 1864, was the date set for the invasion. Information from eastern Kentucky led him to believe that the Rebels would not make an invasion immediately. Burbridge wrote to Halleck that the conspiracy was much more formidable in Indiana, Ohio, and Illinois, than in Kentucky.

On July 22, 1864, six day days after Burbridge issued his Order Number 59, the military authorities took two young men named John Pierman Powell, age 23, and Charles William Thompson, age 18, from the military prison in Louisville to Henderson, Kentucky, to be executed under Order Number 59. Union commander Lieutenant Headington had orders to execute the two young men for the "atrocious attempt of a gang of guerilla scoundrels and marauders. . . to murder in cold blood, Mr. Jas. E. Rankin. . . and for other outrages of late in Henderson and vicinity."[267] Both Powell and Thompson were Confederate soldiers who had been captured on July 12, 1864, about five miles from Owensboro. The two young men claimed they were members of a company

265 *Louisville Daily Journal*, July 20, 1864, Military Order.

266 J. Winston Coleman, Jr., *Lexington During the Civil War*, (Commercial Printing Company, Lexington, Kentucky, 1938), 46.

267 Carl Runyon, "Without Cause or Trial:" The Story of the Reprisal Execution of Two Confederate Soldiers at Henderson," Kentucky, Owensboro Community and Technical College, (*Journal for the Liberal Arts and Sciences*, Vol. 8,) 20.

commanded by Confederate Captain Dick Yates, a commissioned officer who was killed in a skirmish near Owensboro. Originally on a recruiting mission, Yates and the two young men met some Federal soldiers and some 100 home guards on Ruff Creek, killing 11 and routing the rest. Thompson and Powell unfortunately became separated from the rest of the company and were captured by the Union forces. On July 20, Union soldiers moved the two men to the Henderson County jail to await their execution.[268] The reason for Powell and Thompson's order for execution stemmed from an incident that occurred on July 11, 1864, in Henderson. A band of outlaws looted the establishment of Mr. James Rankin of Henderson. The leader of the group ordered the robbers to leave. Rankin hid in a back room on the third floor. The leader returned with a group of other men and found Mr. Rankin. They demanded he open the safe, but Rankin told the men he did not have all the pieces to assemble the combination key. As Mr. Rankin descended the stairs to see if he could find the pieces for the lock, one of the outlaws shot him in the back of his neck and beat him with the butt of his gun. Rankin ran to a nearby store. The outlaws chased him into another store. William Lewis, a store clerk, begged for Mr. Rankin's life. The outlaws turned and left.[269] Although severely wounded, Mr. Rankin refused to receive any part of the $18,000 forcibly collected from his neighbors to pay him his losses by guerillas.[270] Mr. Rankin sent a note requesting that Lieutenant Headington spare the two young men. Two prominent citizens from Henderson, Archibald Dixon and Mayor Banks, sent a telegram to Union General Hugh Ewing requesting a stay of execution because the citizens of the town feared retribution from the outlaws and the two young men claimed they were not robbers but sworn Confederate soldiers. General Ewing agreed to delay the execution until he spoke with General Burbridge.

On July 20, 1864, the steamer Palestine transported William Thompson and Powell from the Henderson County jail to the site of their execution. Thompson wrote a letter to his father and mother stating that he was on the

> "road to be shot. By taking your advice I would have staid at home. I listened to my friend before I did to you, took their advice and went with them. Bear it patiently. Take care of yourself dear father and not work too hard. Bear everything patiently. Take care of Mother as long as you can and not let it overpower her constitution. Ever since the officers told

268 Byron Crawford, "Two Executions in Kentucky aided neither Union nor unity," *The Louisville Courier-Journal*, May 2, 1980.

269 Runyon, 20.

270 Robert McDowell, *City of Conflict*. (Louisville: Louisville Civil War Roundtable Publishers, 1962), 166.

> me I was to be shot I have been praying and fasting that I might see you once more in this world. Dear sister, You bear it patiently and take care of yourself. Don't fret Mother and Father any more than you can help. Tell Johnny to stay with Mother and Father as long as he can. Tell him to take care of himself and remember me. Pray that we meet in Heaven if we cannot meet here. Tell all of my friends that they have better stay home as long as possible. I wish you would settle up my debts. Tell Father to send John to school as long as he is able to.
>
> Tell all of my relatives to pray for me that we all may meet in Heaven some day together. Pay Jim Cissel one dollar borrowed money, Andrew Gough two dollars, John Blanford one dollar and seventy five cents.
>
> Give Johnny my colt, bridle, and saddle. Tell him to take care of him and keep him as long as he lives. Give Rosy, Fanny, Tell her to keep her in remembrance of me. Good Father and Joe Heayden, Come to Henderson immediately when you get this news.
>
> I don't know when I am to be shot but come immediately. Pierman (Powell) sends you the same.
>
> Goodbye, Farewell, We part forever, William Thompson.
>
> P.S.
>
> I haven't suffered anything more than uneasiness on account of Mother since I got the news. Have been well taken care of. Have had plenty to eat along till now and I don't want much. I have kept well and was well satisfied until heard the news. I was in great hope that I would see you again until I got that news. I am in hopes that I will get to see Father yet.
>
> Tell Rosa and Mother that it is not worth while for them to come. But Father start immediately and come in haste double quick until he gets there. If I am dead when he comes get both our bodies and carry us and put us in the grave yard.[271]

Unfortunately, the letter that William Thompson sent to his parents arrived to his home long after his execution.

On July 21, a group of about 40 to 100 rebel guerillas placed themselves outside of Henderson and demanded the town to surrender and release the prisoners. Lieutenant Colonel Soery told Lieutenant Headington that Powell and Thompson were under his command. Headington refused to surrender the town or the prisoners. Colonel Sypert, the Confederate commander, told Headington he had one hour to clear the town of women and children.

271 Byron Crawford, "Two Executions in Kentucky aided neither Union nor unity," *The Louisville Courier-Journal*, May 2, 1980.

Strangely, the Confederates did not attack and rode away from the town.

On July 22, Colonel Headington received orders from Burbridge to proceed with the execution, but not for the attack on Rankin but for the murder of Colonel James Poole. Both Powell and Thompson were placed in two chairs with their arms fastened to fence boards. Union soldiers blindfolded them. Headington shed tears before giving the command to fire.[272] Twelve Union soldiers fired a volley into the body of Powell and then Thompson. After the execution, Headington handed over both bodies to the local citizens who cleaned them and sent them to their friends in Curdsville, Daviess County, Kentucky. After arriving in Daviess County, Powell and Thompson were laid to rest in double graves at the St. Alfonsus Parish Catholic Cemetery, at St. Joseph's Church. In the later part of July, James Rankin died of his wounds.[273]

During the month of July guerilla bands attacked the Louisville & Nashville Railroad employees to the point where the trains could no longer operate on a regular basis. James Guthrie, president of the railroad, asked Secretary of War Stanton for 300 Henry repeating rifles. Burbridge supported the application for rifles made by Guthrie to Stanton. Burbridge sent the 26th and 48th Kentucky to clear out the country west of the Louisville and Nashville Railroad.

On July 26, 1864, Burbridge issued Order Number 61, in which he stated that citizens who had been banished from Missouri and other states on account of their Rebel sympathies and other acts that weaken the authority of the United States government and those who encouraged Confederate soldiers who fought against the United States were to leave the district within 20 days and not to return to Kentucky. Burbridge ordered all military officers and provost marshals to arrest and send to his headquarters for transportation beyond the limits of the United States all persons failing to comply with his order. [274]

The next day, on July 27, Burbridge sent eight Confederate prisoners from the jail on Water Street in Lexington, Kentucky, and sent them out of the city in various directions to be shot. He sent a detail of soldiers to Eagle Creek, Scott County, near the Owen County line with two captured guerillas, B. Grisley Wooten and William Woods. Wooten was a member of Company C, 2nd Kentucky Cavalry, who was captured in Elizabethtown, Kentucky, on July 23, 1864. Woods was from Edgefield, South Carolina. Union Captain J. E. Merritt

272 Byron Crawford, "Two executions in Kentucky aided neither Union nor unity," *The Louisville Courier-Journal*, May 2, 1980.

273 Runyon, 22.

274 O.R.--Series I--Volume XXXIX/2 [S# 78] Union Correspondence, Orders, and Returns Relating to Operations in Kentucky, Southwest Virginia, Tennessee, Mississippi, Alabama, and North Georgia (The Atlanta Campaign Excepted), from May 1, 1864, to September 30, 1864.(*)--#9, General Order Number 61, 205.

and a squadron of Federal soldiers purchased two coffins and shot Wooten and Woods on the spot where Mr. Robinson, a Union supporter, was killed by guerillas at his home on Eagle Creek.[275] The sad part of the story is that Robinson later turned out to be unharmed.[276]

The next day on July 28, 1864, General Joseph Holt wrote to Secretary of War Stanton that he gave Burbridge permission to raise two black regiments. General George Thomas endorsed the idea. Holt stressed to Stanton that the raising of the black regiments was very important. These regiments were composed of men almost "raised on horseback," of uncompromising loyalty, and had an intimate knowledge of the topography of the country. He stated that the black regiments would prove a powerful instrument in ridding Kentucky of the guerilla bands of robbers and murders which infested and oppressed the entire state. He also stated that the black regiments' presence in the different counties would create a positive influence in favor of the government's policy of employing black troops. That same day, Secretary of War Stanton authorized Burbridge to raise two regiments of black cavalry, to be mounted from horses procured by seizure from Kentucky citizens, giving them certificates of payment, payable at the end of the war, to all loyal citizens who continue to remain loyal during the war. The price for the horses should not exceed the price paid by the purchasing officers of the Kentucky government,[277] an order that would upset the Kentucky horse owners and slave owners.

As Burbridge dealt with the guerilla warfare and stepped up his harsh retribution, he decided to influence the state elections to make sure that only loyal Union radicals won the election. On July 29, three days before the annual state elections, General Burbridge tried to influence the election by issuing an order to every sheriff in the 2nd appellate district that Alvin Duvall was not allowed to appear on any poll books as a candidate for office.

On that same day, two alleged guerillas were sent from the prison in Louisville, Kentucky, to Russellville, Logan County, to be shot on the spot where a Mr. Porter died from wounds while resisting the outrages of guerillas. Union soldiers chose only Harvey Thomas of Company C, 2nd Kentucky Cavalry, 23 years old, from Williamson County, Tennessee, to be executed. Union soldiers ordered the stores in Russellville closed and for the business owners to be present for the execution. At sundown, 12 soldiers from Captain Page's Company

275 Collins, *History of Kentucky*, 137; Jim Reis, "The Ugly Side of War," *The Kentucky Post*.

276 J. Winston Coleman, Jr., 47; James Head, *The Atonement of John Brooks*, (Florida: Heritage Press, 2001), 199.

277 Ibid.

E, 26th Kentucky Infantry fired six bullets into the body of Harvey Thomas.[278]

On July 30, 1864, Burbridge acted on information he had gathered on a secret conspiracy in Kentucky. He ordered the arrest of the leading members in Louisville, Kentucky, who belonged to the Sons of Liberty. Burbridge also ordered the arrest of Chief Justice for the State of Kentucky Joshua Bullitt. As the ferry between Jeffersonville, Indiana, and Louisville, Kentucky, prepared to leave the wharf, Federal agents arrested Bullitt. During the next two weeks, military authorities arrested Dr. Henry F. Kalfus, W.K. Thomas, Alfred Harris, G. S. G. Payne, Joseph R. Buchanan, Thomas Jeffries, J. J. Paul, John Hines, John Colgan, Henry Stickrod, Michael Carroll, William Fitzhenry, Erwin Bell, A. J. Brannon, Thomas Miller, A. J. Mitchell, John Rudd, Charles J. Clarke, B. C. Redford, John H. Talbott and W. G. Gray, who were residents of Jefferson County and Louisville, Kentucky. On July 28, 1864, Union spy, Felix Stidger, learned in Indianapolis that a day had been set for an armed uprising by the Sons of Liberty. Alarmed by the news Stidger met with Union General Henry Carrington, Governor Oliver Morton of Indiana, Governor Thomas Bramlette, Burbridge, and Colonel Fairleigh. Stidger told the assembly that 1,500 trained and well armed men were ready to attack Camp Morton at Indianapolis and free 6,000 Confederate prisoners. Nearby, he also reminded them that the state and Federal arsenals had enough arms to equip 6,000 men. In Kentucky, Stidger told the council that a band of members were waiting for the signal to set the whole city of Louisville afire. Seven regiments of seasoned Confederate soldiers were hiding their arms, waiting to assemble on the day of the uprising.[279]

On July 31, 1864, Judge Advocate General Joseph Holt gave his report to Secretary of War Stanton. Holt met with Governor Bramlette, General Burbridge, and General Hugh Ewing, Colonel Fairleigh, Major Sidell, and others connected with the civil and military administration. He also had interviews with various prominent and well instructed citizens upon the public affairs in the state. He reported that Kentucky was in a deplorable state. He wrote to Stanton that a very large part of the state was completely overrun with guerillas who plundered farm houses, and fields, and villages at will, and murdered helpless victims of their robberies. These thieves and murders moved in small bodies of from four or five to 20 men. They were mounted on the best horses and armed with weapons which they concealed in boots and under their clothes. They encountered no opposition. With the exception of a single guerilla, who was shot while trying to force his way into a store at Bardstown, Kentucky, the guerillas had met no resistance on the part of the citizens. The citizens feared a

278 Collins, *History of Kentucky*, 137; James Head, *The Atonement of John Brooks*, 200.
279 Robert McDowell, *City of Conflict*, 166-167.

greater calamity would fall upon them if they resisted, rather than submitting to the guerillas. They preferred giving up their horses, goods, and other portable valuables than to having their houses burned over their heads, and their lives sacrificed, which would occur if they tried to defend themselves. The guerilla bands were the fruit of Lincoln's amnesty proclamation. Burbridge wrote a letter to Holt expressing his opinion that nine-tenths of the guerillas infesting Kentucky had taken the oath under the amnesty proclamation.[280]

According to Holt, the Rebels do not regard any oath administered to them by Federal authority. He stated that the guerillas mocked the oaths, which they take only because "they can make them instrumental in advancing their personal interests and treasonable enterprises."[281] The rebels used the proclamation and the oath as a means of returning to Kentucky, visiting their friends, making observations on the Union military affairs, and then arming, mounting, and equipping themselves either for the Confederate service or for the career of robbers and cut throats. General Burbridge urged for the suspension of the proclamation in Kentucky and Holt supported Burbridge's recommendation. Holt stated that the existence of a conspiracy in Kentucky and the adjoining states for an armed cooperation with the Rebels furnished an additional and powerful reason why Burbridge's proposal to end the proclamation should be requested. In Holt's opinion, the government was too weak in Kentucky to justify the state to allow the build up of active treasonable elements, which was a result of the proclamation. He added that that recent orders from Burbridge in enforcing compensation from rebel sympathizers for the thefts and robberies of guerillas and directing the execution of guerilla prisoners in retaliation for murders committed by the guerilla bands, produced the "happiest effect in mitigating the committed atrocities."[282] According to Holt, a number of executions had already taken place and no murder by guerillas had occurred since the executions. He pointed out that the outlaws banded together in the same interests and were animated by the same spirit, and sought the accomplishment of the same guilty ends. "They are a brotherhood of traitors and felons, and the public safety demands that they should be held responsible for their crimes of each and all of their members."[283] Burbridge's executions had inspired a most "wholesome terror" and Holt hoped that the stern but necessary policy

280 O.R.--Series I--Volume XXXIX/2 [S# 78] Union Correspondence, Orders, and Returns Relating to Operations in Kentucky, Southwest Virginia, Tennessee, Mississippi, Alabama, and North Georgia (The Atlanta Campaign Excepted), from May 1, 1864, to September 30, 1864.(*)--#9, 215.

281 Ibid.

282 Ibid.

283 Ibid.

inaugurated by Burbridge would not be relaxed.[284]

According to Holt, the recruiting of black troops in Kentucky proceeded at a satisfactory rate. He reported that 10,000 blacks had already enlisted into the Union army and would double in 60 days. He reported that the black soldiers exhibited courage, loyalty, and zeal and were the "noblest and most cheering signs of the times."[285] Since the start of the recruitment of black troops in Kentucky those who supported slavery and treason carried out outrages on the black enlistees. According to Holt's sources, slaves escaping their masters with a view of entering the military service were beaten, maimed, and murdered, but the horrible conditions had changed under an improved public sentiment and from the vigor and success with which the government had continued to press the black enlistment policy. Holt stated that the feeble opposition to the recruitment of black troops in Kentucky was carried out by mainly unscrupulous politicians who hope to make out of this "popular irritation a certain amount of political capital to be invested in the approaching Presidential election."[286] Holt believed that the recruitment of black troops in Kentucky was a success.

Holt stated that after careful investigation, he revealed the existence of a treasonable association in Kentucky, with ramifications that extended throughout the states of Ohio, Illinois, and Indiana, and possibly Missouri. He claimed that the society was secretive, had passwords, ritual, and aims, through a cooperation with the Confederates, in striking at General Sherman's communications, or trying to overthrow the government. According to Holt, a large number of influential men in Kentucky, including the highest positions under the state government, were found to be members and officers in the association or conspiracy. General Burbridge proceeded to deal with the most prominent members of the conspiracy in Kentucky in a "manner demanded by the public peril and justified by the precedents of history."[287] He stated that the conspirators should not be allowed to operate in a state that had vast military operations. Holt stated that Burbridge had the complete support of the Federal government. He had faith that Burbridge would not only cut up the conspiracy in Kentucky by the roots, but would also make treason in Kentucky socially infamous. He also wrote that Burbridge's action would be a marked departure from the policy of conciliation. "Such an open abandonment of a policy that has faded after sacrifices of blood and treasure, would be hailed with universal satisfaction."[288]

On August 1, 1864, Burbridge wrote to General Sherman regarding what

284 Ibid.
285 Ibid.
286 Ibid.
287 Ibid.
288 Ibid.

he was to do with the men arrested as aiders or guerillas. He had a lot. He asked Sherman if the guerillas and aiders should be sent to South America or the Tortugas. He had already arrested members of the Sons of Liberty. He wrote that there was no reason to try them for their crimes. Burbridge suggested that he must imprison the guerillas or send them away. General Sherman wrote to Burbridge that in order to send the prisoners to the Dry Tortugas, he had to secure permission from the Secretary of War. Sherman assured Burbridge that he had his full consent and wanted Burbridge to thoroughly clear Kentucky of all suspicious men.[289]

On August 1, the election for sheriffs and some minor county or precinct officers took place in the 2nd District. Alvin Duvall was a candidate for re-election. Duvall had been on the bench since 1856 and had been chief justice. Because of Burbridge's order, Duvall's name had to be removed from the polls. Burbridge's order forced Duvall to flee the state and avoid arrest. He received a large vote in three counties which did not receive Burbridge's order. The Unconditional Union Party thought that the path had been cleared for their candidate Mortimer M. Benton to win the election in the 2nd District, since Duvall was out of the way. The Democrats nominated Judge George Robertson, a former chief justice, as a candidate and telegraphed his name to all the polling booths on the morning of the election. Before Burbridge learned that Robertson had been added to the polls and could issue another order to remove Robertson's name, military authorities allowed Robertson's name to appear on the ballots. Robertson won the election. During the election only 11,000 votes were cast from a possible 45,000, which indicated that the army had completely demoralized and intimidated the citizens of the 2nd District.[290]

For the first time, Governor Bramlette broke rank with General Burbridge and asked if the sheriffs and officers received any order from any military commander requesting them to exclude from the poll books any candidate's name and if they did, they were to send him the order. If they obeyed the order, they were to supply the name of the candidate who benefited from order. He also asked how many votes the excluded candidate would have received. He also asked if the judges were overawed by the presence or menacing actions of soldiers who interfered with the free and equal election.[291]

On August 6, Burbridge wrote to Secretary of War Stanton informing him

289 O.R.--Series I--Volume XXXIX/2 [S# 78] Union Correspondence, Orders, and Returns Relating to Operations in Kentucky, Southwest Virginia, Tennessee, Mississippi, Alabama, and North Georgia (The Atlanta Campaign Excepted), from May 1, 1864, to September 30, 1864.(*)--#9, 217.

290 Collins, *History of Kentucky*, 137-138; E. Merton Coulter, *The Civil War and Readjustment in Kentucky*, (Chapel Hill: University of North Carolina Press, 1921), 184.

291 Collins, *History of Kentucky*, 137-138.

that he arrested leading members of the Sons of Liberty in Kentucky and had the names of leading members in Indiana and Illinois. He suggested that Union General Samuel Heintzelman be ordered to arrest these men in Indiana and Illinois. He also suggested that the prisoners at Rock Island and Indianapolis be removed to a safe point farther north, since a danger existed that the prisoners might be released by armed traitors.[292] The next day, Secretary of War Stanton wrote to Burbridge that his actions against the disloyal persons in his command were approved. He also authorized Burbridge to establish his headquarters in Louisville. He could re-enlist for general service for one year all the cavalry he could mount. General Ulysses S. Grant suggested that the new organizations, white and black, should be enlisted as infantry, and mounted. His mode of mounting cavalry by seizing horses from disloyal citizens was approved, and he authorized him to seize all he could lay his hands on. He also placed the State of Kentucky under his order.

On August 10, 1864, the *Louisville Democrat* reported that "a large number of political prisoners are confined in the military barracks here, and the number is being increased daily by the arrival of prisoners arrested in other portions of the state."

With the arrests of Judge Bullitt and many prominent Louisville citizens, Governor Bramlette felt the heat and tried to convince Burbridge to release the Sons of Liberty conspirators. On August 12, Governor Bramlette wrote to Burbridge that he was satisfied that some of the men who were urging him to make arrests and would have had them made to the greatest extremes are now turned against him, and seeking popularity by denouncing Burbridge's arrests. The governor told Burbridge that if he were in his place, he would release upon bond all those arrested unless in Indiana and Ohio and the leaders of the conspiracy who were arrested. The governor stated that in his interview with Burbridge, Burbridge said that they were in no danger from the Sons of Liberty in Kentucky. The chief danger came from those states north of the Ohio. Bramlette stated that the arrests placed Burbridge in a false position, since he only arrested men in Kentucky and allowed the conspirators to go untouched in other states where they were more extensively and dangerously organized. Bramlette stated that men north of the river who were seeking to make for themselves political capital at Burbridge's expense and to the endangerment of their own quiet was, in the Governor's opinion, "iniquitous." Bramlette

292 O.R.--Series I--Volume XXXIX/2 [S# 78], Union Correspondence, Orders, and Returns Relating to Operations in Kentucky, Southwest Virginia, Tennessee, Mississippi, Alabama, and North Georgia (The Atlanta Campaign Excepted), from May 1, 1864, to September 30, 1864.(*)--#10, Letter from General Stephen Burbridge to Secretary of War Edwin Stanton, August 6, 1864, 228.

stated that those men "would crush you and your people for their own political aggrandizement."[293]

Bramlette wrote to Burbridge that, "By letting these men off upon bond for their good behavior and legal conduct, it will let you off without any serious effect anyway and will leave the responsibility upon those who urged forward the movement. If the authorities in Ohio and Indiana fail or refuse to act, it will raise a clamor against you in Kentucky – men will naturally ask why deal with Kentucky more harshly then with other States, especially as in the other states the conspirators are far more dangerous? I make these suggestions for your serious consideration as your friend."[294]

On August 11, 1864 Burbridge wrote to General Sherman stating that Kentucky had 3,000 head of cattle, which in the event of invasion would probably fall into Confederate hands. He suggested to Sherman that his commissary department purchase all the cattle he could and send them to the front, saving transportation from the north, and putting them "where the enemy can derive no benefit from them." Sherman wrote to Burbridge that if 3,000 cattle were not safe in Kentucky, they would hardly be safe on the road to the front. Sherman wrote that the owners of the cattle should drive them to a place of safety.[295]

On that same day, General Sherman wrote to Union General Leslie Combs, in Frankfort, Kentucky, defending Burbridge's actions. Sherman stated that he did not wish to harm any inoffensive person in the world. In ordinary times, Sherman would like to see the lives and property, the liberties and rights, political and religious, protected and insured, but the country had fallen on troublesome times. He stated that there were people in Kentucky who were "utterly callous and forgetful of the rights of others, and who will on all occasions thrust their offensive opinions and acts upon the rest of the community. Not content with sending their sons and all they could influence into a hostile army, they continue to reside in Kentucky and by secret acts and letters keep alive the spirit of hostility, keeping up an uncertain, feverish state of things, actually

---

293 Letter from Governor Thomas Bramlette to General S. G. Burbridge, August 12, 1864, Stephen Gano Burbridge Letter 1862-1865, University of Kentucky Special Collections and Digital Programs, Lexington, Kentucky.

294 Ibid.

295 Major General William T. Sherman to Major General Stephen G. Burbridge, August 11, 1864, Lexington, Kentucky, O.R.--Series I--Volume XXXIX/2 [S# 78]Union Correspondence, Orders, and Returns Relating to Operations in Kentucky, Southwest Virginia, Tennessee, Mississippi, Alabama, and North Georgia (The Atlanta Campaign Excepted), from May 1, 1864, to September 30, 1864.(*)--#10, 239.

more hurtful to the peace of the state than if they were openly hostile."[296] He wrote to General Combs that he could not believe General Burbridge would commit acts of wanton cruelty that General Combs described to General Sherman. Nor could Sherman believe that General Combs asked him to leave the field and give the state of Kentucky his personal attention, nor should he give orders based upon General Combs' simple assertions. Sherman sent General Combs' letter to General Burbridge so he could undo an act of injustice if committed on false information. Sherman was aware that military power, when unchecked, may do grievous wrongs, but Sherman posed the question to General Combs on how it was to be avoided? He asked General Combs whether the military should trust the grand juries in rebellion. Sherman agreed with Combs that Kentucky had inexplicable families and state factions, that the "veriest murdered, and horse-thief, and dirty dog, if arrested can forthwith produce credentials of respectability."[297] Sherman stated that respectable families in Lexington and Frankfort, blind to interests of the industrious classes of the state, had and continued to encourage the public enemy in every way. He hoped that General Burbridge would send to the Dry Tortugas, or Brazil, every one of these men, women, and children, and encourage a new breed. He hoped Burbridge would not do a single act of injustice, but "he is human and not infallible. No act will be done which cannot be recalled. Still for the time being, they must go away."[298] Sherman hoped that the blow would fall on no friend of General Combs, but should Burbridge arrest one of his men, Sherman pledged his honor when the South ceases the war, Sherman would be open to mercy and a restoration to home and peace and happiness to anyone who lost them because of his acts.[299]

On August 12, 1864, Burbridge's Order Number 59 continued to be carried out. Union soldiers took four guerillas from Eminence, Kentucky, to some point in the adjoining county to be shot.[300]

During the months of July and August, Burbridge set out to build more fortifications in Kentucky. As Sherman marched through Georgia, Kentucky no longer faced the threat from a Confederate army, but Burbridge felt the need to build earth works. Burbridge received permission from Union General John Schofield to build fortifications in Mount Sterling, Lexington, Frankfort,

---

296 Major General William T. Sherman to General Leslie Combs, August 11, 1864, in the field near Atlanta, Ga. O.R.--Series I--Volume XXXIX/2 [S# 78] Union Correspondence, Orders, and Returns Relating to Operations in Kentucky, Southwest Virginia, Tennessee, Mississippi, Alabama, and North Georgia (The Atlanta Campaign Excepted), from May 1, 1864, to September 30, 1864.(*)--#10, 240.

297 Ibid.

298 Ibid.

299 Ibid.

300 Collins, *History of Kentucky*, 138.

and Louisville. The plans furnished for each location to have a small enclosed field work of about 200 yards along the interior crest, with the exception of Louisville, which would be 500 yards. Other earthworks would follow in Louisville as opportunity and the means available would allow. All the works were to be built by soldiers, except at Frankfort, where the works were performed by the state and at Louisville by the city. Lt. Colonel. J. H. Simpson, of the Federal Engineers, furnished the plans and engineering force. Lt. Colonel Simpson also rebuilt the stockade defending the bridges on the Kentucky Central Railroad, burned by Morgan's force in his June 1864 raid, with two stockades being built at each location including Keller's bridge, Kimbrough's bridge, and Townsend's Bridge.[301]

On that same day, General Burbridge issued Order Number 63 which stopped all shipments of produce or goods of any kind, either in or though or into the state, except those who carried a special permit, issued for four months, to persons whom Burbridge thought to have "well known loyalty." A board of five advisers established the loyalty of those who applied. After receiving their permit they would have to swear an oath that they would not give aid or comfort to the rebellion and through conversation and action, they would do all they could to discourage, discountenance, and overthrow the rebellion and help to restore the authority of the U.S. government over those states in rebellion. Those who transported goods without the permit would be arrested and imprisoned and the goods seized and the owner's names reported to General Burbridge for further orders.[302]

On August 14, 1864, Sherman again defended Burbridge's actions. Sherman wrote to James Guthrie, president of the Louisville and Nashville Railroad, that he regretted the arrest of many citizens in Kentucky and still more that they gave cause for their arrest. Sherman could not personally look into the arrests, but had to leave them to Burbridge. Sherman stated that when the national integrity was threatened and the very fundamental principles of all government endangered, minor issues should not be made by Judge Joshua Bullitt and others. Sherman stated that citizens should waive and abate their private notions of right and policy to those who were duly appointed as agents of the government, certain that if they were in error the time would reveal the real principles. Sherman noticed that in Kentucky, the people had a disposition to cry against the tyranny and oppression of the Union government. He wrote

301 O.R.--Series I--Volume XXXIX/2 [S# 78] Union Correspondence, Orders, and Returns Relating to Operations in Kentucky, Southwest Virginia, Tennessee, Mississippi, Alabama, and North Georgia (The Atlanta Campaign Excepted), from May 1, 1864, to September 30, 1864.(*)--#10, 244-245.

302 Collins, *History of Kentucky*, 138.

to Guthrie that if it were not for the war, tyranny would not exist in the government. Any acts of tyranny were the result of war, and he stated that the Rebels had made the war. Sherman stated that the citizens forgot the strong facts of the beginning of the war. Long before the North or the Federal government dreamed of war, the South seized the arsenals, forts, mints, and custom houses, and made prisoners of war the garrisons sent to protect them against Indians, Mexicans, and blacks. He also reminded Guthrie as to who burned his bridges, or forced Union men to give up their slaves to work on the Rebel forts at Bowling Green, Kentucky. He also reminded Guthrie who burned their houses when they differed with the Confederate's opinion. When Sherman did not allow his men to burn fence rails for fire or gather fruit or vegetables even though his men were hungry, the Confederates seized them as their property. He stated that his men restrained themselves to protect property and law. According to Sherman, the Rebels first introduced terror as a part of their system and forced contributions to diminish their wagon trains and increase the mobility and efficiency of their columns. During the Kentucky Campaign, in 1862, when Union General Don Carlos Buell moved slowly with his vast wagon trains, Confederate General Braxton Bragg moved swiftly, living off the land. Sherman claimed that the Union army was forced in self defense to imitate the Confederates example. Sherman stated that the Union army must be governed by law. He stated that the Confederates dared the Union army into war. The Union army accepted and must fight the war to its end. "War is the remedy our enemies have chosen. . . . They wanted war, and I say let us give them all they want, not a word of argument, not a sign of let up, no cave in till we are whipped or they are."[303] According to Sherman, the side issues of blacks, states rights, conciliation, outrages, cruelty, barbarity, bankruptcy, subjugation were, in his opinion, idle and nonsensical.[304]

Sherman wished Guthrie well in Kentucky. He wanted to push the main Rebel army far from Kentucky and root out the other class, who, under the plea of being soldiers, were regarded by the Union army as "common vagabonds and thieves."[305] He stated that Confederate General Joseph Johnston would not sanction "such dogs as call themselves guerillas in Kentucky, nor would Lee or Bragg, or any other man who thinks he is fighting to establish a new and independent government better suited to their interests and honor."[306]

303 Major General William T. Sherman to James Guthrie, August 14, 1864, O.R.--Series I--Volume XXXIX/2 [S# 78] Union Correspondence, Orders, and Returns Relating to Operations in Kentucky, Southwest Virginia, Tennessee, Mississippi, Alabama, and North Georgia (The Atlanta Campaign Excepted), from May 1, 1864, to September 30, 1864.(*)--#10, 249.

304 Ibid.

305 Ibid.

306 Ibid.

Sherman stated that he would sustain General Burbridge if satisfied that he was not influenced by mere personal motives and nothing in Sherman's opinion had occurred to suggest anything of the kind. Sherman suggested that Judge Joshua Bullitt and the rest of his Sons of Liberty must spend time abroad and reflect on the great theory of self-government. He would like Governor Bramlette and the real "thinking men of Kentucky"[307] to know the kindly feelings Sherman entertained toward them, and how he wished to insure tranquility and peace.[308]

As August came to a close, guerrilla warfare continued unabated in Kentucky. On August 15, 1864, Confederate General Adam Rankin Johnson led a raid into the state. He seized three steamers, crossed near Shawneetown, Illinois, with 1,500 men. On that same day, Union General E. A. Paine, of Paducah, reported that guerillas took 275 cattle from a boat at Caseyville. Guerillas fired into the boats and killed one man. Several days later on August 20, Union Captain E. H. Samuels from Covington, Kentucky, reported guerillas committing depredations in Covington and Campbell, including stealing horses from Union men.

On August 15, Burbridge ordered George W. Wainscott, William Lingen felter, and John W. Lingenfelter executed at Williamstown, Grant County, in retaliation for the murder by guerillas of Joel Skirvin and Andrew Simpson. All three men were members of Company E, 3rd Battalion, Mounted Rifles. A company of the 30th Kentucky Infantry, under Colonel Alexander shot the men. Burbridge also ordered Richmond Berry and May Hamilton to be taken to Bloomfield, Nelson County, to be executed for the killing of J. R. Jones. Berry had been a member in Colonel Hollis's regiment and Hamilton had been a member of Company G, 7th Confederate Cavalry Battalion. Both men were shot by a squad of the 8th Kentucky Cavalry, under Colonel Bristow.[309]

On August 20, 1864, Brigadier General Hugh Ewing ordered the post commander in Louisville to select four guerillas and send them to Franklin, Kentucky, to be publicly shot for the murder of Union men. Union soldiers only took three men to Franklin. Union soldiers shot J. Bloom and W. B. McGlassin for the death of Mr. Harvey Travelated, a Union citizen of Simpson County, Kentucky, who was shot and killed by "the notorious scoundrel Harper."[310]

At the Democratic Convention in Chicago, representatives at the conventions read spirited letters from two Kentucky delegates, John W. Leathers from Covington and Dr. Joseph R. Buchanan. They could not attend because both candidates had been arrested and confined as political prisoners at Louisville.

307 Ibid.
308 Ibid.
309 Collins, 138; James Head, *The Atonement of John Brooks*, 200.
310 James Head, *The Atonement of John Brooks*, 200-201.

Former Governor Charles Wickliffe of Kentucky read in his speech that "many of the best and most loyal citizens of Kentucky–among them twenty or thirty ladies–are now imprisoned by the military in Louisville, in damp and dirty cells, with only straw to lie upon, and the coarsest fare; and the newspapers of Louisville are forbidden to make the slightest allusion to this terrible state of affairs. I proclaim it here and now–at the risk of my liberty, perhaps my life."[311] Dr. E.O. Brown, surgeon in charge, denied Wickliffe's allegations and stated that the female prisoners are not confined in "damp, dark, and filthy cells," but good dwelling houses, which were well ventilated and dry.[312]

On September 2, 1864 Burbridge heard about the murder of Mr. David Henry of Meade County, Kentucky. He ordered Union Lieutenant Colonel Fairleigh, Post Commander at Louisville, to select four guerillas from Thomas Dupoyster's men and send them to Brandenburg to be publicly shot in retaliation for the murder of David Henry. Union Lieutenant Colonel Fairleigh took John Brooks of Jackson, Mississippi, Robert Blinco of Hawesville, Frank Holmes of Cloverport, and Julius Bradis of Louisville, to Brandenburg. All the prisoners were regular Confederate soldiers. Brandis stated he was a soldier from Company L, 2nd Kentucky Cavalry. Confederate Captain Rolla sought recruits for his command and enlisted Frank Holmes into his small band of 25 men. Lieutenant John Brooks belonged to the 8th Kentucky Infantry, Company A, then the 10th Kentucky Partisan Rangers, Company C and later made Captain in the 16th Kentucky Cavalry in August of 1864. The prisoners were unlucky to draw black beans from a box containing hundreds of white beans.[313]

A resident of Meade County, David Henry was an ardent Union supporter and prominent farmer. A guerilla leader known only as Captain Bryant and seven of his men arrived at Henry's home in late August of 1864 and demanded to be fed dinner and feed their horses. As they rode away, Henry shot at the guerillas and shouted for a Union lieutenant to flank the guerillas from the rear. Bryant and his men thought that the Yankee cavalry was hot on their trail and headed for safety. Captain Bryant realized he had been tricked. There were no Union cavalry in the area, and he swore revenge upon Henry. On August 28, 1864, Captain John Bryant and 35 men surrounded Henry's house and demanded that he come out of his house. Henry, who hid upstairs, heard

311 Collins, *History of Kentucky*, 139.

312 Ibid.

313 Marshal Myers, Dr. "Civil War Incidents in and around Meade County, Kentucky, The Terror of the Black Flag: Guerilla Warfare in Meade County." 2003, published by Jane Marlow Willis Wordsmith, Brandenburg, Kentucky; *Louisville Daily Journal*, September 6, 1864, "Execution of Guerillas in Meade County"; James Head, *The Atonement of John Brooks*, (Florida: Heritage Press, 2001), 2.

his daughter pleading with the guerillas to spare her father's life. After awhile, Henry decided to head downstairs, while Bryant waited on the back porch. When Henry came within range of Bryant's pistol, he fired and killed Henry. When the prisoners arrived at Brandenburg, Lieutenant John Enoch of the 54th Ohio Infantry took charge of the prisoners and escorted them to the Henry farm. George Prentice, editor of the *Louisville Journal*, described the four young unmarried men as having received "many advantages in younger days."[314] The pastor of the Brandenburg Baptist Church, George H. Hicks accompanied the four men to the Henry farm. At 2:00 p.m., September 4, 1864, the four men knelt and thanked their captors for their gentle kindness. Twenty Union soldiers were divided into four squads with five men each, with each squad having a gun loaded with a blank. Each prisoner folded his hands across his chest and kept his eyes closed. As the shots rang out, each man fell to the ground without a groan.[315] Four more men lost their lives to Order Number 59. After the execution, the bodies were placed in a wagon and taken back to Brandenburg. The citizens volunteered to take care of the bodies and preserve them for the friends of the deceased. Lieutenant Enoch accepted their offer and took his men aboard a steamer and headed back for Louisville.[316] One of the sad aspects of the story of these men is that Burbridge did not have to execute these men. On September 1, Captain Dupoyster's men rode into Meade County. They first robbed a general mercantile store of about $1,000 and then hit Mr. Trent's store taking money and goods. Later that day, Duyposter's men attacked the residence of Mr. Calvin Murry. After robbing several other homes they arrived at Joe Coonas' residence. Captain Bryant approached Mr. Coonas, but when Mr. Coonas saw Bryant wearing a rebel flag on his hat band, he opened fire. A hale of gunfire erupted between the men and when the smoke cleared, Captain Bryant lay dying on floor. He died two hours later. On September 16, 1864, the *Louisville Daily Journal* reported that a guerilla named Hedge killed Captain Dupoyster in the streets of Taylorsville, Spencer County, Kentucky.[317]

By September 11, 1864, Burbridge reported to Union Major General Schofield that Confederate guerrillas under Confederate General Adam Rankin Johnson and Colonel George M. Jessee had been routed and dispersed. He reported Kentucky quiet. He proposed a raid against the salt works in southwestern Virginia and hoped that General Schofield would direct the forces in east Tennessee to cooperate with his raid. Union Brigadier General Alvan Gillem reported to Burbridge that the Confederates could not concentrate 2,500

314 "Execution of Guerillas in Meade County." *Louisville Daily Journal*, Sept. 6, 1864.

315 Ibid.

316 Ibid.

317 James Head, *The Atonement of John Brooks*, 152-153.

men in southwest Virginia and east Tennessee combined. The principal part of the Confederate force was at Jonesboro, Tennessee. Confederate General John Hunt Morgan concentrated all his available force at Greenville, where General Gillem surprised and defeated Morgan on September 4, 1864. He reported that Morgan's men were discouraged. He also reported that there were only 200 men at the salt works. He wrote to Burbridge that the loss of the works "would be a terrible blow to the rebellion."

On September 13, Burbridge began his move against the Home Guard of Kentucky, which would eventually bring the demise of General Burbridge's career. The Kentucky Home Guard was Governor Bramlette's pet project and he was not going to let General Burbridge interfere with his troops, but Burbridge went ahead and issued Order Number 3, in which he stated that he was pained to hear that in various portions of his command, squads of Federal soldiers and companies of men calling themselves State Guards, Home Guards, or Independent Companies were roving around the country committing outrages on citizens, seizing their horses and property without authority, insulting and mistreating them. He expected such behavior from guerillas, but not from men armed in the Union cause. He issued the order that all property seized or taken without authority by any persons whatsoever for military purposes would be restored to the owners and no property of any kind would be seized or taken from peaceable, law abiding citizens of his command without authority in writing from his headquarters or from some one of the division or brigade commanders, except when absolutely necessary in the actual and immediate pursuit of the enemy, or where provisions and forage were needed and it was impossible to obtain them in the regular way. In all such cases, the property, other than provisions and forage, was to be returned to the owners. The officers of his command were directed to strictly and vigorously enforce his order, and should any companies fail or refuse to obey it, the nearest officer of his command would, in case of Home Guards, or Independent Companies, disarm, disband the men, seize the property they have taken illegally, restore it to their owners, arrest the officers, and send them to the nearest brigade commander, with a statement of the facts and circumstances. Should the offenders be regularly organized under the laws of Kentucky as "State Guards" the facts would be reported to the Governor.[318]

On September 13, 1864, Captain J. Bates Dickson, Burbridge's assistant,

318 General Order Number 3, Major General Stephen G. Burbridge, Headquarters Lexington, Kentucky, September 11, 1864, O.R.--Series I--Volume XXXIX/2 [S# 78] Union Correspondence, Orders, and Returns Relating to Operations in Kentucky, Southwest Virginia, Tennessee, Mississippi, Alabama, and North Georgia (The Atlanta Campaign Excepted), from May 1, 1864, to September 30, 1864.(*)--#16, 375.

ordered General McLean to send William Deal, alias William Master, and John Lancaster to Colonel Mims, in Louisa, Kentucky, to be publicly shot for the murder of a Union citizen. Master, whose real name was William LaMaster was a member of Company L, 14th Kentucky Cavalry. LaMaster escaped the execution.[319]

As September came to an end, General Burbridge continued to be supported by General Sherman and the radicals in the state. So far, he had pleased his superiors. On September 24, 1864, Dr. Robert Breckinridge made a speech in Lexington supporting Burbridge's executions and unwarranted arrests. He told the crowd, "as to these [illegal and unwarranted military executions], all the fault I have to find is, that more should not have been arrested than were; and many of those that were arrested were set at liberty too soon. . . . When Simon de Monfort was slaughtering the Protestants in the south of France he was appealed to by certain persons-declaring that his men were mistaken, that they were killing many who were good Catholics. To which he replied, "Kill them all; God knows his own." And this is the way we should deal with these fellows; treat them all alike; and if there are any among them who are not rebel at heart, God will take care of them and save them at least."[320] The radicals in the state still supported his efforts, but a division was slowly forming between Burbridge and Governor Bramlette over election manipulation and the Home Guard. Guerrilla warfare continued to wreak havoc in the state. To restore some glory to his career, Burbridge decided to attack the salt works in southwest Virginia. The President, the Secretary of War, General Sherman all showered praise on Burbridge when he defeated General Morgan's forces. If he destroyed the salt works in Virginia, maybe he could restore his glory and his problems with guerrilla warfare and the Kentuckians distaste for his recruitment of black regiments would go away. If he took his black regiments into combat and they won glory, maybe Burbridge hoped that the people of Kentucky would see how black men could be used to fight alongside white men. Unfortunately, Burbridge's plans to destroy the salt works would not go as he planned and his goals for glory would elude him. When he returned to Kentucky after his raid, his problems still faced him.

319 James Head, *The Atonement of John Brooks*, 202.
320 *Military History of Kentucky*, 220.

Chapter 8

The Saltville Massacre

By the end of September 1864, General Burbridge decided to make another raid into southwest Virginia and destroy the salt works. Burbridge had high hopes for his raid. He hoped that it would strike a major blow against the Confederacy. He also hoped to impress his superiors by taking his black regiments into battle. Secretary of War Edwin Stanton gave permission for Burbridge to equip himself with horses from disloyal citizens of Kentucky and he supplied Burbridge with equipment for the horses. Burbridge had a lot riding on the success of his raid.

By September 17, 1864, Union General Alvan Gillem reported to Burbridge that he was ready to move out. He reported that the Confederates were demoralized. The salt works were at the mercy of the Union forces. His destruction of the salt works and the Virginia Railroad would relieve east Tennessee and east Kentucky from Confederate raids. Three days later, Union General John Schofield wrote to Union Major General William T. Sherman that he had consulted with General Burbridge and decided to let Burbridge make his expedition into southwestern Virginia and arranged with General Jacob Ammen and General Gillem to cooperate with Burbridge. Burbridge hoped a military success would offset, in his superiors' minds, civilian grumblings about his highhandedness and ineptitude.[321] Burbridge would take three old regiments and the remainder of the twelve month's Kentucky troops. One of the regiments that Burbridge would take with him was the 5th United States Colored Cavalry. Union Colonel James Brisbin was commander of the 5th USCC. Captain Thomas Bunch of the 5th USCC confiscated slaves for the regiment and accepted bribes from their owners for their return. Bunch threatened many slave owners with violence if they failed to accept his terms of $100. He gave enlistment papers to the slave owners and kept the slaves for the regiment. Unfortunately, many of the black soldiers who rode with Burbridge on his expedition were unorganized, given untrained horses, and Enfield rifles instead

321 Michael Jennings, "The Lost Regiment," *Louisville Courier-Journal*, February 15, 1996.

of carbines.[322] When the 5th USCC arrived in Prestonburg to join Burbridge's command, they did not receive a friendly welcome. Colonel Brisbin reported that while they were on the march, "the colored soldiers, as well as their white officers, were made the subject of much ridicule and many insulting remarks by the white troops, and in some instances petty outrages, such as the pulling off the caps of colored soldiers, stealing their horses, etc."[323] He also reported that the black cavalrymen made no response to white soldiers' taunts.

Burbridge rode out with three separate columns. Union General Nathaniel McLean's Kentucky Division rode directly toward the salt works, while Union General Jacob Ammen's 800 men rode to Bull's Gap, Tennessee, and General Alvan C. Gillem advanced on Jonesboro, Tennessee, with 1,650 men. Ammen and Gillem would join Burbridge for the raid on Saltville.[324] Saltville was the Confederacy's most important salt works. Located along the north fork of the Holston River in Smyth County, Virginia, the salt mines were essential to the preservation of meat for the southern armies.[325]

On September 29, 1864, General William T. Sherman wrote to General Ammen, commander of the East Tennessee District, that he needed to send a message to Burbridge. Sherman wanted to recall Burbridge's forces and report to Nashville or the nearest point on the Louisville and Nashville Railroad. Sherman wanted Burbridge to move against Confederate General Nathan Bedford Forrest in middle Tennessee. Unfortunately, Sherman's order would come too late. Burbridge was already on his way to the salt works.[326]

On that same day, on September 29, 1864, General Burbridge forced the Confederates, under Confederate Colonel Henry Giltner's Kentucky Cavalry Brigade, consisting of the 4th Kentucky Cavalry, 10th Kentucky Cavalry, 10th Kentucky Mounted Rifles, 64th Virginia Mounted Infantry and two unattached companies, from Clinch Mountain and Laurel Gap. On October 1, 1864, Burbridge pushed the Confederates three and a half miles from Saltville. Colonel Giltner and the local militia occupied the town. Instead of attacking, Burbridge made a major flaw and camped for the night.

---

322 Thomas Mays, *The Saltville Massacre* (McWhiney Foundation Press, Abilene, Texas, 1998), 26.

323 Michael Jennings, "The Lost Regiment," *Louisville Courier-Journal*, February 15, 1996.

324 Mays, *The Saltville Massacre*, 30.

325 Michael Jennings, "The Lost Regiment," *Louisville Courier-Journal*, February 15, 1996.

326 O.R. Series I, Vol. XXXIX/2 [#79] Confederate Correspondence, Orders, Returns relating to operations in Kentucky, Southwest Virginia, Tennessee, Mississippi, Alabama, and North Georgia (The Atlanta campaign excepted) from October 1, 1864 to November 13, 1864, General William T. Sherman to Brig. Gen. Ammen, Sept. 29, 1864, 524.

The next day, Confederate General John Echols managed to pull together 2,800 men to face Burbridge's 4,500 men. Confederate General John Williams took personal command of the defense of Saltville. Williams strongly entrenched the Confederate troops on the bluffs, under the command of General Echols and Vaughn. Burbridge used only a portion of his command and attacked the Confederates with only 2,500 men and drove Giltner's brigade back to the main Confederate line. Giltner passed through Colonel Robert Smith's 13th Battalion of Virginia Reserves. Burbridge attacked Smith's position. Two thousand Federals charged and overran Smith's men. Smith fell back to the main Confederate line.

Burbridge attacked the Confederate right along Chestnut Ridge. Confederate General Felix Robertson and George Dibrell's small brigades faced the 5th USCC and two white regiments. After two unsuccessful attacks upon Chestnut Ridge, Union Colonel Robert Ratliff's brigade prepared for a final charge. The 5th USCC and the 12th Ohio Cavalry and the 11th Michigan cavalry dismounted. The 5th USCC assembled on the Federal left. Ratliff's brigade advanced toward Chestnut Ridge. Confederate sentinels heard a Union officer urging the black soldiers to fight well and telling them the destruction of the salt works would be worth more than the capture of Richmond: the Confederate capital.[327] The Federals advanced under heavy fire through briars and scrub brush which slowed down the Federal advance. According to Confederate Colonel George Dibrell, commander of the Tennessee brigade, the black soldiers had been placed in front of the white regiments and "driven through the briars."[328] When the Confederates saw black troops advancing toward their works, they became enraged at the sight, left their breastworks, and charged. The fighting went on for three hours, with Dibrell's and Robertson's men concentrating their fire on the black troops. The Confederates were driven back to a line of ditches atop the ridge. The Confederates abandoned the ridge and retreated to a new line in front of the town. The Federals found a gap between Confederate Robertson's brigade on the left and some reserves on the right. Robertson withdrew and left Dibrell surrounded and a large gap opened up on the Confederate center. The Rebels fired grape shot and canister at the oncoming black troops, but the 5th USCC kept advancing and took the Confederate works.[329]

The next Federal attack came on the Confederate center. The Federals

---

327 Michael Jennings, "The Lost Regiment," *Louisville Courier-Journal*, February 15, 1996.

328 Ibid.

329 Thomas Mays, *The Saltville Massacre* (McWhiney Foundation Press, Abilene, Texas, 1998), 51.; Michael Jennings, "The Lost Regiment," *Louisville Courier-Journal*, February 15, 1996.

drove Colonel Giltner from the ford as he attempted to form his brigade. The Confederates fell back and tried to hold their line in a clearing in front of a log church. The Confederates advanced to within 50 feet of the Federal line and fired a volley, and then fell back to the church. Colonel Trimble of the 10th Kentucky Cavalry was killed and his men fell back to the safety of the Confederate batteries.

The two Federal assaults came to a halt. Colonel Charles Hanson's 37th Kentucky Cavalry dismounted and marched to Little Mountain. Hanson planned to take the Confederate left flank. The final Federal assault under Colonel Hanson failed and cost Burbridge 100 casualties, including Colonel Hanson, who was severely wounded.[330]

The Confederate lines held off the remaining Federal assaults, and at 5:00 p.m. Burbridge decided to retreat. Ratliff's Cavalry, including the 5th USCC, held the Confederate works until dark. Burbridge left most of his dead and wounded on the battlefield, including the men of the 5th USCC.

As Burbridge withdrew, Confederate General John C. Breckinridge arrived with John Echols. Other Confederate reinforcements arrived, including the cavalry brigades under General Basil Duke, George Cosby and John Vaughn. The Confederates won the battle and managed to save the salt works.

According to Burbridge, he "whipped" the Confederates at every point and forced them back to their main works. According to Burbridge, the occupation of the works was prevented only by the lack of ammunition. He estimated the Confederates at 6,000 to 8,000 and General Breckinridge was reinforced with 4,000 from Lynchburg. General Gillem did not participate in the battle, because his men had been recalled to protect Sherman's supply lines around Atlanta, although Burbridge did not know Gillem had been recalled. Burbridge estimated his loss at 350 men. On October 3, 1864, General Burbridge received his orders from General Sherman to return to Kentucky.[331]

After the battle, the black wounded soldiers found themselves facing enraged Confederate soldiers. One of the worst atrocities of the war would occur the day after the Battle of Saltville. On October 3, 1864, Confederate General Felix Robertson told Guerrant that he had killed all the black soldiers. Robertson and his command saw no reason to take any black prisoners. Confederate trooper Private George Mosgrove of the 4th Kentucky Cavalry awoke at dawn amid dense fog. He wrote in a post-war memoir: "Presently I heard a shot,

330 Mays, 52.

331 O.R. Series I, Vol. XXXIX/1 [#77] Sept. 20-Oct. 17, 1864-Raids from Kentucky and East Tennessee into Southwestern Virginia. No. 1 Reports of Bvt. Gen. Stephen G. Burbridge, U.S. Army, commanding District of Kentucky.

then another and another until the firing swelled to the volume of that of a skirmish line."[332] He mounted his horse and arrived in front of Dibrell's and Robertson's brigades on Chestnut Ridge and found the Tennessee soldiers killing black soldiers. Mosgrove wrote that the Tennesseans were "mad and excited to the highest degree. They were shooting every wounded negro they could find. . . . It was horrible, most horrible."[333] When the black Union soldiers tried to run, the Confederates shot them down. Mosgrove wrote: "It was bang, bang, bang, all over the field-negroes dropping everywhere."[334] Confederate Captain Edwin Guerrant noted in his diary that his men took no black prisoners. Private Harry Shocker, a wounded Union soldier from the 12th Ohio Cavalry, watched as Confederate guerilla Champ Ferguson walked around the battlefield killing white Union prisoners along with the black Union soldiers. Shocker crawled off and hid just in time as he watched as Ferguson killed Union soldier Crawford Hazelwood. Shocker witnessed Ferguson kill four black soldiers at a cabin on Sander's house. Many of the wounded soldiers from Ratliff's command had been placed in the house. Mosgrove found seven or eight wounded black soldiers in a cabin. He saw a boy around sixteen with a pistol in each hand shooting every black prisoner in the room. Captain Orange Sells of the 12th Ohio Cavalry was in the cabin at the time and witnessed the murders. Lieutenant George W. Carter of the 11th Michigan Cavalry witnessed eight or nine blacks murdered.[335]

Champ Ferguson

When General Breckinridge saw the Confederate soldiers killing black Union soldiers he became enraged and ordered the massacre to stop, but as soon as he rode away the killing continued. None of the other Confederate generals did anything to stop the killing. Breckinridge's aide, James B. Clay, Jr., grandson of the Great Compromiser Henry Clay, wrote to his mother that "it

332 Michael Jennings, "The Lost Regiment," *Louisville Courier-Journal*, February 15, 1996.

333 Ibid.

334 Ibid.

335 Thomas Mays, *The Saltville Massacre* (McWhiney Foundation Press, Abilene, Texas, 1998), 55-60.

was a great pleasure. . . to go over the field & see so many. . . of the African descent lying mangled and bleeding on the hills around our salt works."[336]

But the killing did not stop at the battlefield. Surgeon William Gardner, of the 30th Kentucky Volunteer Infantry, was left with the wounded on the battlefield and was captured on October 3, 1864, but General Breckinridge paroled him. He reported that on October 3, several armed men arrived at his field hospital and took five black Union soldiers, who were wounded, and shot them dead. On October 7, several of the Union wounded prisoners from the battle of Saltville were taken to the Emory and Henry College Hospital, in Washington County, Virginia. Several armed men entered the hospital at 10:00 p.m. and went up into the rooms occupied by the Federal wounded prisoners and shot two of the wounded black soldiers in their beds.

On October 8, at Emory and Henry College Hospital, several armed men under Champ Ferguson, wearing Confederate uniforms entered the hospital at 4:00 p.m., overpowered the guard that had been placed by the surgeon in charge, went up into the rooms occupied by the Federal wounded prisoners. Champ Ferguson shot Lieutenant E. C. Smith, 13th Kentucky Cavalry, in the head. Smith was in his bed, where he lay severely wounded. Ferguson later claimed he was avenging Smith's murder of Confederate guerillas captured in Kentucky. Ferguson called out for other Federal officers confined there, particularly Colonel Charles Hanson, 37th Kentucky Cavalry and Captain Degenfield, 12th Ohio Cavalry, swearing that he intended to kill all of them. Surgeon Murfree, the surgeon in charge, the steward, Mr. Acres, and other attendants of the hospital prevented the killing by risking their own lives. Surgeon Murfree assisted in removing Hanson, Degenfeld, and Surgeon William Gardner to a place of safety.[337] Although statistics vary, about 100 black soldiers and white officers were murdered after the battle of Saltville.

After the battle, General Breckinridge ordered his men to pursue General Burbridge's men. He ordered Colonel Giltner's brigade to follow Burbridge, while General Basil Duke, Cosby, Vaughn, Dibrell, and Robertson followed a parallel route to Hayter's Gap to cut off the Federal retreat, but Burbridge managed to outrun the pursuing Confederates and make his way back to Kentucky.

When Burbridge arrived in Kentucky, he ordered the arrest of Champ Ferguson. Under a flag of truce, Burbridge informed Basil Duke that he considered the murder of Lieutenant Smith "one of the most diabolical acts of the

---

336 Jennings, "The Lost Regiment," *Louisville Courier-Journal*, February 15, 1996.

337 O.R. Series I, Vol. XXXIX/1 [#77] Sept. 20-Oct. 17, 1864-Raids from Kentucky and East Tennessee into Southwestern Virginia. No. 3 Reports of Surgeon William H. Gardner, 13th Kentucky Infantry, of the shooting of Union prisoner.

The execution of Confederate guerilla Champ Ferguson on October 20, 1865, at Nashville, Tennessee, as sketched by J.M. Arnold.

war."[338] He also warned that if the Federals captured Ferguson and his men, they would not be treated as prisoners.[339] Union General N. C. McLean suggested that the Confederate Government deliver Champ Ferguson and his men to the Union government for punishment, and if the Confederate government refused, immediate retaliation should be enforced upon Confederate prisoners, man for man. Burbridge endorsed the recommendation.[340]

General Breckinridge ordered the arrest of Champ Ferguson, but Ferguson escaped capture by leaving his department. The Federal authorities caught up with Ferguson and captured him. The Federal courts charged Ferguson with 53 counts of murder, including 14 at Saltville. He was convicted, and on

338 O.R.--Series I--Volume XLIX/1 [S# 103] Union Correspondence, Orders, and Returns Relating to Operations in Kentucky, Southwestern Virginia, Tennessee, Northern and Central Georgia, Mississippi, Alabama, and West Florida, from January 1 to March 15, 1865. (*)--#8, Letter from Brevet General S. G. Burbridge to Brig. Gen. B.W. Duke, C. S. Army, February 24, 1865, 765.

339 Ibid.

340 Thomas Mays, *The Saltville Massacre* (McWhiney Foundation Press, Abilene, Texas, 1998), 68.; O.R. Series I, Vol. XXXIX/1 [#77] Sept. 20-Oct. 17, 1864-Raids from Kentucky and East Tennessee into Southwestern Virginia. No. 3 Reports of Surg. William H. Gardner, 13th Kentucky Infantry, of the shooting of Union prisoners.

October 20, 1865, Ferguson was hanged in Nashville, Tennessee. As for General Robertson, Federal authorities never charged him with the massacre and he lived to be the last surviving Confederate general.

Union Colonel James Brisbin paid tribute to the black soldiers who fought at Saltville. He wrote: "I have seen white troops fight in twenty-seven battles, and I never saw any fight better." When the black soldiers, their ammunition gone, finally withdrew from the hilltop they had captured, he wrote, "those who had scoffed at the colored troops on the march out were silent." Kentucky Adjutant General Lorenzo Thomas reported that the 5th USCC had performed better than any other regiment in the battle. "They charged the rifle pits and carried them after two repulses by the enemy of our white troops."[341] General Burbridge "spoke in the highest terms of the gallantry of the Fifth Colored Cavalry-they doing better service than any other regiment."[342]

Burbridge returned to Kentucky from his failed expedition to Saltville. He had hoped his expedition would boost his image, but he had to return to Kentucky to face ever more criticism. As the fall and winter months of 1864 arrived, Burbridge would have to fight to keep his command in Kentucky. Some of his allies began to turn against him, including the President of the United States.

341 Jennings, A9.

342 O.R. Series I, Vol. XXXIX/2 [#79] Union Correspondence, Orders, and Returns to Operations in Kentucky, Southwest Virginia, Tennessee, Mississippi, Alabama, and North Georgia (the Atlanta Campaign excepted) from October 1, 1864 to November 13, 1864.

Chapter Nine
The Great Hog Swindle and the Election of 1864

When Burbridge arrived in Kentucky from his failed expedition into southwest Virginia, he returned to a state overrun with guerrillas. His strict policy did not stop the killings and plundering. Criticism against his command continued to rise. That criticism reached President Lincoln's ears and Governor Thomas Bramlette of Kentucky lost favor with Burbridge. Burbridge's superiors no longer supported him. Burbridge had embroiled himself in the Great Hog Swindle of 1864 and had influenced the outcome of President Lincoln's election. Although Burbridge thought he helped Lincoln by doing everything in his power to make sure Lincoln won the election, he only brought on the wrath of the citizens of Kentucky. By the end of 1864, Burbridge's hold on Kentucky slipped through his fingers.

While Burbridge fought at the Battle of Saltville, Union General John Schofield paid Kentucky a visit and reported on the military conditions there. On October 3, 1864, he sent a letter to Union General William T. Sherman expressing his displeasure with the military affairs in Kentucky. He wrote that there was a criminal looseness and gross corruption in the administration of military justice. He stated that public enemies received their freedom by paying large fees to lawyers who had influence with commanding officers, while innocent citizens had been kept in prison without trial. The provost marshal's department at Louisville and the military police of the District of Kentucky were engaged in the trading of black substitutes and extorting fines for violation of petty regulations. He reported that the police officers appeared to perform all the duties of public prosecutors, judge, and receiver of money. The charges relative to corruption in the release of prisoners involved Burbridge. He stated that Burbridge acted in reference to the arrest and disposition of disloyal persons under direct orders from Sherman. Schofield did not investigate the charges, since Burbridge was under the orders of Sherman.[343]

To make matters worse, Burbridge began to arrest Union officers for disloyalty. Secretary of War Edwin Stanton relieved officers of command under

343 Ibid.

Brigadier General Allen. Stanton sent Quartermaster Terry to New Orleans and reduced his rank to Captain. The Secretary of War requested that if Burbridge was willing to furnish the names of any officer in his department who was disloyal or using their influence, personal or official, against the government, Stanton would relieve them from duty. Union Judge Advocate General Joseph Holt suggested that supplying the names of disloyal officers would be "a great service to the country."[344]

On October 16, 1864, Burbridge wrote to Judge Advocate Joseph Holt that when he returned to Kentucky from his expedition he found that during his absence his actions, motives, and character had come under attack. He found that the citizens of Kentucky accused him to be guilty of bribery and corruption. Burbridge wrote to Holt that his position in Kentucky was an "unenviable one and that is impossible for me to please every Union man." He determined to do what he considered right in every case, trusting that those who placed him in command would do the same by him, and whatever may be their action he would have the proud consciousness of having done what he honestly considered the good of the cause since he had been in the service. He felt that he was surrounded by petty annoyances that he had no power to remove. Burbridge felt that three officers in his command injured him personally and the Union cause, by their acts and assertions, for which the public held him responsible. Union Captain H. B. Grant, of the 27th Kentucky Infantry, inspector general of the district, Captain Stephen Jones, aide-de-camp and commissary general of prisoners for the district, and Lieutenant Colonel J. H. Hammond, assistant adjutant general, in charge of the draft attacked Burbridge. Captain Grant and Captain Jones were Union General George B. McClellan's men. McClellan was running against Abraham Lincoln for President. Both men used their influence and position against Burbridge, in his effort to carry the state for Mr. Lincoln. He felt that the public did not understand that he had no power to remove them and consequently the public accused Burbridge of double dealing by keeping Captains Grant and Jones in their positions. He wanted both men to be removed from the district. He wrote that Lieutenant Colonel Hammond was with Burbridge in politics, energetic and capable, but lacked in moral integrity. He was ambitious, interfering, and selfish. He grasped at the prosperity or misfortunes of his friends to elevate himself to a higher position and power. He also asked for Hammond to be removed.

Burbridge became alarmed at the conditions in Kentucky. He sent six

344 John Scott Papers, 1821 to 1915, Reel 1F59-M-301, Letter from Judge Advocate General Holt to Major General S. G. Burbridge, October 1, 1864, University of Kentucky, Margaret King Library, Lexington, Kentucky.

regiments of black troops out of the state and five white regiments to Nashville, and five other regiments would be mustered out, reducing his force to 16 regiments. He was convinced the Confederates would throw a large cavalry force into the state in small detachments, scattering them across the state to interfere with the election, and then to concentrate their detachments and join Breckinridge's main force for a grand raid over the state. He needed troops to protect the polling booths and to prevent any raid. With the placement of the proper troops, Kentucky could be carried for Lincoln. He stated that Kentucky had a strong Union element, especially in the districts that had been overrun by guerillas, yet he claimed every effort of the opposition was being made to defeat him. Burbridge stated that the opposition's candidates and electors traveled over the part of the state infested by guerillas in safety, while the Union electors were obliged to take a strong guard with them, showing where the sympathy for McClellan came from.

He suggested that the commissioners appointed to settle claims of loyal men for blacks who had gone into the army be sent to Kentucky at once and work until after the election. He stated that Kentucky must be held for Lincoln. He had used every means in his power to accomplish the task. He claimed that he had been assailed by those who in name support the administration, but are actually selfish. He gave some government patronage to prominent influential men, who were not loyal and had doubtful politics, securing them and their influence for the administration, which otherwise would have been used against the Union. He made favors, if he could secure a vote for Lincoln.[345]

By October 17, Burbridge feared that he would be attacked by Confederate General Hylan Benton Lyon. Lyon took Eddyville, Kentucky, and placed his batteries to prevent the passage of river boats on the Cumberland River. Colonel Chenoweth, reinforced by General Nathan Bedford Forrest, moved on Mayfield, Kentucky, and Lexington, Kentucky. Burbridge asked Union General Henry Halleck for reinforcements, since four regiments were sent to Nashville and 6,000 of his black troops were sent to other points. General Halleck wrote to Burbridge that no troops were available to reinforce Paducah.

On October 25, in retaliation for the shooting of a Union soldier by Confederate guerrilla Sue Mundy's men, near Brunerstown, present day Jeffersontown, Jefferson County. Wilson Lilly, a member of Company G, 1st Missouri Volunteer Infantry, Sherwood Hatley, a 70-year-old Presbyterian minister,

345 Letter from Burbridge to Judge Advocate General Holt, October 16, 1864, O.R. Series I, Vol. XXXIX/2 [#79] Union Correspondence, Orders, and Returns to Operations in Kentucky, Southwest Virginia, Tennessee, Mississippi, Alabama, and North Georgia (the Atlanta Campaign excepted) from October 1, 1864 to November 13, 1864.

Lindsey Duke Buckner, a Confederate captain in Colonel Chenoweth's regiment, and William Blincoe, a member of Company D, 2nd Kentucky Cavalry, were taken from a military prison by Captain Rowland E. Hackett and 50 Union soldiers of the 26th Kentucky Union Infantry, and taken to the spot where a Federal soldier was killed and all four men were shot by Captain Hackett and his men.[346] While seated on his coffin, awaiting execution, Captain Buckner wrote his farewell letter to his sister, Mrs. Louisa J. Edwards. Buckner wrote that he was "under sentence of death and for what, I do not know. My sentence is not yet made known. My dear sister, I have always loved you and will in my dying breath. It is a hard thing to be chained and shot in this way; and if it was not for the hope I have of meeting you all in Heaven, I would be miserable indeed."[347]

The next day, Colonel Sam Johnson, commander of the 48th Kentucky Infantry, took Lieutenant Colonel James Brewer, a volunteer aide de camp to John C. Breckinridge and Private Thomas Bassett, Company K, 1st Kentucky Cavalry, to be executed in Hopkinsville, Kentucky. Colonel Sam Johnson had been a Methodist preacher in Logan County, but quit the pulpit to join the Union army. He hated Southern soldiers and sympathizers. When Johnson's men brought Brewer in as a prisoner, the Union soldiers asked Johnson what to do with him. He exclaimed: "By God, get a squad and take him down to the river bank and shoot him. . . . Go down to the jail and get that d—ed fellow Bassett and shoot him too." The Union soldiers directed both Brewer and Bassett to kneel with their backs to the squad. Bassett turned his back sobbing. Brewer stood erect and said, "I never turn my back to the enemy. I only ask that you do not shoot me in the face." Colonel Johnson sat on his horse nearby while his men shot and killed both men.[348]

On October 26, 1864, Burbridge issued Order Number 7, in which he expressed his knowledge that citizens in the military district, during public speeches were encouraging their friends to go to the polls armed at the upcoming election, under the false pretense that the military mediated illegal interference. He thought the citizens coming armed to the polls was a well-devised, effectual means of inciting the large rebel element in their midst to acts of violence and of deterring peaceable and orderly citizens from attending the polls. Burbridge wanted to have a fair and free election, and to this end every aid would be afforded to the officers of the election in enforcing the state laws

346 Collins, Lewis & Collins, Richard, *History of Kentucky*, Vol. 1, 1874, 144.

347 James Head, *The Atonement of John Brooks, The Story of the True Johnny "Reb" Who Did Not Come Marching Home*, (Florida: Heritage Press, 2001), 217-218.

348 James Head, *The Atonement of John Brooks*, 203.

upon the subject, both as to the admission of qualified voters and the exclusion of those who were disqualified. The rebel element in his midst, whether resident or coming from other states, had no right to interfere in the state elections, and those who were known as supporters of the rebellion would not be permitted to indulge in "seditious discussions, attend political meetings, or the places of voting on election-day. They must remain quiet or leave the state." In his order, Burbridge quoted the act of the Kentucky State Legislature of March 11, 1862, which he stated must be the test of political rights to all such, and neither false oaths nor the culpable connivance of partisan officers of election would shield from punishment those who violated it. Burbridge referred to the act of amendment Chapter 15 of the Revised Statutes, entitled citizen's expatriation and aliens. In Section 1, the amendment stated that any Kentucky citizen who entered into the Confederate service, in either a civil or military capacity, or enter into the provisional Kentucky Confederate government, in either a civil or military capacity, or having entered service of either the Confederate states or provisional government, or should continue in the Confederate service after the act took effect, or should take up or continue in arms against the United States military or the state of Kentucky, or should give voluntary aid and assistance to those in arms against the U.S. forces, would be deemed to have expatriated themselves and no longer be citizens of Kentucky, nor would they be given citizenship except by permission of the legislature.[349]

In section two of the amendment, anyone who attempted or was called on, to exercise any of the constitutional or loyal rights and privileges belonging only to citizens of Kentucky, could be required to negative, on oath, the expatriation provided in the first section of the act, and upon his failure or refusal to do so would not be permitted to exercise any right or privilege.[350]

In section three, all acts voluntarily done by a citizen and designed by him to aid or assist those in arms against the United States or Kentucky were embraced by the statute. Aid and assistance would be given to those in arms by words as well as acts, as for instance by giving valuable information, persuading and inducing persons to enlist in the Confederate service. Discreet and patriotic officers of the election could easily distinguish under the terms of the law legal and disfranchised voters. Those officers, and not suspected persons applying to vote, were the judges both of the sense of the oath to be

---

349 General Order Number 7, Major General Stephen Gano Burbridge, October 26, 1864, O.R.–Series I–Volume XXXIX/2 [S# 79] Union Correspondence, Orders, and Returns Relating to Operations in Kentucky, Southwest Virginia, Tennessee, Mississippi, Alabama, and North Georgia (The Atlanta Campaign Excepted), from October 1, 1864, to November 13, 1864. (*)--#19, 457.

350 Ibid.

administered, of the proper questions to be put and answered, and of the legal effect of the effect of the facts disclosed. Officers within his command would arrest every one violating the order, and citizens were requested to communicate infractions of it to the nearest military authority.[351]

On that same day, Burbridge issued Order Number 8, in which he stated that irregular bands of armed men within his lines, disconnected from the Rebel army, who prowled through the country and subsisted by destroying the property of citizens and the government are guerrillas, and would be treated as such. Burbridge stated that they were without an idea of permanent occupancy, or with a reasonable hope of seriously injuring his communications. They formed no part of the original army of the rebellion, and when captured were not entitled to the treatment prescribed for regular soldiers, but by the laws of war, they have forfeited their lives. Frequent robberies and murders committed by these outlaws demanded that the laws of war be stringently meted out to them. Burbridge declared that from "hereafter no guerillas will be received as prisoners, and any officer who may capture such and extend to them the courtesies due prisoners of war will be held accountable for disobedience of orders."[352]

On October 27, 1864, President Abraham Lincoln wrote to General Burbridge expressing his concern with his collection of a considerable amount of money from the citizens of Allen and Barren counties to compensate Union men for the depredations committed upon them by Confederates. Lincoln ordered Burbridge to refund the money. Lincoln wrote that he would have to hear both sides, and in his opinion, that in some extreme cases, "this class of proceedings becomes a necessity; but that it is liable to almost inseparable from-great abuses, and therefore should only be sparingly resorted to, and be conducted with great caution; that you, in your department, must be the judge of the proper locations and occasions for applying it; and that it will be well for you to see that your subordinates be at all times ready to account for every dollar, as to why collected, of whom, and how applied–Without this, you will soon find some of them making assessments and collections merely to put money in their own pockets–and it will also be impossible to correct errors in future and better times."[353]

---

351 Order No. 7. October 26, 1864, Lexington, Kentucky, O.R. Series I, Vol. XXXIX/2 [#79] Union Correspondence, Orders, and Returns to Operations in Kentucky, Southwest Virginia, Tennessee, Mississippi, Alabama, and North Georgia (the Atlanta Campaign excepted) from October 1, 1864 to November 13, 1864.

352 Order No. 8, October 26, 1864, O.R. Series I, Vol. XXXIX/2 [#79] Union Correspondence, Orders, and Returns to Operations in Kentucky, Southwest Virginia, Tennessee, Mississippi, Alabama, and North Georgia (the Atlanta Campaign excepted) from October 1, 1864 to November 13, 1864, 457.

353 Abraham Lincoln to Stephen Burbridge, October 27, 1864, Abraham Lincoln Papers, Library of Congress, Washington, D.C.

On October 28, 1864, Burbridge asked Brigadier General Hugh Ewing whether four guerrillas from Henderson and four guerillas at Keysburg, Logan County, had been executed. If he had not executed them, he was to carry out the order immediately. Three days later, Burbridge wrote to Colonel Maxwell Cicero at Bowling Green, Kentucky, to arrest Mr. Perkins of Elkton and every man in his district who attempted to intimidate Union men from voting, either by threats or intimidation that their property would be destroyed or their lives endangered. Burbridge ordered Colonel Cicero to hold such men in prison until further ordered. For every depredation committed upon Union men Burbridge would retaliate three-fold upon the Copperheads and rebel sympathizers in the area.[354]

On that same day, Burbridge issued a letter from his military headquarters in Lexington, stating that those who owned or feed hogs in Kentucky were informed by the United States government that they wanted to buy surplus hogs in Kentucky. He stated that a fair market value would be paid for all the hogs that were for sale. He hoped that all hogs owners would willingly sell to the government any excess hogs and not allow the excess pork to be packed in the country, which would invite raids for the Confederates to capture the excess pork. He wrote that Major H. C. Symonds, Commissary of Subsistence, in Louisville was instructed with the details of hog buying business and would give all necessary information.[355]

On November 1, 1864, General Ewing wrote to President Lincoln that Burbridge lost Lincoln the vote in Kentucky because of his offensive manner of carrying into effect Lincoln's orders to recruit black troops. General Ewing stated that if Burbridge had pursued a wise and conciliatory course, the order would have prevented dissatisfaction. He stated that if Lincoln made the changes Ewing recommended Union General Thomas Crittenden to replace Burbridge. He stated that Crittenden was a man of good sense to the manner born and would probably be better than anyone Lincoln could appoint to conciliate the people while he execute the laws.[356]

General George Thomas wrote to Burbridge that Major Chambliss, special inspector of cavalry, Military Division of the Mississippi, reported that he seized or issued to black cavalry regiments horses intended for issue to the

354 Brevet Major General Stephen G. Burbridge to Colonel Maxwell Cicero, Lexington, Kentucky October 30, 1864, O.R. Series I, Vol. XXXIX/2 [#79] Union Correspondence, Orders, and Returns to Operations in Kentucky, Southwest Virginia, Tennessee, Mississippi, Alabama, and North Georgia (the Atlanta Campaign excepted) from October 1, 1864 to November 13, 1864.

355 *Military History of Kentucky*, 218-219.

356 Letter from General Ewing to Abraham Lincoln, November 1, 1864, Abraham Lincoln Letters, Library of Congress. Washington, D.C.

Military Division of Mississippi cavalry. He ordered Burbridge to turn over all the horses to the Mississippi division and ordered Burbridge not to interfere with any of the dismounted cavalry regiments sent to Louisville for remount, nor with the horses, horse's equipment, or cavalry ordnance stores, or arms intended for the Mississippi division cavalry. In response, Burbridge wrote to General Thomas on November 8, 1864, that General Meredith demanded for immediate use reinforcements, so he sent, under authority from General Sherman to use any troops that might be in Kentucky in cases of necessity, the 9th and 13th Indiana Cavalry, dismounted, to Paducah. The danger over, they were immediately returned to Louisville. Burbridge claimed he was not aware of having diverted any cavalry, ordnance stores, or horse equipments intended for the front from their destination. Whenever he sent mounted men to Tennessee as cattle guards or otherwise, the men had been returned dismounted.[357]

As night fell on November 1, Confederate guerrilla William Marshal and his men shot and killed Robert Graham, who lived near Peak's Mill, Franklin County. The next day on November 2, Burbridge sent S. Thomas Hunt, a 20-year-old lawyer who joined the Confederate army, who was captured by Union soldiers on his way back to army; Thomas Lafferty, a 42-year-old man and political prisoner; Elijah Horton, 22 years old of Carter and a member of Company M, 10th Kentucky Cavalry; and Captain John Jones of Texas, from the prison in Lexington to the lower corner of Major Hunt's pasture in South Frankfort. Burbridge assembled a small squad of Union soldiers and the soldiers prepared the four men for execution. At the men's request Reverend B. B. Sayre offered a prayer. As soon as he pronounced the "Amen," one of the prisoners, Thornton Lafferty, managed to escape, but soon fell, his body riddled with bullets from the Union soldiers rifles. The other three stood still and the Union soldiers shot them dead and their bodies buried without coffins. Hunt's body was reburied at Maysville, while the others were buried in the Frankfort Cemetery.[358] On that same day, two blacks were killed and in retaliation William Long of Maysville, Mason County, William Tithe of Williamstown, Grant County, William D. Darbrow near Dallesburg, Owen County, and R. W. Yates of Bacon Creek, Hart County were shot at Pleasureville in Henry County. Tithe and Darbrow were members of the 4th Kentucky Cavalry. Yates had been

357 Brevet Major General Stephen G. Burbridge to General George Thomas, November 8, 1864, Lexington, Kentucky, O.R. Series I, Vol. XXXIX/2 [#79] Union Correspondence, Orders, and Returns to Operations in Kentucky, Southwest Virginia, Tennessee, Mississippi, Alabama, and North Georgia (the Atlanta Campaign excepted) from October 1, 1864 to November 13, 1864., 693.

358 Collins, *History of Kentucky*, 146; Kentucky Historical Marker, A Civil War Reprisal, located at the New Capitol Grounds, Frankfort, Kentucky; James Head, *The Atonement of John Brooks*, 204.

turned over to Union authorities for the killing of Mr. Rankin. Sixteen hours after their execution, their bodies were still lying on the floor of the depot, near where they were shot.[359] The people of Pleasureville were afraid to touch the bodies for fear they too would go to prison. Confederate Colonel Jessee and his men took the bodies away and buried them in Eminence. Three of the men were buried in Eminence, while William Long was taken to Maysville for burial.[360]

On November 5, 1864, Union soldiers executed four men named M. Jackson, J. Jackson, G. Rissinger, and N. Adams for the murder of Mr. Adam Harper. Members of Sue Mundy's band of guerillas murdered Harper on November 1, 1864. After the execution the Union soldiers buried the four men in a shallow trench near where they fell. Eventually the men were re-interred in the city cemetery.[361] On that same day, a skirmish took place near Bloomfield, Kentucky, and Union Major Samuel Martin of the 37th Kentucky Infantry, reported that one of his companies surprised some guerillas at Bardstown. Out of the 15 men who had their horses shod and pillaging the town, his men managed to capture three men. Two men managed to escape Martin's men. The men who escaped were none other than the infamous guerillas Sue Mundy and "One-Armed Berry." Martin's men took the three men captured, Tingle or Tindle, Parkhurst and Warford, to headquarters and when the party got to within five miles of Bloomfield, they tried to escape. The Union soldiers opened fire and killed all three men, although historian James Head and Stewart Cruickshank feel that the three men were executed by the Union soldiers. The citizens of Bloomfield took the remains to town for burial, although their exact location is unknown.[362]

On November 8, 1864, two Rebels named Richard Cheney and another man named J. Peters or McDonald or Jones were taken from the military prison in Louisville and shot at Munfordville in Hart County in retaliation for the murder of James Madison Murphy, Company A, 13th Kentucky Infantry, by guerrillas. According to the Provost Marshall of Munfordville, 20 or 30 men dressed in civilian clothing came to the house of David Cavin on the Green River and took Murry out of bed and hauled him into the woods near the home of Murry's brother Benjamin Murry. There, he was shot in the head and thrown into the sink hole in the woods. The next day, two blacks were killed, and

359 Collins, 146.

360 Emily Moses, "Marker Honors memory of killed soldiers." *The Henry County Local*, Sunday, November 5, 2006; James Head, *The Atonement of John Brooks*, 205.

361 James Head, 205; Collins, 146.

362 James Head, *The Atonement of John Brooks*, 205-206.

Burbridge selected James Hopkins, John W. Sipple and Samuel Stagdale to be shot at Bloomfield in Nelson County, Kentucky.[363]

On November 8, 1864, Lincoln was re-elected President of the United States. Although Burbridge tried to influence the election in getting Lincoln elected in Kentucky, Union General George B. McClellan received 61,486 votes, while Lincoln only received 26,592. Lincoln received majorities in 25 counties out of the 101 reporting, and in 56 counties he received over 100 votes. In only eight counties did McClellan receive over 100 votes. Historian E. Merton Coulter stated that there were 54,000 fewer votes cast in the 1864 election, than in 1860, which indicated the great demoralization which prevailed over the state. He wrote that "although military interference was not nearly so glaring as it had been in previous elections, still some of the falling off must be attributed to intimidation by the army, for [Robert] Breckinridge and [General Stephen] Burbridge sedulously worked to create the impression that the test of loyalty, which meant payment for slaves and property seized and freedom from arrest and persecution, would be determined by the way a person voted-if he voted at all. And many, doubtless, considered no record better than a bad one-hence they stayed at home."[364]

On November 9, General George Thomas wrote to Burbridge that if mounted men sent by him to Tennessee or the front had been dismounted, it was done by General Sherman's order. General Sherman also ordered that neither horses nor horse equipment sent to Louisville for the mounted troops of the Military Division of the Mississippi would be diverted to any other purpose. By General Sherman's order, General Thomas had been placed in command of all the troops of the Military Division of the Mississippi not immediately under his command. General Thomas requested that Burbridge comply with the above instructions in the future.[365]

Also on the same day, Governor Thomas Bramlette wrote to General Ulysses S. Grant, asking for the removal of General Burbridge from his command in Kentucky. He bypassed General Sherman because of the "disturbed condition of communications" between him and Sherman. He stated in the letter to Grant that all his "ingenuity and watchfulness have been taxed to the utmost for some time to foil the evil effects of General Burbridge's weakness

---

363 Collins, 146; James Head, 207.

364 E. Merton Coulter, The Civil War and Readjustment in Kentucky, (Chapel Hill: University of North Carolina Press, 1921, reprint 1966), 187-188.

365 General George Thomas to General Burbridge, November 9, 1864, O.R. Series I, Vol. XXXIX/2 [#79] Union Correspondence, Orders, and Returns to Operations in Kentucky, Southwest Virginia, Tennessee, Mississippi, Alabama, and North Georgia (the Atlanta Campaign excepted) from October 1, 1864 to November 13, 1864.

and mischievous acts in this military district."[366] He stated that Burbridge for several weeks irritated and exasperated the minds of the loyal people of Kentucky. "His outrageous and indiscriminate arrests of persons purely on account of their favoring the election of McClellan, treating as rebels all who are opposed to Mr. Lincoln's re-election; threatening and bullying the citizens; and menacing the civil authorities and officers of the State, laying unjust political restrictions upon the business and necessary trade of the country, seeking out inventions by which to harass, oppress, and injure those who differ with him in politics, [have] produced a very bad state of feeling, which has required all my skill to keep from manifesting itself in open violence."[367] Governor Bramlette stated that Burbridge had arrested many citizens on the day before for no other reason except disloyalty, as he termed it, of being opposed to Lincoln's re-election. Burbridge arrested and sent off to the Southern lines, Union General John B. Houston, of Lexington. According to the governor, rumors of many others were being sent to prison because of political vengeance. The governor wrote: "In a word, he is making more enemies to our safety than much prudence can overcome."[368]

The Governor wrote that Burbridge sought to provoke collision with civil authorities, but the governor foiled his plan, because he would not allow such a collision. He used prudence, foresight, wisdom, or any personal sacrifices to prevent collision. He stated that Burbridge "has not the capacity to comprehend the evils which he is prompted to provoke. He is instigated by men who do comprehend and intend them, and who work upon his weakness through his vanity to accomplish them. He is wholly unfit for any command where there is anything at stake which requires either intellect, prudence, firmness of purpose, justice, or the manliness of the soldier to accomplish." Governor Bramlette asked General Grant to arrest the malevolent acts which through the "weakness and vanity of General Burbridge have been and are being inflicted upon the loyal citizens"[369] of Kentucky.

On that same day, Bramlette also wrote President Lincoln stating that General John Houston, a loyal man and prominent citizen, was arrested by Burbridge to be sent off behind Union lines for no other offense than opposition

---

366 Governor Thomas Bramlette to Lt. Gen. Ulysses S. Grant, Frankfort, Kentucky, November 9, 1864., O.R. Series I, Vol. XXXIX/2 [#79] Union Correspondence, Orders, and Returns to Operations in Kentucky, Southwest Virginia, Tennessee, Mississippi, Alabama, and North Georgia (the Atlanta Campaign excepted) from October 1, 1864 to November 13, 1864, 724.

367 Ibid

368 Ibid.

369 Ibid.

to Lincoln's re-election. He asked Lincoln to save his administration and the country from the shame of such iniquities.[370]

Union General Grant wrote to Secretary of War Edwin Stanton that he did not know how far Governor Bramlette ought to be conciliated, but he stated that from the very start he did not trust General Burbridge's ability and fitness. He had selected General Ammen for the command of Kentucky and placed him there with orders, but General Ammen at the time was engaged as a member of a court martial. General Burbridge was available at the time and assigned temporary command, but managed to retain the command. Grant stated that he had unofficial complaints on General Burbridge's course and thought that the best interest of the service required that a more sensible soldier, one free from prejudice and party influence, should be sent to relieve him. Grant recommended General Grenville Dodge to replace Burbridge. Grant sent a staff officer the previous week to investigate the complaints against Burbridge.[371]

The next day, on November 10, 1864, President Lincoln sent a letter to General Burbridge stating that he had received a telegram from Governor Bramlette stating that General John Houston had been arrested and sent beyond Union lines. Lincoln answered the governor with the following telegram: "I can scarcely believe that General John B. Houston has been arrested for no other offense than opposition to my re-election; for if that has been deemed sufficient cause of arrest I should have heard of more than one arrest in Kentucky on election day. If however, General Houston has been arrested for no other cause than opposition to my re-election General Burbridge will discharge him at once, I, sending him a copy of this as an order to that effect." Lincoln immediately wanted a response from Burbridge.[372] Burbridge wrote to Lincoln that Governor Bramlette was wrong in saying that John B. Houston was arrested for no other offense than opposition to his re-election. He stated that Houston's influence and speeches were of a treasonable character and he persisted in making treasonable speeches after several warnings of what would happen if he continued his speeches. Burbridge allowed Houston to return from Covington under oath and bond as long as he did not oppose the

370 Letter from Governor Thomas Bramlette to Abraham Lincoln, November 9, 1864, Frankfort, Kentucky, Abraham Lincoln Letters, Library of Congress.

371 Governor Thomas Bramlette to Lt. Gen. Ulysses S. Grant, Frankfort, Kentucky, November 9, 1864., O.R. Series I, Vol. XXXIX/2 [#79] Union Correspondence, Orders, and Returns to Operations in Kentucky, Southwest Virginia, Tennessee, Mississippi, Alabama, and North Georgia (the Atlanta Campaign excepted) from October 1, 1864 to November 13, 1864, 725.

372 Letter from Abraham Lincoln to General Stephen Burbridge, November 10, 1864, O.R. Series I, Vol. XXXIX/2 [#79] Union Correspondence, Orders, and Returns to Operations in Kentucky, Southwest Virginia, Tennessee, Mississippi, Alabama, and North Georgia (the Atlanta Campaign excepted) from October 1, 1864 to November 13, 1864.

government. Burbridge wrote to Lincoln that a vigorous policy against rebel sympathizers in Kentucky must be pursued, and if he had erred, he feared that he did not make enough arrests.[373]

On November 10, 1864, Burbridge sent a telegram to Governor Bramlette stating that "in the exercise of power delegated to me by the President of the United States I have arrested John B. Houston, and am responsible for my action to my Government. When the civil authorities make no effort to suppress disloyalty the military must and will."[374]

The next day, on November 11, 1864, Union General John Schofield authorized and directed General Burbridge, that his command of the district of Kentucky had been revoked.[375]

On November 12, 1864, General Burbridge wrote to Governor Bramlette that he did not make any insinuations or innuendoes when he wrote that civil authorities made no effort to suppress disloyalty and that the military authorities would. He stated that for months Colonel Frank Wolford, Richard T. Jacob, John Houston, and others made speeches in different parts of the state, reviling the administration, but also endeavored by their remarks to discourage enlistments, and weaken the power of the government in its efforts to suppress the rebellion. He went on to write that the state authorities did nothing to interfere with the speeches and even sanctioned and approved them. Burbridge stated that he did not make any insinuations of dereliction of duty on the part of the civil authorities, but openly spoke out that if the military authorities had received the civil authorities' hearty and cordial support in their efforts to maintain the government and preserve the peace in the state, Kentucky would not be cursed with the presence of guerilla bands and her loyal citizens, would not be outraged by frequent robberies and murders. [376]

Governor Bramlette replied stating that his letter referred to the speeches made by Colonel Wolford, Lt. Governor Richard Jacob, and General John

---

373 Letter to Abraham Lincoln from General Stephen Burbridge, November 11, 1864, Abraham Lincoln Papers, Library of Congress, Washington, D.C.

374 Letter from General Stephen Burbridge to Governor Thomas Bramlette, November 10, 1864, O.R. Series I, Vol. XXXIX/2 [#79] Union Correspondence, Orders, and Returns to Operations in Kentucky, Southwest Virginia, Tennessee, Mississippi, Alabama, and North Georgia (the Atlanta Campaign excepted) from October 1, 1864 to November 13, 1864.

375 Special Field Orders Number 149, Headquarters Army of the Ohio, November 11, 1864, O.R. Series I, Vol. XXXIX/2 [#79] Union Correspondence, Orders, and Returns to Operations in Kentucky, Southwest Virginia, Tennessee, Mississippi, Alabama, and North Georgia (the Atlanta Campaign excepted) from October 1, 1864 to November 13, 1864.

376 Letter from General Burbridge to Governor Thomas Bramlette, November 12, 1864, O.R. Series I, Vol. XXXIX/2 [#79] Union Correspondence, Orders, and Returns to Operations in Kentucky, Southwest Virginia, Tennessee, Mississippi, Alabama, and North Georgia (the Atlanta Campaign excepted) from October 1, 1864 to November 13, 1864.

Houston, and others. He wrote to Burbridge that the Thursday before the election, "without anyone thinking of interfering, enunciated a more reviling charge against the administration than any I have heard of coming from any other source, when you concluded your speech, as reported in the *Frankfort Commonwealth*, with the following words, 'Now, gentlemen, you all want pay for your horses, and niggers, and corn, and your hogs. Be cautious what record you make.' This, to all who heard or read it, was regarded as avowing the purpose to take, without compensation, the property of those who voted against Mr. Lincoln. You, so 'reviling the Administration' by charging it with such infamous purpose, have passed unquestioned. . . . As to the charge that those pure and incorruptible patriots have been endeavoring to discourage enlistments, etc., I believe it to be as untrue in reference to them as I know your charge to be untrue in reference to the state authorities. It is but a shallow pretense, gotten up from false accusations, to afford a pretext for wreaking political vengeance upon them. . . You know that at all times the state authorities have promptly and cordially responded to your calls, and earnestly aided you in all those objects [supporting the government, preserving the peace in the state, and suppressing guerillas bands.] When you desired the militia called into service to aid you, it was promptly done, whenever and wherever you desired it, and for such period as you requested. When you desired the state forces employed at any place, they were promptly sent as requested. And when you were preparing to go upon your Saltville expedition, which resulted so unfortunately to you and the country, the state forces were disposed of as you requested."[377] Bramlette closed his letter by stating that had Burbridge's success been better and matched his means, it would have saved him from attempting to cover up his failures under "calumnious charges against the state authorities, and would have enabled you to respond to a question put for information, with at least a decent regard to gentlemanly courtesy."[378]

After the election, Governor Bramlette wrote President Abraham Lincoln a letter continuing his attack against General Burbridge. He wrote that he regretted that "General Burbridge is pursuing a course calculated to exasperate and infuriate rather than pacify and conciliate. His whole course for weeks past has been such as was most calculated to inaugurate revolt and produce collisions. My utmost powers have been taxed to frustrate the evils of his course, and preserve peace and order. I have thus far succeeded but shall need your cooperation, and assistance to attain that unity and harmony which I desire, but which

377 Collins, *History of Kentucky*, 147.
378 Ibid.

he will defeat, in the blunderings of a weak intellect and over-weaning vanity. Any man in command in Kentucky can easily harmonize with the state authorities if he wishes to do so." He went on to write to Lincoln that he wanted to have the Headquarters of the Commandant in Kentucky at Frankfort where he could have a free interchange of views with the Commandant, which would avoid the evils which resulted from Burbridge's weakness. Matters between Burbridge and the Governor had reached the point where he could not have personal conversations with Burbridge, but kept all correspondence on an official level in writing. He asked to have a commandant with whom he could be on social terms of courtesy and equality. He stated that the system of arrests inaugurated by Burbridge outraged public judgment and should be restricted. "His want of truthfulness enables him unscrupulously to make false charges, to sustain his outrages against public judgment."[379]

Governor Bramlette stated that Burbridge's system of trade permits had been shamefully carried out in some places. The system depreciated the public revenues during the upcoming year. Many loyal men were driven out of business after having paid the tax and obtained a license, and for no other reason than their political preferences. The loyal men would not take out license again unless the restrictions were removed and the government revenues would be diminished without return. Governor Bramlette wrote, "It is certainly better to risk the chances of even a disloyal man trading, than cut off hundreds of loyal men by such regulations and exasperate them and diminish the sources of revenue. A hearty support of the Government by loyal men though differing in views of policy from you is better than a hollow quasi-loyalty purchased of a semi-rebel by a trade permit."[380]

Governor Bramlette also mentioned that the hog farmers of Kentucky had raised a considerable amount of commotion over Burbridge's orders. He mentioned in his letter to President Lincoln, Symonds' agents attempted to force the farmers to let their hogs go to them at greatly less than the market price, by falsely telling them that the Government had fixed the price and unless they received it willingly their hogs would be taken at the price fixed anyhow, and if they attempted to sell, or if packers attempted to purchase and pack their hogs, the meat would be confiscated and the farmers arrested and imprisoned. Some large houses in Louisville that had paid their tax were held in check and cut off from business, although they offered to sell to the Government their hog

---

379 Letter from Governor Thomas Bramlette to President Abraham Lincoln, Monday, November 14, 1864, Abraham Lincoln Papers, Library of Congress, Washington, D.C.

380 Ibid.

product at six dollars less per hundred than the Cincinnati market if permitted to go on with their business.[381]

In the summer of 1864, Major Henry C. Symonds, depot commissary at Louisville, set about a plan in which commissary officers bought hogs directly from Kentucky farmers and packed pork in Louisville for the army. The United States military did not like the idea of packing their own pork. In November of 1863, the pork trader journals reported that there would be a hog shortage and a poor corn crop. A month later groups of provision merchants began to speculate in army mess pork and prime mess in New York, Cincinnati, and Saint Louis. Pork prices began to soar. The country's pork packers were small operations with little capital. The dealers who had the largest financial resources controlled the market outlets of the pork trade. The packers borrowed their working funds from eastern commission men. With no marketing outlets of their own, they simply consigned their pork to the commission house. The army had to bargain with the provision dealers for their pork.[382]

In September 1863, pork mess sold for $17. By 1864 the price rose to $32, which was better than gold in New York. The speculation was wholly at the expense of the government. The army only bought salt pork; rising prices drove out any competition. By August 1864, Cincinnati wanted $45 dollars a barrel for pork. Pork supplies for Union General William T. Sherman's army ran low. Symonds proposed that the army pack their own pork. Symonds approached Powell and Company of Madison, Indiana, Robert Floyd of Cincinnati, and his meat inspector Michael Hargadon to make a bid to pack pork for the army. On September 13, all three businessmen agreed to buy and kill hogs for the army, to supply salt and barrels, and to pack the meat for a commission of $4.35 per hog. Symonds claimed he could pack pork for only $3 per hog. Symonds secured permission from General Burbridge.[383]

On October 14, 1864, Symonds gave a contract to J. Smith Speed and Robert Floyd to pack pork at $3.10 per hog. On October 17, he persuaded General Burbridge on October 28, 1864, to issue an order requiring shippers to obtain permits before sending any hogs out of Kentucky. On November 5, Colonel Wagner Swaine, who commanded Covington and Newport, closed the river crossing to the Cincinnati market. Congressman Robert Mallory met with Symonds and agreed the army had the right to take the hogs, but only at fair market price. With military controlling the railroads, packers found that

381 Letter from Governor Thomas Bramlette to President Abraham Lincoln, Monday, November 14, 1864, Abraham Lincoln Papers, Library of Congress, Washington, D.C.

382 Palmer Boeger, "The Great Hog Swindle of 1864," *The Journal of Southern History*, Vol. 28, No.1 (Feb. 1962), 60.

383 Ibid., 60-61.

moving their pork was impossible and with Burbridge's restrictions on out of state shipping, Kentucky hogs headed straight to the government buyers.[384]

Burbridge's published order on transportation of hogs brought a wave of anger from packers. Most Kentuckians blamed Burbridge for the new pork scheme. Symonds hired six men to buy hogs and to deliver them to the government packers. He did not ask for bids as required from military regulations, but hired men politically acceptable to General Burbridge. Kentucky farmers assumed that there was a corrupt alliance between the agents and certain army officers.[385]

Army contractors paid farmers eight cents a pound for hogs, the going market price, but increased their pressure on farmers and local livestock dealers. The agents bought several thousand hogs directly from farmers at seven and a half cents a pound. When the farmers learned that hogs were bringing ten and a half cents at the Louisville market, they cried out that they had been forced into selling their hogs at the lower price by the army's threat to take their animals by force. A few army officers were trying to line their pockets at the expense of the Kentucky farmer. Newspapers took up the hog farmers' concerns. By November 15, Colonel Charles A. Kilburn, supervisor of the Ohio valley depots and Symonds' superior, issued an order that no hogs would be seized in Kentucky and anyone holding hogs could sell them in any market and to any person. Holders did not need to obtain permits in the event hogs were shipped out of the state. He revoked all restrictions on railroads and steamboats, but he could not rescind Burbridge's order restricting transportation. Burbridge placed guards on the Ohio River stopping the packers from taking any hogs to Cincinnati.[386] Military authorities resented Burbridge for using black soldiers to guard and feed the hogs, which were purchased in outlying districts and held there in pens before being shipped to Louisville.[387]

To control damage, Symonds fired most of the original contractors and agreed to accept hogs directly from any holders. He stopped the monopoly of the agents. He offered to pay nine cents a pound for hogs delivered in Louisville, but still only paid eight cents a pound at the farms. Kentucky farmers began to sell their hogs again.

In his letter of November 14, Governor Bramlette asked President Lincoln to help him to preserve peace and order in Kentucky. He stated that Burbridge would not correct the evils because he had favorites to reward and enemies

---

384 Ibid., 63.
385 Ibid., 63-64.
386 Ibid. 66-67.
387 *Military History of Kentucky*, 219.

to punish and would use his official status to carry out his favoritism and personal vengeance.[388] Although no reply from Lincoln to Governor Bramlette has been located, the War Department ordered Burbridge to revoke his order that attempted to control the price of hogs.[389] On November 28, the railroads and steamboats of Kentucky were available to hog packers and Kentucky hogs could move freely out of the state.

By the end of the war, the Louisville hog project obtained eight million pounds of salt pork, 29,130 barrels at a cost of $34 a barrel. On December 22, pork sold for $39 a barrel. As late as February 1865, pork sold at $38 a barrel. Symonds claimed that he saved the government $200,000 and apologized for not doing better. Governor Bramlette told the Kentucky legislature that Symonds and his corrupt agents had stolen $300,000 from Kentucky farmers. The citizens of Kentucky would not forget the hog affair for an entire generation.[390]

According to historian E. Merton Coulter, the principal result of the feud between General Burbridge and Governor Bramlette over the arrest of General John B. Houston led Kentucky in bitter hostility to Burbridge and the military regime which he represented.[391] The hog swindle, the election tampering, his Order Number 59, the arrest of General John B. Houston, the feud with the Governor Bramlette, brought his superiors to ask Lincoln for the removal of General Burbridge. As November came to a close, Burbridge faced increased criticism not only from Governor Bramlette, but also from the citizens of Kentucky who asked for the President's help. President Lincoln would have no choice but to become involved in the feud between Governor Bramlette and Burbridge, resulting in Burbridge's dismissal.

---

388 Palmer Boeger, The Great Hog Swindle of 1864, *The Journal of Southern History*, Vol. 28, No.1 (Feb. 1962), 66-67.

389 Ibid.

390 Ibid., 70.

391 Coulter, 188.

Chapter 10
Political Relations Break Down

After the election, the feud between Governor Thomas Bramlette and General Stephen G. Burbridge continued to escalate. The citizens of Kentucky wrote to President Lincoln asking for his help to relieve Burbridge. The Governor and many Kentuckians felt that Burbridge went too far in his arrests of Lieutenant Governor Richard Jacob and Colonel Frank Wolford, former commander of the Union 1st Kentucky Cavalry. The radicals in the state made their last ditch effort to save their biggest supporter, but to no avail. By the end of the year Burbridge would be relieved of command.

On November 13, 1864, Burbridge continued to carry out his Order Number 59. He ordered the execution of six guerillas; three of the guerillas were brothers, named Horton, Tom Forrest, Mr. Moore, and John Fry, for the murder of a Union soldier in Henderson County. Colonel Glenn's United States Colored Troops executed the six men. The men were shot on a hill near the river and an old coal shaft. All six men came from Captain Ollie Steele's Company of Hollis regiment. Three days later November 15, 1864, Burbridge ordered the execution of two Confederate soldiers, named Captain McGee and Walter Ferguson. Walter Ferguson was a soldier in Confederate General John Hunt Morgan's command and a native of Lexington. Ferguson's friends and relatives tried to intervene on his behalf, but to no avail. Early in the morning, Federal soldiers took Ferguson and McGee out of the jail on Water Street in Lexington and took them to the fairgrounds in Lexington and hung them.[392] According to George Ranck, who was a witness in Lexington: "many a door and window was tightly closed that dismal day to shut out the horrible sights and sounds of that funeral march, and it was not without the sacred tribute of tears and prayers of the deepest sorrow that the soldiers died."[393]

On November 16, as Burbridge lost favor with his military superiors, the radicals in Kentucky, such as Reverend Robert Breckinridge, tried to keep him in command. Breckinridge wrote to President Lincoln to congratulate him on

392 Collins, 148.
393 J. Winston Coleman, Jr., *Lexington in the Civil War*, 48.

his recent victory in the elections, but he had to tell Lincoln of his betrayal and perilous condition in Kentucky. He stated that the old secession party and the Unionist party were united and took possession of Kentucky. The Unionist party in all official capacity exerted their power. He accused Governor Thomas Bramlette, member of the Unionist Party, of being the leader of the old secessionists. Breckinridge stated to Lincoln that Bramlette and his whole influence, with most of the officials, civil and military, were not to be trusted by loyal men in the state. He asked Lincoln whether the general government should uphold the state authorities who had betrayed the government and Breckinridge's Unconditional Unionist party or would Lincoln uphold the national cause and the Union party in defiance of the state authorities? If Lincoln supported the Unconditional Union party, the state would recover quickly, but if Lincoln did not support the Unconditional Union party, he would have to take the state by arms. He wrote that the state authorities would harm the state and that he did not need Governor Bramlette. He recommended that Lincoln ignore Governor Bramlette, restrain him, and not trust him or anyone around him, civil and military.[394]

Breckinridge stated that any officer who was hostile toward Lincoln could not be safely left in Kentucky. None of the civil authorities should be left in office if they were doubtful or negligent. He stated that the recent arrests made in Kentucky by Burbridge did incalculable good. He wrote that great efforts had been made to have General Burbridge release Judge Joshua Bullitt, Lt. Governor Richard Jacob, Mr. Paul Shipman, who was the associate editor of the *Louisville Journal*, and Colonel Frank Wolford. Breckinridge wrote that if these men were released and General Burbridge removed from his command, the whole national government would be thrown against the national cause in Kentucky. If the government sent General Burbridge to Washington, the result would be that the leading conspirators of the state would follow the lead of the *Louisville Journal* and succumb.[395]

The executions continued in Kentucky. On November 19, Burbridge ordered two separate executions. In Hart County, Burbridge ordered the execution of W. C. Martin, W. B Dunn, John Edmonson, J. M. Jones, W. L. Robinson, John Tomlinson, A. B. Tudor and Sanford Turley for the murders of Pvt. James F. Lile, formerly of Company B, 21st Kentucky Infantry and G. W. Rolston. A feared raid by General Hylan Lyon's men prevented the original men

394 Letter from Robert Breckinridge to Abraham Lincoln, November 16, 1864, Abraham Lincoln Papers, Library of Congress. Washington, D.C.

395 Letter from Robert Breckinridge to Abraham Lincoln, November 16, 1864, Abraham Lincoln Papers, Library of Congress. Washington, D.C.

selected for execution to be shot. Union soldiers drew a second lottery and W. C. Martin and John Tomlinson avoided execution on the second drawing, but Lycurgus Morgan, a soldier famous for his daring, was selected instead. The final six men selected—Lycurgus Morgan, John Henn, A. B. Tudor, W. T. Thornton, W. B. Dunn, and Jacob Baker—were shot to death in Green County.[396]

On November 22, Governor Thomas Bramlette telegraphed President Lincoln that Lt. Governor Richard Jacob and Colonel Frank Wolford were under arrest under the order of the Secret Inquisition. A Kentucky historian wrote in 1874 that a secret cabal of five men in Lexington controlled the actions of General Burbridge. Governor Bramlette asked Lincoln if he would order their release. President Lincoln replied to Bramlette stating that General Suddarth, commander of the Kentucky Home Guard, Mr. Hodges, Secretary of War Edwin Stanton and himself were trying to devise a means of pacification and harmony for Kentucky. Bramlette wired Lincoln back stating that Jacob and Wolford were patriots and devoted to the preservation of the Union and the suppression of the rebellion, but he understood that affidavits made in some "dark corner, extra judicial and ex parte, by men who were afraid to avow their infamy in the face of an open tribunal, face to face with the men they accused, constituted the foundation of their arrest." He wrote to the President that those who "falsely accuse dread the light of an investigation; and therefore, they seek to keep up a secret inquisition, in which to condemn without a trial and punish without a hearing."[397]

On November 22, 1864, Theodore Bell, a Kentucky physician, Unconditional Unionist and president of the Kentucky branch of the U.S. Sanitary Commission, wrote to Judge Advocate Joseph Holt in the case of Lieutenant Richard Jacob and pleaded to keep Burbridge in command. Bell referred to a petition being circulated on the behalf of Richard Jacob. The 47 men who signed the petition claimed to be unconditional Unionists, including Lincoln's friend Joshua Speed. Bell stated that most of the signers were either Rebels in their sympathies or men who were for the Union, provided their conditions were met. He claimed most of the signers were enemies of the administration and sympathized in the violent sentiments expressed by Jacob. The Union men of Kentucky rewarded Jacob by making him Lieutenant Governor. Jacob was a Unionist who organized the 9th Kentucky Cavalry and served as Colonel, but he became an outspoken critic of the Emancipation Proclamation and opposed the election of Union soldiers. He also campaigned for Union General George

396 Collins, *History of Kentucky*, 148; James Head, *The Atonement of John Brooks*, 208.

397 Collins, *History of Kentucky*, 148.

B. McClellan, who was on the Democratic ticket. Bell wrote that Jacob repaid the Unionists with treachery. According to Bell, in Jacob's speech in New Albany, Indiana, he said Kentucky had tolerated the election of Lincoln once, but she would not do it again. The night before the election in Louisville Jacob's "violent in his speech, in uttering his proscriptive policy as Scylla was at Rome. He named Union men in this city who would have to leave, and he said all who entertained similar sentiments should be exiled."[398]

Bell wrote that Burbridge should not be set aside, at the instance of men who hate him because of his loyalty. All appeals for release of the men arrested should be made to Burbridge, "who is faithfully carrying out the policy announced in the orders of General Sherman." The President of the Louisville Union League, O. F. Miner, endorsed Bell's letter and recommended that the matter of Lieutenant Governor Jacob should rest with General Burbridge.[399]

On November 23, 1864, Charles Eginton wrote to President Abraham Lincoln stating that the latest arrests of Lt. Governor Richard Jacob, Colonel Frank Wolford, and others who allegedly made treasonable speeches during the election campaign, were not made at his instance or obtained by him, but with the approval of leading Unionists whose information and patriotism entitled them to every proper consideration, and a summary discharge of the Parties would not only bring the authorities in Kentucky into disrespect, but embolden the enemies of the government to commit further outrages. He had canvassed the Congressional District as the Union Candidate for Elector and he became aware of the violent denunciations and those who opposed Lincoln's election, including Rebels who went to the polls with arms in their hands and used violence if necessary to put down the "Minions of the administration." He stated that evil influence exercised by the Rebels made it dangerous for Union men. He had to remain at his home in Winchester, but felt compelled to spend half his time in Lexington, Kentucky. He felt assured that Radical Republican Dr. Robert Breckinridge, Judge William Goodloe and others would support his views and he called for the most stringent measures to protect the future as well as punish the past.[400]

Judge William Goodloe wrote Lincoln that Kentucky was more disloyal than Tennessee, and if the military forces were not present, no loyal man could remain in the state. He urged that if severe measures were not used toward the leaders, Kentucky would outbreak in 60 days. According to Goodloe, the

398 T. S. Bell to Joseph Holt, November 22, 1864 (Case of Richard Jacob), Abraham Lincoln Papers, Library of Congress, Washington, D. C.

399 Ibid.

400 Letter from William C. Goodloe and Charles Eginton to Abraham Lincoln, Wednesday, November 23, 1864, Abraham Lincoln Papers, Library of Congress, Washington, D.C.

speeches of Lieutenant Governor Richard Jacob, Colonel Frank Wolford, Thomas Bramlette, Harlan, Davis Clay, and John Houston, had aroused the bad passions of the opponents of the administration which would require severe measures. In Louisville, he stated that Lincoln's friends did not canvass and lost the city and country around them. He wrote that General Burbridge was not severe enough and the Union men may have to ask for General Benjamin Butler before loyal men could get any security. Judge Goodloe could not attend a court 12 miles from Lexington without a military guard.[401] Goodloe wrote another letter to the President on the same day stating that the arrest of Lieutenant Governor Jacob and Colonel Frank Wolford by General Burbridge led to great complaints. He stated that the loyal men of Kentucky advised and fully endorsed General Burbridge's actions. In his opinion, Jacob and Wolford were too dangerous for the safety of Kentucky to be permitted to remain in the state making incendiary and treasonable speeches. He hoped that General Burbridge's actions would not be interfered with.[402]

At the end of November Union Assistant Adjutant General E. D. Townsend wrote to General Burbridge that he had received a communication signed by Joseph Clement and others from the Union League of Louisville requesting that rations be issued by the government to the suffering poor of the city, which was forwarded with his recommendation. The chief of staff, General Henry Halleck, recommended that "if Louisville will not support her own poor and destitute, General Burbridge should be authorized to levy a military contribution for that purpose from the disloyal inhabitants of that city." Halleck's recommendation was also approved by Secretary of War Edwin Stanton. On November 30, 1864, Burbridge had no choice but to implement the recommendation. He ordered that all disloyal inhabitants of Louisville contribute for the benefit of the suffering poor.[403] By implementing the policies of his superiors, Burbridge incurred the unpopularity of issuing such orders.[404]

Suffering did not only occur in Louisville, at Camp Nelson, the largest black recruiting camp, Burbridge wrote to Secretary of War Stanton that a large number of black women and children accumulated at Camp Nelson. Many of them were wives and children of the Union black soldiers. He wrote that their would be a lot of suffering among them during the winter, unless shelters

401 Letter from William C. Goodloe and Charles Eginton to Abraham Lincoln, Wednesday, November 23, 1864, Abraham Lincoln Papers, Library of Congress, Washington, D.C.

402 Letter from William Goodloe to President Abraham Lincoln, November 23, 1864, Abraham Lincoln papers, Library of Congress, Washington, D.C.

403 O.R. Series I, Vol. LII/1 [S# 109] Letter from E. D. Townsend Assistant Adjutant General to General Stephen Gano Burbridge with endorsement, November 26, 1864.

404 Louis De Falaise, "Gen. Stephen Gano Burbridge's Command in Kentucky," Kentucky Historical Society, (69, April 1971), 117.

were built and rations issued to them. He pleaded to the Secretary, "for the sake of humanity, I hope you will issue the proper order in this case as soon as possible."[405]

On December 1, 1864, Albert Hodges, editor of the Frankfort, Kentucky, newspaper, *Commonwealth*, wrote to President Lincoln about the affairs in Kentucky. Kentucky citizens became bitterly divided over the policies of General Burbridge. His arrest of prominent citizens, such as Lieutenant Governor Richard Jacob, worsened the already tense relationship between the Lincoln administration and Governor Bramlette. Hodges and General Samuel G. Suddarth, commander of the Kentucky State Militia, met with Lincoln on November 22, 1864, to discuss "means of pacification and harmony for Kentucky." He wrote to Lincoln that had General Burbridge had carried out, in good faith, the instructions given to him by Lincoln and Secretary of War Edwin Stanton, in the matter of raising troops in Kentucky, whether black or white, and the Chief Executive officer of Kentucky consulted, there would have been no difficulty between them. Hodges went to visit General Burbridge to try to bring about harmony between the Governor and Burbridge. Burbridge promised Hodges that he would try to make it convenient to have consultations with the Governor and do everything in his power to harmonize their action. Hodge wrote to Lincoln that General Burbridge did not carry out his promise and never consulted with the Governor on any subject.[406]

Hodges asked Governor Bramlette if he would support General Ambrose Burnside taking command of Kentucky. Governor Bramlette told Hodges that the people of Kentucky would respond with joy. Hodges stated that if Lincoln gave to Kentucky General Burnside, the Governor would have no problem in favoring an amendment to the Constitution for the abolition of slavery throughout the country. Hodges asked Lincoln to remove the permit system, the hog restriction, the restoration of those who had been arrested for expressing improper sentiments during the election, to their restoration of their homes and families, to wipe out old scores, and make a fresh start.[407]

On December 1, 1864, Burbridge ordered the Assistant Adjutant General E. D. Townsend to supply the wants of the black women and children who accumulated at Camp Nelson. A. Schofield of the United States Sanitary Commission wrote that the government would build suitable buildings for the women and children of Camp Nelson and a permanent home would be erected

405 O.R. Series, I, Vol. 45/1 General Stephen Burbridge to Secretary of War Edwin Stanton, November 29, 1864.

406 Albert G. Hodges to Abraham Lincoln, December 1, 1864, Abraham Lincoln Papers, Library of Congress, Washington, D.C.

407 Ibid.

for them so they could be educated and furnished with work. He wrote that two or three hundred women and children would be brought permanently into the school and Camp Nelson "would become the most important place in the State of Kentucky."[408]

The next day, on December 2, 1864, Union General Ulysses Grant wrote to Secretary of War Stanton recommending General Darius Couch to replace Burbridge as commander in Kentucky. Stanton replied to Grant's request and stated that Couch was not a good administrative officer for Kentucky. He preferred General George Stoneman. President Lincoln wanted to see the reports about Burbridge. If the complaints against Burbridge were true, then there was no need to keep him in command, "but if the military authority is surrendered to a sympathizer with Bramlette, Doctor [Robert] Breckinridge says it will be necessary to conquer Kentucky."[409]

On December 7, 1864, Assistant Adjutant General E. H. Ludington wrote a scathing report to Secretary of War Edwin Stanton on the military and civilian affairs in Kentucky. He wrote to Stanton that a delegation of prominent Kentucky citizens were on their way to Washington to urge a change in policy in the military administration of their state. Ludington submitted his report to Stanton stating that Kentucky had scarcely any security for persons or property. In nearly every county guerillas destroyed property and took the lives of anyone who was or had been in the United States army. The citizens were bitterly "arrayed against each other as to afford immunity, if not assistance, to these desperadoes, for each party is glad to see men of the other murdered. From this intestine hatred guerillas have their origin and maintenance."[410]

In his opinion, Kentucky remained in the Union to preserve slavery and avoid becoming the theater of war, although they strongly sympathized with the South. When the government attempted to draft men or enlist blacks into the Union army, they turned against the government. Kentucky citizens resisted Union officers and became more violent in their denunciations of the administration than the Rebels. In his opinion, a large majority of Kentuckians were disloyal.[411]

Ludington stated that the Kentucky forces comprised entirely of regiments raised in the state for the term of one year's service within the state. They were distributed in very small detachments and never served with their

---

408 Sears, *Camp Nelson*, 144-145.

409 O.R. Series I, Vol. XLV/2 [#94] General U. S. Grant to Edwin Stanton, Secretary of War, December 2, 1864. Letter from Edwin Stanton to General Grant December 3, 1864.

410 O.R. Series I, Vol. XLV/2 [#94] Letter from Assistant Adjutant General Ludington to Secretary of War Edwin Stanton, December 7, 1864.

411 Ibid.

regiments. As a rule, their officers had little capacity and were ignorant of their duties. There was no drill, or discipline among the men. In his opinion, they were a uniformed mob. Serving at home with their local prejudices, they regard their own interests instead of the interests of the country. They did little to punish guerillas. They plundered at their own discretion. As a result, their victims, with all their friends, became exasperated against the government and the troops employed to protect them. He suggested that no regiments formed in Kentucky should serve in the state.[412]

In his report, Ludington stated that Governor Bramlette preferred Union to rebellion but loved slavery. In his opinion, Bramlette hoped to gratify his aspirations for election to the U.S. Senate by yielding to the pressure bearing down upon him from the slave interests in Kentucky. He knew the people of Kentucky were disloyal and put qualifications on his Unionism. His advisors did not conceal their hostility to enlist black soldiers. The Governor's policy was "simply self first, State second, Union last. But he has not enough backbone to make a direct issue with the administration; therefore its policy need not be affected in any way by his views."[413]

Ludington stated that General Burbridge relied upon the advice of others. Their prejudices and interests led him astray. His administration had been a good one. In matters military, he appeared to be lax. Everything seemed to be in confusion. After making every allowance for the inefficiency of field and line officers under his command, there was the want of capacity and energy. He was hated by a majority of Kentuckians, but that signified nothing if he pursued a policy of stringency and impartiality. Ludington did not hear rumors for the demand for Burbridge's removal from command, but heard that the substitution of a man stronger in capacity and character would be a better course to follow.[414]

Ludington suggested in his report that all guerillas must be crushed in the state. In order to crush the guerillas, one hundred good Union troops from another state must be placed in each county. All troops raised in Kentucky should be assigned elsewhere. No troops should be allowed in state service. Noisy and active rebel sympathizers and those who supported the rebellion should be dealt with rigorously. Offenses should be clearly proved, and after proof, no relenting. Every distinction should be made in favor of active and tried Union men. The policy of the administration should be rigidly enforced and Kentucky should feel herself governed, as the state was not, either by civilian

412 Ibid.
413 Ibid.
414 Ibid.

or military authorities. If the Governor arrayed himself against the administration, he should be superseded.[415]

On December 10, 1864, Reverend Stuart Robinson wrote to President Lincoln about Burbridge's order to suppress the *True Presbyterian*, which was an ecclesiastical journal. Robinson served on the faculty and was president of the Danville Theological Seminary in Kentucky from 1856 to 1858. General Burbridge twice suppressed the journal in 1863, and again in November of 1864 for reasons that remain unclear. Rev. Robinson moved to Canada in 1863. He also wrote to Lincoln on behalf of his friend Rev. Samuel B. McPheeters of the Pine Street Presbyterian Church of St. Louis, who had been expelled from his pulpit and ordered from Missouri in 1862 because of his alleged Southern sympathies. In December 1863, a petition to reinstate McPheeters arrived at Lincoln's desk, but he stated that he would not involve himself in ecclesiastical affairs. Rev. Robinson again pleaded for Rev. McPheeters and stated that the *True Presbyterian* never contained political or military affairs or even news of political or military affairs, except when they obstructed upon the church. According to Robinson, the suppression of the journal came from Rev. Robert Breckinridge's personal malignity and the administration's theologians were against him. He freely admitted that he did not sustain Lincoln's administration, but he did not wish to be driven into opposition toward him. He hoped Lincoln would countermand Burbridge's "foolish order of suppression." He appealed to his friends, Dr. Phineas Gurley, the pastor of the New York Avenue Presbyterian Church in Washington, D.C., which was attended by the Lincolns, and to Mrs. Margaret Todd Kellogg and Emilie Todd Helm, who were Mrs. Mary Todd Lincoln's half sisters, to his reliability.[416]

On December 11, another radical in the state, Commonwealth Attorney for the 8th District, John Scott wrote to President Lincoln stating that political enemies in Kentucky had tried to remove General Burbridge from command. He stated that if the men succeeded, his removal would be a blow to the loyal people of Kentucky. He wrote that Burbridge's removal would be a triumph for every rebel and guerilla in the state. He stated that all the complaints against General Burbridge did not come from the loyal men of Kentucky, but from the camp of the enemy. [417]

Scott also wrote that on January 4, 1865, the Union Party in Kentucky

---

415 Ibid.

416 Stuart Robinson to Abraham Lincoln [with Lincoln's endorsement], December 10, 1864, Toronto, Canada, Abraham Lincoln Papers, Library of Congress, Washington, D.C. transcribed and annotated by the Lincoln Studies center, Knox college, Galesburg, Illinois.

417 Letter from John Scott to Abraham Lincoln, Lexington, Kentucky, December 11, 1864, Abraham Lincoln papers, Library of Congress, Washington, D.C.

would hold a convention in Frankfort, in which the policies of General Burbridge would be freely discussed and hoped that Lincoln would not take any action to remove Burbridge until after the convention. He had no doubt that the convention would pass the immediate emancipation of slaves in Kentucky.[418]

On December 17, General Burbridge issued an order requiring ferry boats plying the Ohio River to have permits or to know that that the owners had permits, for cattle, produce, and goods crossing the river.[419]

Union General George Stoneman, along with General Burbridge, led another raid in December 1864 against the salt works. Four thousand Union cavalry, including the 5th USCC and the 6th USCC participated in the raid. The cavalrymen suffered from exposure to the cold weather. Numerous deaths occurred resulting from the cold weather. On December 17-18, outnumbering the Confederates four to one, the Federals took on Confederate General John C. Breckinridge's men along the Holston River. After two days of fighting, Breckinridge withdrew. On December 20, 1864, General Stoneman captured Saltville and began destroying the works, lead mines, the Virginia & Tennessee Railroad, and the town of Abington, Wytheville and Bristol.[420] General Burbridge reported that salt works at Saltville and the lead works at Wytheville, Tennessee were in ruins and could not be repaired. But General Breckinridge reported that the damage "can soon be repaired; the enemy are being pursued."[421]

On December 26, 1864, Lieutenant Governor Richard Jacob wrote to Lincoln a letter in his own defense. Jacob stated in his letter to Lincoln that on November 11, General Burbridge arrested Jacob at his country home 25 miles above the city of Louisville. He was taken to Lexington and kept at Union General Nathaniel C. McLean's headquarters, who was the district commander of Kentucky. Jacob was carried under strict guard and expelled through Federal lines under the penalty of death if he returned during the war. He was forced into Confederate lines, to accept hospitality and protection from people he had fought against and after he had shed his blood. He claimed that he was seized as a felon, not permitted to talk with his friends or consult with his friends, not confronted, no charges preferred, and no trial permitted. He had no idea why he was arrested, except through a newspaper clipping from the *Cincinnati Commercial*, which stated that the *Washington Post* stated that the arrest of Jacob would lead to important disclosures of a wide conspiracy to inaugurate a second revolution, the object of which was to make Kentucky

418 Ibid.
419 Collins, *History of Kentucky*, 150.
420 Mays, 68.
421 *Military History of Kentucky*, 217.

independent of the United States government. Jacob stated that he knew nothing of a conspiracy. He was never connected with a conspiracy. He had never belonged to any secret political, military or any other kind of organization in his life. He freely admitted that he was opposed to Lincoln's re-election. He believed that Lincoln's re-election was a misfortune to the country. He had worked with all his energy and intellect to defeat Lincoln. He believed it was his right and duty as an American citizen. Lincoln was re-elected against his wishes and efforts. He was also determined to bow as a good citizen to the verdict of the American people. He did not intend to give Lincoln factious opposition. He was not permitted to remain quiet. Three days after the election he was arrested, but on December 1, 1864, he read in the *Louisville Journal* that Lincoln had consented to the release of Jacob and Colonel Frank Wolford. Jacob wanted to know whether the story was true and whether Lincoln would issue an order for him to be passed through the lines to return to his duties as Lieutenant Governor. He asked that General Burbridge's order be rescinded. Jacob wrote to Lincoln that he had not committed any crime and did not ask for a pardon, but merely asked for justice. Lincoln wrote to Jacob on January 18, 1865, granting him permission to return to Kentucky.[422]

On December 28, 1864, Union Captain J. Bates Dickson, Assistant Adjutant General to General Burbridge, wrote to Lincoln that Lieutenant Governor Jacob's offense was making treasonable and seditious speeches, which were calculated and intended to weaken the power of the government in its efforts to suppress the rebellion. According to Dickson, Jacob's arrest was advised by Reverend Robert Breckinridge and other prominent loyal men of Kentucky.[423]

On December 28, 1864, the commissioners of investigation of black troops in Kentucky, Tennessee, and Alabama issued their report to the Secretary of War Edwin Stanton. They reported that they visited Louisville, Lexington, and Camp Nelson, Kentucky. They reported there was no organized camp for the reception and care of black refugees within the state. That Camp Nelson had been broke up and abandoned, by the order of Brigadier General L. Thomas, Adjutant General. The abandonment of Camp Nelson not only encouraged the hopes of secession sympathizers in Kentucky, but, discouraged enlistments of black men, who would not leave their families to the "tender mercies of

422 Richard Jacob to Abraham Lincoln, December 26, 1864 [with endorsement by Lincoln], December 26, 1864, Richmond, Virginia. Abraham Lincoln Papers, Library of Congress, Washington, D.C.

423 J. Bates Dickson to Abraham Lincoln, December 28, 1864, Abraham Lincoln papers, Library of Congress, Washington, D.C.

Kentucky hospitality, humanity or Christianity."[424] Many of the women and children of the Union black soldiers suffered because they were driven from their homes by their Union-hating masters. Hundreds of refugees from other states congregated to Kentucky for safety and protection. They recommended a camp of reception be instituted for both black and white troops at Camp Nelson. They reported that they found General Burbridge "a gentleman whose sympathies are largely with these distressed people; and the recommendations we here make are strictly in accordance with his views and wishes, and which we sincerely hope may meet with your approval."[425]

On January 2, 1865, General Burbridge returned from his second expedition to Saltville, Virginia. Five hundred black soldiers joined Burbridge along with Union General Alvan Gillem's troops. A battalion of the 6th USCC cavalry, 300 hundred men, attacked and defeated Confederate General Basil Duke's brigade. The Confederates were driven half a mile, with a loss of 30 men killed and wounded. They were on the crest of a hill at Marion, and the black troops charged over open ground, and did not fire a gun until within 30 yards of the Confederates. This was the first time the 6th USCC was under fire.[426]

Although Burbridge and his forces finally took Saltville, his command faced overwhelming criticism from his superiors. Investigations by military commanders concluded that Burbridge had no military control in his state. Guerilla warfare continued to wreak havoc. Although the radicals tried to support their best defender, Burbridge's command was coming to an end. President Lincoln became involved in the criticism against Burbridge and Lincoln did not like what he heard from his informants. Burbridge's days as the military district commander of Kentucky were numbered. By February 1865, Burbridge would leave his command.

---

424 Richard Sears, *Camp Nelson: A Civil War History*, (Lexington: University of Lexington Press, 2002), 160.

425 Ibid.

426 O.R. Series I, Vol. XLV/2 [#94] Letter from L. Thomas, Adjutant General to Secretary of War Edwin Stanton, January 2, 1865.

Chapter 11

A Career Comes to an End

As a new year came to Kentucky, the Civil War was winding down. Union General Ulysses S. Grant pursued Confederate General Robert E. Lee and his Army of Northern Virginia near Richmond, Virginia. Union General William T. Sherman pursued Confederate General Joseph Johnston in the Carolinas. The Confederacy was coming to an end. Burbridge's command was also coming to an end. Even though the radicals in the state petitioned on behalf of Burbridge, the criticism from Governor Thomas Bramlette, his military superiors, such as Union General John Schofield, local Kentuckians, and informants forced President Abraham Lincoln to relieve Burbridge of command. Burbridge's legacy as "Butcher Burbridge" would forever haunt him. Burbridge may have thought he was supporting the Union cause, but he only drove Kentuckians away from the Republican Party and into the Democratic Party.

On January 2, 1865, Governor Thomas Bramlette wrote to Secretary of War Edwin Stanton that the Kentucky legislature authorized him to raise 5,000 men for the defense of the state. He deferred the matter until the condition of affairs demands that Stanton and Brameltte do something to rid the state of guerrillas. He wrote that the troops raised would be for the state's protection. The few state forces he had in the field rendered material assistance to the government in keeping open communication with the Union army at the front and protecting the citizens of Kentucky. He asked the secretary of war to issue him all necessary papers. His troops would cooperate with the Federal authorities in case of invasion and ridding the state of guerrillas. The raising of the 5,000 men would not interfere with enlistments required by the Federal government to fill their quotas. The Secretary of War granted Bramlette's request.[427]

On January 4, 1865, the Radical Union state convention convened in Frankfort. Judge William C. Goodloe, president of the state convention, invited Union General George Thomas and General Burbridge and staff to sit with

427 The Military Department of Kentucky, *Military History of Kentucky*, (The American Guide Series, Works Projects Administration, 1939), 224, 225.

the delegates. The convention recommended to the President that Burbridge be made a Brigadier General in the Regular army and the committee approved "cordially of the most rigorous retaliatory warfare against all guerillas, raiders, and fully endorses the action of the Federal military authorities in the discharge of their duties." During the convention Burbridge explained that the return of Judge Joshua Bullitt was by an exchange of prisoners between Confederate General Nathan Bedford Forrest and Federal General Henry Washburne and if Bullitt returned to Kentucky, Burbridge would arrest him again. He also stated that Bullitt should have been arrested and hung and would have been arrested had he not escaped."[428] Burbridge's statement pleased his radical supporters.

On January 5, 1865, President Lincoln informed General Ulysses Grant to allow Lieutenant Governor Richard Jacob to pass through Union lines and meet him in Washington, D.C.[429]

During Governor Thomas Bramlette's annual message to the Kentucky legislature on January 6, 1865, he again attacked General Burbridge. In his speech he stated that he selected Burbridge to carry out certain agreements, such as preventing unlawful acts growing out of black soldiers recruitment; agreeing to stop recruiting or drafting in each county as soon as its quota was filled, to confine recruiting to the regularly appointed officers for that service, and removing the recruited blacks to camps of instruction outside the state of Kentucky, "instead of doing so, [Burbridge] adopted the most offensive and injurious modes of violating them. . . . He established a system of trade permits in violation of law and to the detriment of the public interests, which, as administered, was a most shameful and corrupt system of partisan political corruption and oppression."[430] He advised the legislature to "collect the facts, showing its corrupt use, and present them to the national authorities, in such form as to secure the abolishment and future prohibition of all such interferences with the lawful and necessary trade of the country." The Governor brought up the hog swindle of the 1864 and stated that Burbridge patronized the swindle which was being carried on by the Commissary Department. Bramlette put an end to the hog swindle, but not before "the farmers had sustained losses to at least $300,000, yet in time to save them the loss of over $1,000,000. It is due to the honest farmers of the state that you collate, or provide for so doing, the facts bearing upon this attempted and partially executed fraud, and present them also in connection with the military trade regulations." Bramlette stated that the

428 Collins, Lewis & Collins, Richard, *History of Kentucky*, Vol. 1 , 1874., 151.

429 O.R. Series II, vol. VIII [#121] Letter from President Lincoln to General Ulysses S. Grant.

430 Collins, *History of Kentucky*, 151.

gravest matter of military outrages occurred when loyal citizens were arrested, imprisoned, and banished without a hearing or without even knowing what charges were put against them. The governor stated that many of the arrests were for partisan political vengeance and the arrested were forced to pay heavy sums of money for their release and stated that "how the spoils, so infamously extorted, are divided, has not transpired to the public information." The governor recommended that the limitation to actions for malicious arrest and false imprisonment be repealed. He also recommended that the offense of causing or obtaining arrests under malicious or false imprisonment be a felony or high misdemeanor.[431] After Bramlette's speech, great indignation of the citizens of Kentucky fell over the state because of the hog swindle. The citizens were not only upset at the military authorities who had used their power and threats to carry the hog swindle, but also at the private individuals who were suspected, or more than suspected, of "sharing in the spoils of the plunder."[432]

On January 8, 1865, President Lincoln set aside Burbridge's order of December 17, 1864, restricting trade with Kentucky. Burbridge's adjutant general, J. Bates Dickson denied that any such order was ever given by Burbridge.[433]

In a special message to the legislature, Governor Bramlette on January 11, 1865, told of a telegram he had received from the "general commanding," referring to General Burbridge, which directed him to take immediate steps for the mustering out of state troops, in compliance with the orders from the war department. The Governor told the legislature that he intended to go forward and encourage the organization of companies for one year state service, under the act of February 20, 1864. He stated that the commander of the district prohibited him from recruiting the state troops. Bramlette stated the "malevolent opposition to the employment of the necessary means for defense of the citizens of the state and this unwarrantable assumption of control over the civil authorities of the state, and the effort by military threats to nullify a law of the state, should be ended."[434] Bramlette appointed a committee by the General Assembly to go to Washington to see the President and try to revoke the order, since the safety of Kentucky citizens required Federal troops in the absence of state troops.

On January 12, 1865, Captain Charles M. Keyser, Acting Assistant Adjutant General, wrote to General Burbridge informing him that the general commanding desired information on whether the state troops had been mustered

431 Collins, 151.
432 Ibid., 153.
433 Ibid., 152.
434 Ibid., 152.

out of service, in compliance with an order received from the War Department. If not, Burbridge was to take immediate steps to muster out and to prevent by order any further recruiting in such organizations.[435]

On that same day, January 12, 1865, Confederate Major General John C. Breckinridge wrote to General Burbridge that he had received information that Burbridge held in irons at Lexington, Kentucky, Colonel John D. Morris, Lt. Colonel C. K. Johnson, and Major Theophilus Steele, who were to be executed. Breckinridge informed Burbridge that Morris and Steele were regularly recognized officers of the Confederate Army from his command, and Johnson was a regularly commissioned officer. Breckinridge was not going to argue with Burbridge over legality, but he demanded for the prisoners to be treated as prisoners of war, and if they were executed, he would resort to extreme measures to secure justice to the officers and men of his command. Breckinridge's aim was to alleviate the necessary hardships and suffering of prisoners of war. Any exceptional treatment of those who had fallen into his hands had been in violation of his orders and had promptly received necessary attention. He had the right to claim that prisoners of war from his command be treated as prisoners of war. Breckinridge held three Union officers of equal rank from Burbridge's command, whose treatment would be regulated by Burbridge's treatment of Breckinridge's officers. If Burbridge changed the status of his prisoners from guerillas to prisoners of war, Breckinridge would do the same for his prisoners.[436]

On January 20, 1865, a military commission condemned Nathaniel Marks, Company G, 7th Confederate Cavalry, as a guerilla. Marks protested his innocence, but to no avail. Union soldiers executed Marks in Louisville, Kentucky.[437]

On January 21, 1865, Union Brigadier General H. W. Wessells, Inspector General of Prisoners, wrote to General Burbridge that he requested that Colonel J.D. Morris and Major Steele to be immediately released and forwarded under guard to Lieutenant Colonel John E. Mulford, agent for exchange of prisoners, Fort Monroe, Virginia.[438]

On February 4, 1865, H. T. Martin, President of the Union League in

435 O.R. Series I, Vol. XLV/2 [#94] Letter from Capt. Chas. M. Keyser to Major General Burbridge, January 12, 1865.

436 O.R. Series II, Vol. VIII [#121] Union and Confederate Correspondence, Orders, Etc., relating to prisoners of war and state from January 1, 1865 to the end. Letter from John C. Breckinridge to General Burbridge.

437 James Head, *The Atonement of John Brooks*, 209.

438 O.R. Series II, Vol. VIII [#121] Union and Confederate Correspondence, Orders, Etc., relating to prisoners of war and state from January 1, 1865 to the end. Letter from General H. W. Wessells to General Stephen Burbridge.

Louisville, Kentucky, wrote to General Burbridge asking him to help the destitute and suffering families of Union soldiers. He also asked to help the widows and orphans of husbands and fathers who had died during the war. He stated: "Can we do nothing to alleviate their pressing and present wants? Is there no way by which their necessary wants could be supplied from the subsistence department? If not, humanity demands, that some other plan should be devised or immediate steps taken to relieve their wants. General, you are aware, no doubt, of the fact that the city of Louisville, in her incorporate capacity, has never taken a step or made an effort toward providing for this class of our destitute citizens. Neither has there been any organized effort on the part of citizens in their behalf." Martin suggested that since the majority of citizens of Louisville had grown rich by their operations and were Southern sympathizers, they should give up their ill gotten gains to be applied to the suffering for the poor. The Union League was gratified that Burbridge commanded the military department of Kentucky and approved and appreciated his past services.[439]

On February 5, 1865, C. J. Lawton wrote to General Burbridge that on January 22, 1865, a company of about 40 men, equipped in Federal uniforms, came to Hartford, Kentucky, claiming they were from the 4th Missouri Cavalry and had been detached to hunt guerillas. The captain of the outfit was Captain Jerome Clarke. Clarke deceived Colonel Shanks and Lawton, who regarded Clarke as a true Federal officer. Clarke asked for a guide to lead him to the Ohio River, where the guerillas were present. They recommended Liuetenant Barnett, who was a recruiting officer of the 125th U.S. Colored Infantry. W. B. Lawton, a soldier from an Indiana regiment who was in Hartford to see his family on leave and wished to return to Evansville, Indiana, to join his regiment, also left with Clarke, after he told Lawton he was going to Owensboro, Kentucky, and would provide Lawton safe passage. W. Lownsley, a discharged soldier of the Union 3rd Kentucky Cavalry, also joined Clarke. About three miles from Hartford, near the Hawsville Road, Captain Clarke hung Lownsley. He was found in the woods a week later. They shot Lawton and Barnett and their bodies were later recovered along side the road. Captain Jerome Clarke was none other than the notorious guerilla, Sue Mundy.[440]

---

439 O.R. Series I, Vol. XLIX {#103] Union Correspondence, Orders, and Returns relating to operations in Kentucky, Southwestern Virginia, Tennessee, Northern and Central Georgia, Mississippi, Alabama, and West Florida, from January 1 to March 15, 1865 #4, Letter from H. T. Martin to General Stephen Burbridge, February 4, 1865.

440 O.R. Series I, Vol. XLIX {#103] Union Correspondence, Orders, and Returns relating to operations in Kentucky, Southwestern Virginia, Tennessee, Northern and Central Georgia, Mississippi, Alabama, and West Florida, from January 1 to March 15, 1865 #4, Letter from H. T. Martin to General Stephen Burbridge, February 4, 1865.

Martin wrote to General Burbridge that every gang of guerillas who visited Hartford, Kentucky, inquired for the men who voted for Lincoln. The citizens had to save their lives by hiding in the brush and hiding out until the guerillas left. They rejoiced when Burbridge announced that men in every county would clean out the guerillas. Colonel Q. C. Shanks recruited a company for the county. People in Hartford were completely subjugated and dared not to speak their sentiments if they were for the policy of the administration. They could have carried the election for Lincoln if it had not been for the guerillas. Lawton was a member of the Unconditional Union Convention held in Louisville in May 1864. Lawton stated that the true loyal men of Hartford all had their eyes turned toward Burbridge, believing he would save them from their unhappy and dangerous position.[441]

On February 6, 1865, Burbridge issued General Order Number 5, stating that President Lincoln had declared martial law in Kentucky. The organizing, equipping, and maintaining of troops under state authority was deemed unlawful and all troops organized, equipped, and maintained were to be disbanded. Commanding officers of state troops were to make sure that all arms were returned to the state arsenal or delivered to the nearest United States quartermaster.[442]

The next day, Governor Bramlette wrote to Secretary of War Edwin Stanton, that the ordered issued by General Burbridge was an "unwarranted assumption of power by an imbecile commander." In the governor's opinion, General Burbridge's order was instigated by men who had long sought to provoke an issue with the state.[443]

On February 7, 1865, Secretary of War Stanton wrote to Burbridge that his General Order Number 5 had been under the immediate consideration of President Lincoln, but he considered Burbridge's action in issuing the order as premature and that he should have waited until the President's determination had been communicated to Burbridge. He ordered Burbridge to revoke his Order Number 5 and abstain from making any other upon the subject until further instructed by the President or by his order.[444]

By this point, President Lincoln had enough of Burbridge. The next day on February 7, 1865, Secretary of War Stanton wrote to Major General John Palmer that President Lincoln had assigned him to command the Department

441 Ibid.

442 O.R. Series I, Vol. XLIX [#103] Letter from Bramlette to Secretary of War Edwin Stanton.

443 O.R. Series I, Vol. XLIX [#103] Letter from Bramlette to Secretary of War Edwin Stanton.

444 O.R. Series I, Vol. XLIX [#103] Letter from Secretary of War Edwin Stanton to Major General Stephen G. Burbridge.

of the Ohio, including the state of Kentucky. The President desired Palmer to focus his attention on Kentucky. The reason was that the Kentucky state troops were disorganized and undisciplined which rendered them almost completely useless against rebel military forces. Palmer was to place his troops, both white and black, in a state of discipline and organization. Major General Burbridge was to be relieved of command and ordered to report to Major General George Thomas for duty in the field.[445]

General Palmer was to continue in the recruiting of black soldiers. President Lincoln was "grieved to be informed that much hostility still exists in the minds of some evil disposed persons in the State of Kentucky against the enlistment of colored soldiers, and that, in order to discourage their enlistment, many cases have occurred of their cruel and barbarous treatment and murder." Palmer was to stop all outrages against black recruiting. The destitute women and children of soldiers in U.S. service, without regard to color, should be given protection and support. He was to ration food, clothing and fuel and shelter to the helpless women and children. A separate account was to be kept by proper officers of all issues to the women and children, so that war expenditures were to be kept separate from civilian expenditures. Refugees from Rebel territory who fled to his department would also receive adequate supplies as well as transportation to enable them to enter the Northern states.[446]

According to Secretary of War Edwin Stanton, guerrillas infested Kentucky. Some of the guerillas were made up of rebels, who had sometime or other been in the Confederate military forces, and of their sympathizers at home. Guerillas were plundering and murdering peaceable citizens. He ordered General Palmer that all such persons were to be treated as "enemies of the human race, and no effort spared to root out and destroy them in the most prompt and effectual manner. You will deal with them in such way as in your judgment will be most effective for the accomplishment of that purpose."[447]

Stanton instructed Palmer to protect all loyal citizens and their property. His department should be diligently and constantly employed and kept in a state of action for the repression of disorders and the restoration of peace and security within his command. The President also declared martial law in Kentucky.[448]

The President also declared that any enlistment of soldiers to be employed within the limits of the state made by the legislative and executive authorities of Kentucky was prohibited. Only the general government could raise troops

445 O.R. Series I, Vol. XLVI/2 [#96] Letter from Secretary of War Edwin Stanton to Major General John Palmer.

446 Ibid.

447 Ibid.

448 Ibid.

to protect the state from domestic insurrection and violence.[449] Even though Governor Bramlette received his wish to replace Burbridge, Lincoln did not approve of his order to raise state troops for his own purpose. According to Stanton, General Palmer still carried on Burbridge's policy to execute all guerillas. Not much changed in the official policy as to how to treat guerillas, but the scandals, the corruption, the inefficiency of Burbridge's administration finally forced President Lincoln to relieve him of command.

Stanton ordered General Palmer to cultivate a friendly and harmonious spirit between the Federal and state government. He was to work with Governor Bramlette and the state authorities, solicit their cooperation, and administer his department so as to give no indication that he offended anyone. He was to make sure that the Governor knew that his mission was to protect all of Kentucky's loyal citizens and subdue the government's enemies.[450]

On February 8, 1865, General Burbridge wrote to Secretary of War Stanton that he had received his dispatch to revoke General Order Number 5. He was under the impression that Stanton wanted his instructions for the state troops to be disbanded. He stated the state troops were plundering and marauding. He had acted after receiving inflammatory handbills, calling for recruits to operate against guerillas and deprive the people of their liberty and private rights. Burbridge ordered U.S. troops to replace state troops. He asked Stanton to tell the President that he would agree to the President's orders.

For his last order, Burbridge ordered the 30th Wisconsin Infantry to camp near the vicinity of Frankfort and track the movements of guerillas and send detachments in pursuit of any guerilla bands in the neighborhood and take no prisoners. Guerillas could attack the state arsenal located at Frankfort and the railroad bridge spanning the river at Frankfort. All troops, whether state or national, at Frankfort were under Major John Clowney, commander of the 30th Wisconsin.[451]

On February 9, 1865, C. T. Worley wrote to President Lincoln asking him if he had sold the "true people to the Union cause" to Governor Bramlette and the Copperheads. He stated that General Burbridge was the leader of the Union party and they would not be led by Bramlette. In his opinion, the withholding of Burbridge's order in regard to abolishing state troops was a complete victory for copperheads and rebels. The Union party depended on Lincoln. If Burbridge was kept in command of Kentucky, "the Union party

449 Ibid.
450 Ibid.
451 O.R. Series I, Vol. XLVI/2 [#96] Letter from Burbridge to Major John Clowney, 30th Wisconsin Infantry.

will be triumphant. If not, the copperheads will triumph, and Kentucky is gone forever, and who will be to blame?"[452]

On February 10, word reached the newspapers that General Burbridge had been relieved of command by General Palmer. One Kentucky newspaper wrote: "Maj. Gen. John M. Palmer, of Illinois, has been appointed to command in Kentucky. Thank God and President Lincoln."[453]

Another member of the radical Union party and friend of R. S. Todd, a member of the Kentucky legislature, D. L. Price, wrote to Lincoln on February 11, 1865, stating that the President's enemies were jubilant and his friends despondent over the removal of General Burbridge. He stated that with Burbridge in command slavery would be eradicated from the state. His removal would decide and embitter the Union party which would lead to their defeat at the next August election. He pleaded for the President to give them Burbridge back and the Union party would give Lincoln emancipation and loyalty.[454]

On February 14, 1865, Burbridge wrote to General Breckinridge that the officers referred to by him were captured far within Union lines, without a command and engaged in recruiting for and obtaining information for the benefit of the Confederates and that Breckinridge had no officers of Burbridge's command captured under similar circumstances in Breckinridge's possession. Burbridge sent to Fortress Monroe, for exchange, Colonel Morris and Major Steele. Burbridge had no information that C. K. Johnson was a lieutenant colonel in the Confederacy. Burbridge tried Johnson as a spy and he was being held in close confinement awaiting corroborative evidence from Breckinridge that he was an officer in the Confederacy.[455]

Burbridge wrote to Breckinridge that he could not recognize as prisoners of war officers and men belonging to the Confederate service captured in a loyal state not attached to any recognized portion of the Confederate army and engaged in assisting and inciting to acts of murder and robbery the roving bands of outlaws and guerillas now infesting Kentucky. Nor did Burbridge recognize Breckinridge's right to regulate the treatment of any officer of his command who he did not consider an officer and the circumstances attending whose arrest are not such that entitle him to the privileges of a prisoner of war. If Breckinridge held any officer of his command as hostage for him, he would consider it his duty to retaliate in a like manner.[456]

---

452 O.R. Series I, Vol. XLVI/2 [#96] Letter from C. T. Worley to President Lincoln.

453 *Military History of Kentucky*, 227.

454 Letter from D. L. Price to President Lincoln, Abraham Lincoln Papers, Library of Congress, Washington, D.C.

455 O.R. Series II, Vol. VIII [#121] Union and Confederate Correspondence, Orders, Etc., relating to prisoners of war and state from January 1, 1865 to the end.

456 Ibid.

Months later, Colonel John D. Morris wrote about his experiences as a prisoner of war in Kentucky and his exchange. According to Morris, in the middle of October 1864, he rode with Colonel R. J. Breckinridge and Major Steele. When they reached Owen County, Kentucky, Morris separated from Breckinridge and Steele while they recruited for the Confederacy. Jessee wanted Morris to join him. Federal soldiers captured Morris and he was well aware of General Burbridge's order requiring all officers and men caught without their commands to be shot on the spot and not brought in as prisoners. The Federal soldiers took Morris to Owenton and confined him in the court house under a heavy guard with 18 other men. The major in command told Morris that he and the 18 men would be shot in the morning. He was taken to a small cell with eight men. The cell amounted to only eight feet by six feet. The walls and floor were made of iron. The air was so foul that Morris vomited repeatedly and a guard took him from his cell and back to the court house. The next morning a party of men were detailed for the execution. Morris convinced Major Mahoney that he should be taken to Lexington to meet with General Burbridge. One man who had been brought into the town the evening before had already been executed. The Federals said he was a guerilla, although the man claimed he was a Confederate soldier. Morris was allowed to ride a horse while the other prisoners rode in a wagon. When Morris reached Frankfort, he was paroled with instructions to report to the railroad depot. At Lexington, Morris arrived at the provost marshal's office and the provost marshal sent him to the prison, which was an old warehouse. About 120 men were housed in the prison, including Yankee deserters, men belonging to General Grant's army who had been sent through the lines by the Confederate government and captured in Kentucky, men who belonged to the guerilla bands, bounty jumpers, disaffected citizens, and Confederate soldiers. One Lieutenant Vance entered the room and picked out 15 men. They were taken downstairs, and later, five returned. They had drawn lots for their lives; the other 10 men were taken out and shot. The next day, six others were carried out and executed. Three men who were brought in belonged to Jessee's command, but within four hours after their arrival, they were carried out and hung. Twenty-eight men, all Confederate soldiers, were killed. None of the men were tried before a military commission or court martial. They were simply selected by the provost marshal without any reference to the guilt or innocence of the parties.[457]

While Colonel Morris was a prisoner, he saw many of the men fall sick to

457 O.R. Series II, Vol. VIII [s# 121] Union and confederate Corespondence, Orders, Etc., relating to prisoners of war and state from January 1, 1865 to the end, Letter from Col. J. D. Morris to the committee of the Confederate Senate.

measles, mumps, diphtheria, typhoid fever, erysipelas, and pneumonia. No one was taken to a hospital until he was almost at the point of death, and many of them did die. After remaining in the prisoner for six weeks he was transferred to another prison, where smallpox spread throughout the prison, eventually affecting Morris. Many of the men in the small pox ward died. Luckily, Morris survived. He was taken to Louisville for exchange and then to Fort Monroe.

On February 20, 1865, Governor Bramlette wrote to President Lincoln, informing him that Major General John Palmer had arrived in Kentucky. Every opinion stated that his appointment would lead to harmony in the state. The governor stated that the good Lincoln did for Kentucky and the national cause by giving Palmer "will exceed your most sanguine hopes." He thanked President Lincoln for assigning Palmer to command the department of Kentucky. President Lincoln's administration would no longer be presented in a false light to his people, by the "wrongful actions of others."[458]

On February 22, 1865, Major General Palmer, under General Order Number 2, relieved General Burbridge from the command of Kentucky and is "ordered to report to Major General Thomas, commanding Department of the Cumberland, for duty in the field." His staff would accompany him.

The next day, General Burbridge asked Secretary of War Edwin Stanton for a thirty days' leave of absence so he could make provisions for his family before taking the field. On February 27, 1865, Major General George Thomas wrote to Burbridge that after his leave of absence expired, he would remain in Lexington, Kentucky, and await further orders. There was no command for Burbridge in his department.[459] Burbridge had no command and stayed in a state that did not want him.

Burbridge's reign of terror in the state of Kentucky came to an end. He took a long journey from being Colonel of the 26th Kentucky Infantry to brevet Major General. He had won great fame at the Battle of Arkansas Post and during the Vicksburg Campaign he became friends with General William T. Sherman. He defeated Confederate General John Hunt Morgan and gained the praise from Sherman, Secretary of War Stanton, and the President. His friends in the Unconditional Unionist Party and Governor Thomas Bramlette came to his support and helped him in securing his position as district commander in the state of Kentucky. Unfortunately, these same people brought Burbridge's downfall. General Sherman let Burbridge believe that he could do anything in his power to stop guerilla warfare. He listened to the radicals who

---

458 Letter from Governor Bramlette to President Lincoln, February 20, 1865, Abraham Lincoln Papers, Library of Congress, Washington, D.C.

459 O.R. Series I, Vol. XLV/1.

used him to settle vendettas and wanted him to make sure only radicals were elected to office, even if he had to tamper with the state elections. He listened to the Governor and used Kentucky's own laws to stop guerilla warfare, but put him at odds with the citizens of Kentucky. Burbridge thought that the President and the Governor would support him if he did everything in his power to make sure that Lincoln was elected in 1864, even if he used bribery or threats. Although he tried to please his superiors by recruiting and arming black soldiers, he only brought on the wrath of the Governor and the slave owning citizens of Kentucky, who erroneously thought that slavery would be preserved in Kentucky. Burbridge thought that he pleased his superiors by implementing Order Number 59. Burbridge was left alone, with no command and hated in his home state.

Chapter 12
Leaving the State and A Legacy

After Burbridge returned from his leave, he spent the rest of the year in Louisville awaiting orders from his superiors. On April 24, 1865, at Camp Nelson, the 56th United States Colored Cavalry presented General Burbridge with a sword and belt and spurs worth $1,000. General James Brisbin made the presentation speech, in which he spoke of General Burbridge as "the pioneer of freedom to the slaves of Kentucky."[460] Burbridge said "the war is over with the rebels, and he expected and hoped soon to see our colored troops sent into Mexico."[461] While in Louisville, he watched as Major General John Palmer laid a "stern grasp"[462] upon Kentucky. Although Burbridge no longer held a command in Kentucky, those who hated him while he was commander brought charges against him. On October 27, 1865, Winn Gunn wrote to General Burbridge that he was on a grand jury of the Federal Court for the district of Kentucky in February 1865 and saw in public prints charges made against him while he was a commander. The judge told the jury that it was their duty to look into the conduct of all Federal officers and see if they had been guilty of charges publicly made in newspapers, and if guilty they should indite all officers involved. After 16 days of deliberation with a large number of witnesses, the jury found no grounds for the charges against Burbridge. Gunn took the list of witnesses who examined the charges of bribery and corruption made in releasing prisoners and the hog contracts, but Gunn lost his memorandum and only could recollect those of General Jeremiah Boyle, Colonel Marcellus Munday, and Mr. and Mrs. Meade. He was impressed with the plain candid statement of facts by General Boyle. Boyle, former district commander of Kentucky before Burbridge took command, did not want to conceal anything from the jury. He and Colonel Munday both gave their opinion that no man approached Burbridge with a bribe, and if he did, they thought that it would be at the peril of his life.

460 De Falaise, Louis, "Gen. Stephen Gano Burbridge's Command in Kentucky," *Kentucky Historical Society*, (69, April 1971), 123.

461 Collins, Lewis & Collins, Richard, *History of Kentucky*, Vol. 1 , 1874, 159.

462 Letter from Governor Bramlette to President Lincoln, March 2, 1865, Abraham Lincoln papers, Library of Congress, Washington, D.C.

He told him to preserve his letter and hand it down to his children as coming from one who owned a number of slaves but was willing to give up all like Burbridge did for the good of his country and from one that never held an office of any kind except one given him by the Lincoln and it had no pay attached to it and that was Commissioner of Alotments to the Kentucky volunteers.[463]

While Burbridge remained in Kentucky awaiting orders, he received a number of letters from his brother Colonel Oscar H. Burbridge. On May 12, 1865, his brother proposed opening a lumber business in Memphis, Tennessee. He needed capital to start his business. He thought he could monopolize the business. The rebel farmers were returning daily to their farms and there was a daily demand for purchasing stock that was destroyed in the war. All the mills in the back country for hundreds of miles had been destroyed and lumber would have to be furnished from Memphis for the entire back country for the 200-mile railroad which was being opened. He noticed that Stanton was reducing the size of the army and thought that Burbridge would be ready to enter into business with his brother. He wanted his brother to come to Memphis and buy a nice place of his own. He mentioned in the letter that they could both buy the finest cotton land for eight to ten dollars an acre.[464]

On May 23, 1865, Oscar H. Burbridge heard nothing from his brother. He became worried that he had not heard good or bad information about affairs in Kentucky. He wrote that he was nearly crazy from not hearing from his brother. He stated that he was doing all he could to work out their difficulties and felt as if he could never show his face in Kentucky until he returned independent. He hoped that his brother would close up all of their outstanding matters. He hoped that by the fall his arrangements would bring them $15,000 and his stock and crops arrangements fixed so that no one could interfere.[465]

On July 11, 1865, his brother O.H. Burbridge wrote to Stephen Burbridge that he was in New Orleans trying to get some Rebel cotton, since he thought there was a fortune to be made in cotton. He could buy cotton at 12 cents a pound if he had the money. He was trying to sell their boat. The plantation business was the thing and that could be operated successfully if they can get the stock. He could get the supplies in New Orleans. Cotton would be high

463 Letter from Winn Gunn to General Burbridge, Bloomington, Indiana, October 25, 1865, The Stephen Burbridge Collection, One Microfilm roll, Margaret King Library, University of Kentucky, Lexington, Kentucky.

464 Letter from O.H. Burbridge to General Stephen Burbridge, Memphis, Tennessee, May 12, 1865, The Stephen Burbridge Collection, One Microfilm roll, Margaret King Library, University of Kentucky, Lexington, Kentucky.

465 Letter from O.H. Burbridge to General Stephen Burbridge, New Orleans, Tennessee, May 23, 1865, The Stephen Burbridge Collection, One Microfilm roll, Margaret King Library, University of Kentucky, Lexington, Kentucky.

next year. Another business partner, John Clary, would furnish the stock, and he would furnish the land.[466]

On July 17, O.H. Burbridge wrote to his brother that he must leave at once for Berlin. He had a claim for 170 bales of cotton. He planned to leave on the steamer Indian Star. He wanted authority to bring out of Texas 2,000 bales of cotton. The 170 bales of cotton would bring $34,000. He hoped that Judge Kellogg would give them the commission to take charge of all government cotton in Texas. He would get authority to bring out 2,000 bales of government cotton.[467]

By the end of 1865, General Burbridge resigned his commission, became a civilian, and moved to Covington, Kentucky. Although Burbridge left the military service, his actions while military district commanding continued to haunt him. On November 22, 1865, General James Brisbin published a letter in the *Cincinnati Commerical* verbally abusing Kentucky and the citizens of Kentucky. He tried to defend Burbridge by stating that himself, adjutant general J. Bates Dickson, and Robert Breckinridge had influenced Burbridge. He stated that Breckinridge "was, throughout his administration, Burbridge's adviser and friend, he was frequently summoned to headquarters, and Burbridge often went miles to consult with the wise old Doctor. I was present at several of those interviews, and know that General Burbridge regarded Robert J. Breckinridge as the wisest and ablest man in Kentucky. He was not alone in his high opinion of the venerable Doctor's wisdom in military as well as civilian matters; for while in command in this part of Kentucky, I relied upon the advice and counsel of the Doctor more than any other man."[468] The letter did not help Burbridge in defending his actions as commander of Kentucky. If anything, it made matters worse.

In a personal altercation, in Covington, Kentucky, Colonel Oscar Burbridge shot Major A. J. Morey, editor of the *Cynthiana News*; the ball passed through his right arm and into his side, inflicting a dangerous wound, and paralyzing his arm so that the pistol he was trying to use fell from his hands. Burbridge had first struck Morey with his cane, and Morey was trying to get his pistol from his pocket when Burbridge shot him. Violent language had passed between the two men, in consequence of Burbridge demanding the author of and threatening to hold Morey responsible for a bitter and abusive article in the *Cynthiana News* about his brother Stephen Burbridge. The recent attempted vindication

466 Letter from O.H. Burbridge to General Stephen Burbridge, New Orleans, July 11, 1865, The Stephen Burbridge Collection, One Microfilm roll, Margaret King Library, University of Kentucky, Lexington, Kentucky.

467 Letter from O.H. Burbridge to General Stephen Burbridge, New Orleans, July 17, 1865, The Stephen Burbridge Collection, one microfilm roll, Margaret King Library, University of Kentucky, Lexington, Kentucky.

468 Collins, 182.

by the two generals was the article which stated: "Does not the ghost of Walter Ferguson haunt Mr. Burbridge? Can he forget the appeals of the ladies of Lexington made to him on behalf of this youth, and how he spurned them from his presence, and doomed him to an infamous death? Can he have forgotten so early how he sent young Jameson and Reese, of Harrison County to eternity for no other reason than that they were rebel soldiers? Has the death of Thornt. Lafferty passed out of his mention? If he has, let him be assured the people have not filled their places yet; and that their homes are desolate and dreary today on account of their absence, and that their memory is fresh and green in the hearts of the people of Kentucky."[469]

General Burbridge published a letter addressed to General Brisbin, in which he asked him to support his defense that he never issued an order stopping the pork, that he never abused, banished, imprisoned, and punished innocent people, in violation of the laws of war, that he never executed without trial, guerillas, rebel soldiers, or citizens, that he never conspired with government contractors to make large sums of money for himself, and that he never made illegal assessments upon citizens and took their private property away and either used them himself or gave them to friends. Brisbin replied that the hog order was issued at the request of the U.S. commissary officers against his judgment. In the *True Kentuckian*, Brisbin's defense of Burbridge did not lead to much credence. The newspaper wrote: "To disprove the accusations against him, he has called upon one who had been so violent in his course and so intemperate in his language, as to render his defense of less weight than if it had proceeded from some source less obnoxious to our people. Moreover, General Brisbin was on General Burbridge's staff, and in a measure identified with his administration of affairs while in command of this military department; he is, of course, anxious to present the actions of his superior officer in a favorable light as possible."[470] The paper gave their opinion that if Burbridge gave the names of those who pretended to be his friends, who were his advisers, who extorted "blood money," who used Burbridge as an instrument to satiate their own "cravings for human blood," then the people of Kentucky would move their indignation from him to those to who were really guilty.[471]

On December 11, 1867 the Kentucky House of Representatives introduced two bills. John W. Leathers, of Kenton County, offered the first bill which gathered information from all citizens arrested, imprisoned, expelled or killed outside of battle by a military commander. John T. Allunut of Louisville

469 Collins, *History of Kentucky*, 182.
470 Collins, 183.
471 Collins, 183.

introduced the second bill which stated that through the public press General Burbridge was charged with causing many citizens of Kentucky and other states to be murdered under military authority and while commander he was guilty of many other atrocities in Kentucky; which Burbridge denied. Allnut went onto to state that "now that the country may be fully informed of the verity or falsehood of said publications, and that the said Burbridge may have a full and fair investigation of his acts and conduct" while commander. A committee of investigation, called the Federal Relations, composed of three representatives and two senators was appointed by the legislature to hear evidence and report to the general assembly the results of their investigation.[472] In 1868, the Kentucky legislature began their investigation into Burbridge's rule as commander of Kentucky, but never completed it.[473]

Burbridge asked General William T. Sherman to help in his defense. On February 19, 1867, Sherman wrote to Burbridge that he had sent him a copy of the letter he addressed to Burbridge on June 21, 1864, in which "the instructions contained in that letter were commands to you, binding on you under the Articles of War, and for which you were no more responsible than for the execution of any other order. I alone am responsible; and I have no fear but my orders were right and appropriate."[474] He concluded that no one should blame Burbridge, for many had found him too lenient.[475] Although Sherman and Brisbin tried to support Burbridge, Kentucky ostracized him and in 1867, he wrote to Robert Breckinridge that he was persecuted and hunted almost like a wild animal and was not "able to live in safety or do business in Kentucky."[476] He wrote to his friend General Brisbin: "My services to my country have caused me to be exiled from my home, and made my wife and children wanderers, while the Government for which I fought seems to care little whether they have bread or not."[477] He bitterly resented the treatment he was receiving from his native state for doing what he considered his duty, patriotically and fearlessly rendered. Burbridge had no choice but to leave his native state.

In 1870, Governor John W. Stevenson, Senator Thomas McCreery, and Representative Thomas Jones ran for governor. Being a friend of Burbridge was used like a weapon for political advancement. During the political campaign, Stevenson accused McCreery that he had recommended Burbridge for

472 Collins, *History of Kentucky*, 183.

473 E. Merton Coulter, *The Civil War and Readjustment in Kentucky*, (Chapel Hill: University of North Carolina Press, 1921, reprint 1966), 292; *Cincinnati Semi-Weekly Gazette*, March 17, passim, 1868.

474 Collins, *History of Kentucky*, 184.

475 De Falaise, 126.

476 Coulter, 393; *Lexington Observer and Reporter*, November 20, 1867.

477 Coulter, 393.

an appointment in the Federal revenue service. A challenge to a duel arose between the two men, but both decided not to take each other up on the challenge. The *New York World* newspaper stated: "The name of Burbridge has been a fire-brand in this state since the days his harsh and bloody rule here as Commander of the Military Department of Kentucky."[478]

Although Kentucky newspapers, citizens, and political leaders continued to harass Burbridge, the black Union veterans supported him. In 1871, local black veterans asked Burbridge to be a guest speaker at a black Methodist church in Covington, Kentucky.

In 1882, the *Louisville Commercial* allowed Burbridge to defend himself. He stated in the article that Thomas Green of Maysville in the *Cincinnati Commercial* and James Blackburn of Frankfort in the *Louisville Courier-Journal* attacked his character as a man and soldier. The men accused Burbridge of causing the death of three recruits for the Confederate army, that he secured for his brother profits from the pork-packing house in Maysville, that he accepted $500 for the release of Captain Peter Everett. Burbridge accused the newspaper press of being controlled by Confederate influence, who "have never missed an occasion to heap the grossest abuse upon me and I know too well the ostracism that must follow any man who, even at this late day–more than 17 years subsequent to the events to which I shall call attention in this communication took place, dares to differ with the verdict pronounced by the guerilla politician of Kentucky." In his defense, he points first to General Ulysses S. Grant's Order Number 4, from November 5, 1863, which stated that rebel raiding parties who visited towns, villages, and farms, where there were no Union forces, and pillaged Union families, department commanders would take steps to stop the evil, or make the loss from the raids the responsibility of secession sympathizers who lived in the neighborhood. For every act of violence to the person of an unarmed Union citizen, a secessionist would be arrested and held as hostage for the delivery of the offender. For every dollar's worth of property taken from Union citizens, or destroyed by the raiders, the secessionists would have to pay money to the sufferers. If the secessionists could not pay in money, land would be taken. Wealthy secessionists would pay money and provisions in support of Union refugees.[479]

Burbridge also referred to Order Number 29, issued March 8, 1863 from Grant's headquarters. The acts of the Kentucky legislature were published and informed Burbridge on February 27, 1864, that Kentucky was exempt from Order Number 4, the civil law would be extensively relied on in cases such as

478 Coulter, 393.

479 "Gen. Burbridge's Defense: The Hog Order, of the hanging of guerillas and other historical matters discussed," *Louisville Commercial*, February 5, 1882.

were intended to be reached by General Order Number 4.[480]

He wrote that after Grant revoked his order, "a reign of lawlessness set in" Kentucky. According to Burbridge, the military was paralyzed by the order of General Grant revoking the authority given it by his previous order. Members of the "Knights of the Golden Circle," "The Sons of Liberty," and other organizations, with "midnight assassins," known as "scouts," "partisan rangers, " or guerillas and Confederate cavalry roamed Ohio, Illinois, Indiana and Kentucky. He stated that he was required to preserve the railroad communications, preserve peace and to supply the army with new troops, horses, mules and beef. He stated that for the good of the state, he would not instate half measures in dealing with the state's enemies. When President Lincoln declared martial law and by the order of Secretary of War Edwin Stanton, Grant's order was restored and Burbridge was charged to carry out the order.[481]

Burbridge addressed the hog swindle of 1864. He claimed that he had no control over Major H. C. Symonds, since he fell under General William T. Sherman's command. The order from the Commissary General to Major Symonds to pack 100,000 hogs came from the Secretary of War and Burbridge stated that he was only following orders. He stated that his only involvement was his order from November 1, 1864, which stated that no more hogs were to be shipped out of the state. He also stated that he did not make any arrangements for his brother with Meisrs, Coons & Company, the company contracted to pack the hogs for the army. During Oscar Burbridge's absence in New Orleans, he asked Stephen Burbridge to collect and forward to him any funds arising from his connections with Meisrs, Coons, & Company, which "in doing I seem to have inadvertently signed my name officially, a mistake which any officer who has had occasion to sign a multiplicity of papers daily will readily pardon."[482]

He addressed guerilla warfare, in which he referred to General Basil Duke's *History of Morgan's Cavalry*, in which Duke stated that after Morgan's raid in 1864, many of the Confederate cavalrymen left their command "altogether and became guerillas." "Kentucky was at one time, and before the close of the war, teeming with these guerillas. It was no use to threaten them with punishment they had no idea of being caught. Besides, Burbridge shot all that he could lay his hands on." Burbridge brought up the bank robbery at Mount Sterling and the robbery of citizens from Cynthiana and Lexington. He also stated that his black soldiers who guarded cattle were shot down after their capture. Soldiers from the army in front on leave were murdered. On the two expeditions

480 Ibid.
481 Ibid.
482 Ibid.

beyond the Cumberland Mountains his black soldiers who were left sick on the road were "mercilessly shot and left by the roadside and those left wounded at Saltville were shot on the battlefield and in their beds." Burbridge stated that with Kentucky overrun with marauding bands of outlaws, who could not be threatened with punishment, he determined to give them a chance to transfer their "deviltry to the South." He gave them 20 days to leave the state. A majority of Morgan's men had been scattered across the state, which presented a terror to the citizens and isolated commands.[483]

He stated that military commissions were appointed to try guerillas whenever caught and many under sentence of death were confined in the jails, at Lexington, Louisville, and other parts of southern Kentucky. His orders to his officers were explicit to hang four of these condemned guerillas in retaliation for the murder by guerillas of citizens or soldiers in the same neighborhood in which the murder was committed. Burbridge stated that frequent appeals for clemency reached his office and he "took great pleasure in extending it. All the prisoners taken in battle at Mount Sterling, Cynthiana, and Virginia were sent South for exchange." He also stated that most of the guerillas who were caught were in Union uniforms.[484] Burbridge did not tell the truth when he stated that a military commission tried the guerillas. Captain Lindsey Buckner's letter to his sister plainly stated that he did not know why he was being executed. As historians James Head and Carl Runyon pointed out, most if not all, were executed without a trial. He plainly stated to Sherman that he had no use for trials. What Burbridge failed to realize was that he was not apprehending the men who committed the murders of Union soldiers and citizens, but executing men who had nothing to do with the crime. Burbridge still did not see the difference between the legitimate Confederate soldier and the guerilla. In his eyes, General John Hunt Morgan's men and Colonel Adam Rankin Johnson's partisan rangers were no different than the guerilla.

Burbridge stated that when he recruited black soldiers for the Union army, slaveholders arrayed against the government and in their rage they included not only the makers of the law but the officers who enforced it. Many Union men, headed by the Governor, were arrayed in open hostility to the measure. Men who opposed secession and whose loyalty to the government was beyond reproach gave incendiary speeches in order to influence the masses against his authority. Burbridge stated that General Grant, General Sherman, General John Schofield, and Secretary of War Edwin Stanton ordered their arrest. Again, Burbridge is correct that Stanton ordered the arrest of Colonel Frank Wolford,

483 Ibid.
484 Ibid.

but some of the arrests, such as Alvin Duvall, were motivated by Radical Republicans. Burbridge in his own words stated that he would do anything in his power to make sure Lincoln was re-elected and he used his influence to arrest those who opposed the government. Burbridge claimed that he nipped the rebellion in the bud, but hostility to him remained to gather strength, as the guerillas "settled down and became citizens."[485]

In the last part of the article, Burbridge addressed the accusation that he put to death three innocent boys and took bribes. He claimed he did not remember the three boys executed from Mason County and he never took a bribe.

Burbridge ended his defense by stating that Kentucky proclaimed their loyalty to the Union government. The Kentucky Legislature stated that any Kentuckian who took up arms against the government and invaded her soil to make war upon her people was "guilty of treason and deserving death." He stated that when the Confederates deserted the army and became "murders and thieves," they were warned of the penalty. Burbridge stated that "too few guerillas were executed. The execution of a few hundred more there would have been productive of good to the peaceable citizens of the State."[486]

Burbridge's past continued to haunt him wherever he went. He tried to live a normal life but his life was filled with failure. His application to be Marshal of the District of Columbia and later Commissioner of Internal Revenue Service were denied. On December 2, 1894, Burbridge died in Brooklyn, New York.

After Burbridge's death what kind of legacy did he leave for Kentucky? Odis Lee Harris on his article on Burbridge wrote that his treatment of captured guerillas was "probably no worse than those of other generals, such as Union General William Tecumseh Sherman and Confederate General Nathan Bedford Forrest."[487] He stated that Burbridge's military operations in Kentucky were successful, overall, in promoting the Union cause. Louisville, Kentucky, historian Robert McDowell disagreed with Harris, stating that Burbridge's retaliatory measures succeeded in arousing sympathy for guerillas. He wrote that as for the guerillas, the knowledge "that that they could expect no mercy caused them to abandon what little self imposed restraint they had previously exhibited. Their actions became more desperate and vicious."[488] McDowell stated that after the war, the citizens of Louisville were "sick of the butchery, sick of the greed of profiteers, sick of rowdy, drunken soldiers, sick of being treated like an occupied city by the Union of which she was supposed to be a part. The

485 Ibid.

486 Ibid.

487 Odis Lee Harris, "Union General Stephen Gano Burbridge Brought Hate and Terror to his Kentucky," *The Kentucky Explorer*, 1995.

488 Robert McDowell, *Louisville in the Civil War*, 180.

only real combat soldiers she knew were Union soldiers, and these had been inflicted on her for four years."[489] The city of Louisville, like many other cities in Kentucky, embraced the returning Confederate soldiers, who had no home, were hungry, and had no money. The citizen of Louisville, as many other citizens in other Kentucky cities, regarded the Yankee soldier with distaste. Confederate General Basil Duke best summed up the feelings toward Burbridge after the war. He wrote in his book *Reminiscences of Basil W. Duke* that "the emancipation of the slaves and the horrible atrocities perpetuated by two Federal generals: Burbridge and Paine, the former a native Kentuckian–who under the guise of military executions murdered nearly 200 citizens and Confederate prisoners, had caused a great revulsion of feeling in that element of the population which had originally staunchly adhered to the Union. Reinforced by these recruits those who had always entertained Southern proclivities, suddenly the post-bellum democracy of Kentucky began its career with a majority that could be scarcely counted. The gubernatorial term of John S. Helm, who was elected in 1867, was the first of a succession of Democratic administrations which continued until 1895."[490] Historian Louis DeFalaise pondered the question as to whether Burbridge was the source of the minority status of the Republican Party in the state up to modern times.

An important lesson can be learned from General Burbridge and the Lincoln administration. Lincoln suspended habeas corpus. Burbridge's military superior, General William T. Sherman told Burbridge to treat guerillas as "wild animals." He wrote to Burbridge to gather up men, women, and children, who were rebel sympathizers in prisons and send them to their own colony. Burbridge shot and killed innocent Confederate soldiers, who never were brought to trial. Burbridge randomly selected four prisoners in Louisville and executed them without trial for every Union soldier killed by a guerilla. Burbridge tried to influence state and federal elections to support the Union cause. As General Sherman told James Guthrie of Kentucky, if civil authorities could not control their affairs, the military had the duty to step in. In a time of war there are many abuses and Americans must reflect and step back to make sure that their liberties guaranteed by the Constitution are not trampled upon by overzealous politicians and military authorities who are protecting their citizens from terrorists. General Burbridge's command reflected how citizens must band together to make sure that they are protected from military abuses and not rush to pass laws that limit their freedoms.

---

489 McDowell, 204.

490 Basil Wilson Duke, *Reminiscences of General Basil W. Duke* (New York: Doubleday, 1911), 478-479.

References

Books

Beach, Damian, *Civil War Battles, Skirmishes, and Events in Kentucky*. Louisville, Kentucky: Different Drummer Books, 1995.

Brown, Dee, *Morgan's Raiders*. New York: Konecky & Konecky, 1959.

Bush, Bryan, *The Civil War Battles of the Western Theater*. Paducah, Kentucky: Turner Publishing, 1998, reprint 2000.

Butler, Lorine, *John Morgan and His Men*. Philadelphia: Dorrance & Company, 1960.

Clark, Thomas, *A History of Kentucky*. Lexington, Kentucky: The John Bradford Press, 1954.

Clotter, James, *The Breckinridges of Kentucky*. Lexington, Kentucky: 1986, The Kentucky Encyclopedia. University of Kentucky Press, 1992.

Coleman, Winston, J., Jr., *Lexington During the Civil War*. Lexington, Kentucky: Commercial Printing Company, 1938.

Collins, Lewis & Collins, Richard, *History of Kentucky, Vol. 1*, 1874.

Coulter, Merton, E.., *The Civil War and Readjustment in Kentucky*. University Press of North Carolina Press, 1926, reprinted 1966.

Davis, William C., *Breckinridge: Statesman, Soldier, Symbol*. New Orleans & London: Louisiana State University Press, 1992.

Duke, Basil Wilson, *Reminiscences of General Basil W. Duke*. New York: Doubleday, 1911.

Evans, Clement, *Confederate Military History Extended Edition: A Library of Confederate States History Written by Distinguished Men of the South*. Wilmington, N.C.: Broadfoot Publishing Company, 1988.

Harrison, Lowell, *The Civil War in Kentucky*. Lexington, Kentucky: University Press of Kentucky, 1975.

Head, James, *The Atonement of John Brooks: The Story of the True Johnny "Reb" Who Did Not Come Marching Home*. Florida: Heritage Press, 2001.

Horn, Stanley, *The Army of Tennessee*. University of Oklahoma Press, reprint edition, 1993.

Jordan, Thomas & Pryor, J. P., *The Campaigns of General Nathan Bedford Forrest and of Forrest's Cavalry*. NewYork: Da Capo Press, 1996.

Johnson, Robert & Buel, Clarence, *Battles & Leaders of the Civil War*. 4 Volumes, New York: Thomas Yosekoff, 1956.

Korn, Jerry, *War on the Mississippi: Grant's Vicksburg Campaign*. Alexandria, Virginia, Time Life Books, 1985.

McClain, Lee, G. *The Military History of Kentucky*. Federal Writers Project of the Works Progress Administration for the State of Kentucky, State Journal, Frankfort, Kentucky, 1939.

McDowell, Robert, *City of Conflict: Louisville in the Civil War*. Louisville, Kentucky: Louisville Civil War Roundtable Publishers, 1962.

McKnight, Brian, *Contested Borderland: The Civil War in Appalachian Kentucky and Virginia*. Lexington, Kentucky: The University Press of Kentucky, 2006.

Mays, Thomas, *The Saltville Massacre*. Abilene, Texas: McWhiney Foundation Press, 1998.

Ramage, James, *Rebel Raider: The Life of General John Hunt Morgan*. Lexington, Kentucky: University of Kentucky Press, 1986.

Rose, Jerlene, ed., *Kentucky's Civil War 1861-1865*. Clay City: Back Home in Kentucky, Inc., 2005.

Sears, Richard, *Camp Nelson: A Civil War History*. Lexington, Kentucky: University Press of Kentucky, 2002.

Sherman, William T., *Memoirs of General W. T. Sherman*. New York: The Library of America, 1990.

Smith, Timothy, *Champion Hill: Decisive Battle for Vicksburg*. New York: Savas Beatie LLC, 2004.

Speed, Thomas, *Union Cause in Kentucky*. New York & London: G. P. Putnam's Son's, 1907.

Stevens, James Darwin, *Reflections: A Portrait-A Biography of the Kentucky Military Institute* [1845-1971] Volume One, 1991.

Woodworth, Steven, *No Band of Brothers: Problems of the Rebel High Command*. Columbia, Mo., and London: University of Missouri Press, 1999.

The War of the Rebellion: A Compilation of the Official Records of the Union and Confederate Armies, 128 Volumes, Government Printing Office, Washington, D.C., 1880-1901.

Articles

Boeger, Palmer, "The Great Hog Swindle of 1864," *The Journal of Southern History*, Vol. 28, No.1 (Feb. 1962).

De Falaise, Louis, "Gen. Stephen Gano Burbridge's Command in Kentucky," *Kentucky Historical Society*, (69, April 1971).

Emily Moses, "Marker Honors memory of killed soldiers." *The Henry County Local*, Sunday, November 5, 2006.

Harris, Odis Lee, "Union General Burbridge Brought Hate and Terror to his Kentucky," *The Kentucky Explorer*, (February 1995).

Jim Reis, "The Ugly Side of War: Executions swift when Rebel raiders caught in Kentucky," *The Kentucky Post* (June 6, 1998).

Marshal Myers, Dr. "Civil War Incidents in and around Meade County, Kentucky, The Terror of the Black Flag: Guerilla Warfare in Meade County." 2003, published by Jane Marlow Willis Wordsmith, Brandenburg, Kentucky.

Carl Runyon, "Without Cause or Trial:" The Story of the Reprisal Execution of Two Confederate Soldiers at Henderson, *Kentucky, Journal of Arts and Sciences*, Vol. 8, No. 3.

Jennings, Michael, "The Lost Regiment," *The Courier-Journal*, February 15, 1996.

Newspapers

The Daily Dispatch, Richmond, Virginia
The Louisville Courier.
The Louisville Commercial
Louisville Daily Journal
The Louisville Courier-Journal

Collections

Library of Congress, Abraham Lincoln Papers, Transcribed and Annotated by the Lincoln Studies Center, Knox College, Galesburg, Illinois.

The Margaret King Library, University of Kentucky Special Collections, Lexington, Kentucky, Stephen G. Burbridge Papers.

The Filson Club Historical Society, Louisville, Kentucky.

National Archives and Records Administration, Washington, D.C.

Compiled Service Records of Volunteer Union Soldiers from the State of Kentucky, National Archives, 1934.

Other

Civil War Heritage Trail

Index

Symbols

1st Arkansas 29
1st Kentucky 81
1st Kentucky Cavalry 75, 106, 153, 168
1st Ky. Heavy Artillery (Colored) 78
1st Kentucky Union Cavalry 112
1st La. Cavalry 69
1st Michigan Colored Regiment 71
1st Missouri Volunteer Infantry 152
2nd Ill. Cavalry 52
2nd Ky. Cavalry 81, 126-127, 138, 153
2nd Ohio 23
3rd Kentucky Union Infantry Regiment 16, 73, 77, 184
3rd Mississippi Infantry Battalion 28
4th Ind. Cavalry 36
4th Kentucky 77, 89, 91, 143, 145, 157
4th Louisiana 29
4th Mo. Cavalry 184
5th United States Colored Cavalry 142-145, 149, 177
6th Missouri Cavalry 41, 51-52
6th United States Colored Cavalry 177, 179
7th Confederate Cav. Batt. 137, 183
7th Ky. Infantry 22
7th Ohio Cavalry 95
7th Tenn. Cavalry 78
8th Iowa 29
8th Ky. Cavalry 137
8th Ky. Infantry 138
9th Ind. Cavalry 157
9th Ky. Cavalry 170
9th Ohio Infantry 26
10th Indiana 26
10th Ky. Cavalry 36, 143, 145, 157
10th Ky. Mounted Rifles 143
10th Kentucky Partisan Rangers 138
10th Texas 50
11th Kentucky 31
11th Michigan Cavalry 86, 90, 146
11th Mich. Reg. 83, 86-87, 90, 144, 146
12th Ohio Cavalry 90, 144, 146-147
13th Battalion of Virginia Reserves 144
13th Corps 40, 65
13th Ind. Cav. 157
13th Ky. Cavalry 147
13th Ky. Infantry 147-148, 158
13th Louisiana 29
13th Ohio 31-32
13th Tenn. Inf. 27
14th Brigade 28, 31-33
14th Iowa 29
14th Ky. Cavalry 141
14th Ohio 22
14th Wisconsin 31
16th Indiana Infantry 47-49, 53, 55, 59-61, 64
16th Ky. Infantry 23, 78, 138
17th Ky. Cavalry 23
17th Ohio Battery 41, 47-48, 51, 55-57, 59, 66-67
18th Ky. Infantry 36
19th Kentucky 49, 57
19th Louisiana 29
21st Ky. Infantry 169
22nd Ky. Infantry 91
23rd Wisc. 47, 49, 51, 55, 59-61, 68
25th Missouri 28
26th Ky. Union Volunteer Infantry 7, 20, 23, 28, 30-33, 126, 128, 153, 190
27th Ky. Infantry 151
30th Ky. Infantry 137
30th Ky. Volunteer Infantry 147
30th Tennessee 27
30th Wisc. Inf. 187
31st Indiana 29
33rd Indiana 22
37th Ky. 86, 88, 90, 145, 147, 158

37th Ky. Mounted Infantry 86
39th Ky. 86, 88, 90
40th Ky. 71, 88, 90
40th Ky. Mounted Infantry 71
45th Kentucky 87, 90
45th Ohio 63
47th Kentucky 93
48th Kentucky 111, 126, 153
52nd Ky. 88, 93-94
54th Ohio Inf. 139
55th Ky. Infantry 85
56th United States Colored Cavalry 192
60th Ind. Inf. 47-49
60th Tenn. Reg. 58
64th Virginia Mounted Infantry 143
67th Ind. Inf. 47-49, 55, 59-60, 66-67
69th Ohio 47-48
77th Illinois 57
83rd Ohio 47-49, 52, 55, 59-61, 64, 67
96th Ohio 48
97th Illinois 49
118th Illinois Mounted Infantry 66-67
125th U.S. Colored Infantry 184
127th Illinois Infantry 78
168th Ohio 92-93
171st Ohio 92-93

A

Abington, Va. 82, 95-96, 105, 177
Alexander, Col. 137
Allen, B.H. 105
Allen, Robert 118, 151
Allnut, John T. 196
Allunut, John T. 195
Alston, R.A. 96, 105
Ammen, Jacob 30, 71-72, 142-143, 161
Amnesty Proclamation 108, 110
Anderson, Ben 16
Anderson, Lucius 111
Anderson, Robert 16, 20
Appler, Jesse 28
Arkansas Post 7, 43-48, 50, 190
Arkansas River 43, 46
Army of Kentucky 36
Army of Mississippi 34
Army of Tennessee 19, 21, 42
Army of the Ohio 28, 30, 34, 106, 162
Asper, Joel F. 92-93
Averell, William 87

B

Baker, Jacob 170
Baldwin, Lt. Col. 48
Banks, Mayor 124
Banks, Nathaniel 40, 46, 65
Bardstown, Ky. 35, 89, 128, 158
Barnett 184
Bartlett 31
Bassett, Thomas 153
Baton Rouge, La. 19, 40, 64
Bayou Teche Campaign 62-65, 69-70
Beauregard, P.G.T. 16, 29-31, 33
Beech Grove, Ky. 26
Bell, Erwin 128
Bell, T.H. 77
Bell, Theodore S. 109-110, 170-171
Belmont, Mo. 20
Belt, Captain 24
Benton, Mortimer M. 9, 131
Benton, William 60-61
Berry, G.W. 94
Berry, Richmond 137
Big Bayou Pierre 56
Big Black River 56, 58-59
Big Eagle Bridge 36
Blackburn, James 197
Blair, Francis 56, 58
Blincoe, William 153
Blinco, Robert 138
Bloomfield, Ky. 137, 158-159
Bloom, J. 137
Blount, Capt. 41, 48
Boggy Bayou 51
Bolivar 51-52
Bondurant 23
Bowen, John 56
Bowling Green, Ky. 22, 25-27, 136, 156
Boyle, Jeremiah T. 71, 192
Bradis, Julius 138
Bragg, Braxton 28-30, 34-37, 81, 87, 106, 136
Brandenburg, Ky. 138-139, 204
Brannon, A.J. 128
Breathitt 23
Breckinridge, John C. 16, 29, 37, 82, 145-148, 152-153, 177, 183, 188
Breckinridge, Rev. Robert 7, 10, 13, 75-76, 111, 121, 141, 159, 168-169, 171, 174, 176, 178, 194, 196
Breckinridge, R.J. 189
Brewer, James 153
Brisbin, James 142-143, 149, 192, 194-196
Bristol, Tenn. 177
Bristow, Benjamin H. 111, 137
Brooks, John 138
Brown, Dr. E.O. 138
Brown, John Mason 87-88, 90, 94-95
Brown, Scott 18
Brownson 17
Bryant, John 138
Buchanan, Joseph R. 128, 137
Buckland, Ralph 84
Buckner, Judge 38
Buckner, Lindsey Duke 153, 199
Buckner, Simon 17, 22, 27, 35, 37, 86
Buehler, Theodore 67
Buell, Don Carlos 28-37, 136
Buford, Absolom 77-79
Bullitt, Joshua 9, 128, 132, 135, 137, 169, 181
Bunch, Thomas 142
Burbridge, Oscar H. 193-194, 198
Burnam, Curtis 111
Burnside, Ambrose 173
Butler, Benjamin 172
Butler, J.S. 92
Byrne, E.P. 106

C

Cahill, Captain 71
Cairo, Ill. 20, 22, 40
Cameron, Robert 16, 68
Cameron, Simon 16
Campbell, Ky. 137
Camp Boone 19, 22
Camp Burnside 113
Camp Clay 19
Camp Dick Robinson 19-20, 37
Camp Joe Holt 19
Camp Morton 128
Camp Nelson 71, 83, 113, 118-119, 172-174, 178-179, 192
Camp Trousdale 22
Carlisle, Ky. 94-95
Carnahan, Capt. 64
Carr, Eugene 60-61
Carrington, Henry 128
Carrion Crow Bayou 65-66, 68
Carroll, Michael 128
Carter, George 146
Carter, Samuel P. 26
Carthage 54-55
Caseyville, Ky. 122, 137
Cassell, Major 93
Castelman, Humphrey 106
Catlettsburg, Ky. 86
Cayuga 56
Chalmers 30
Chambers, Capt. 51
Chambliss, Maj. 156
Champion's Hill 7, 55, 57-58
Chattanooga, Tenn. 34, 84, 87
Cheatham 28-29
Cheney, Richard 158
Chenoweth, Major 90, 93, 152-153
Chestnut Ridge, Va. 144, 146
Chetlain, Augustus 120
Chicago Mercantile Battery 57, 61
Chickasaw Bayou 41-42
Chickasaw Bluffs 40, 42, 46
Churchill, Thomas 44, 49
Cicero, Maxwell 156
Cincinnati, Ohio 11, 17, 20, 35, 86, 90, 165-166
Clarke, Charles 128
Clarke, Jerome 184
Clarksville, Tenn. 83
Clary, John 194
Clay, Davis 172
Clay, James Jr. 146
Claysville, Ky. 95
Cleburne 28, 30, 35
Clement, Joseph 172
Clowney, John 187
Colgan, John 128
Colquitt, Peyton 57
Columbus, Ky. 20-22, 26-27
Columbus, Tenn. 77
Combs, Leslie 133-134
Conover, Lt. 53, 58
Coonas, Joe 139
Cooper, Capt. 91, 94
Cooper, Wickliffe 91
Copperheads 121, 156, 187-188
Corinth, Miss. 28, 31, 33
Cosby, George 145, 147
Couch, Darius 174
Covington & Lexington Railroad 87
Covington, Ky. 17, 35-37, 118, 137, 161, 165, 194, 197
Cowan, Major 69
Crittenden, George B. 25
Crittenden, John 16
Crittenden, Ky. 85
Crittenden, Thomas 25-26, 28, 35, 156
Cromwell, Ky. 23-24
Crook, George 87
Crossland, Edward 17
Cumberland Gap 22, 26, 37, 82, 87
Cumberland River 25-26, 79-80, 112, 152
Cunningham 112-114
Cynthiana, Ky. 7, 10, 36, 86, 92-96, 100, 106, 117-118, 194, 198-199
Cypress Bayou 51
Cypress Bend, Ark. 50-51

D

Dallas 40-41
Darbrow, William 157
Davis, Garrett 17, 19
Davis, Jefferson 20-21, 33, 106
Davis, Gen. Jeff 35
Deal, William 141
Deer Creek 50-54
Degenfield, Captain 147
Delhi, La. 40-42
Department of Missouri 26
Department of the Cumberland 20, 190
Department of the Ohio 83, 185
Desha, Joe 16
Dibrell, George 144, 146-147
Dickenson, Judge 53
Dickson, J. Bates 90-91, 95, 110-112, 140, 178, 182, 194
District of Kentucky 71, 82, 106, 122, 145, 150
Dixon, Archibald 76, 124
Dodge, Grenville 161
Donaldsonville 64
Donelson 22, 26-28
Doniphan, Lt. 24
Duckworth, W.L. 78
Dudley, Peter 17
Duke, Basil 145, 147, 179, 198, 201
Dumont 35
Duncan, Blanton 17
Dunnington, John 44
Dunn, W.B. 169-170
Dupeire, Major 68
Dupoyster, Thomas 138-139
Duvall, Alvin 9, 127, 131, 200

E

Echols, John 144-145
Eddyville, Ky. 79-80, 152
Edmonson, John 169
Edwards Station 56-58
Eginton, Charles 171
Elizabethtown, Ky. 81, 126
Emerson, Col. 48-49
Eminence, Ky. 134, 158
Enoch, John 139
Evansville, Ind. 184
Everett, Peter 89, 94, 197

Ewing, Hugh 111, 124, 128, 137, 156

F

Fairleigh 128, 138
Falmouth, Ky. 93
Ferguson, Champ 146-148
Ferguson, S.W. 51
Ferguson, Lt. Col. 80
Ferguson, Walter 168, 195
Fitch, Le Roy 112, 122
Fitzhenry, William 128
Flemingsburg, Ky. 95
Flint, J.P. 83
Floyd, John 27
Fonda, Colonel 66-67
Foote, Andrew 26-27
Forrest, Nathan Bedford 14, 27, 30, 77-80, 82, 84-85, 143, 152, 181, 200
Forrest, Tom 168
Fort Anderson 78
Fort Clay 91
Fort Donelson 22, 26-27
Fort Henry 22, 26-27
Fort Hindman 43-48, 50
Fort Holt 21
Fort Monroe 183, 190
Fort Pickering 84
Fort Pillow 84
Fort Robinson 94
Fort Sumter 16, 20
Fournet, V.A. 68
Frankfort, Ky. 16, 21, 35-37, 70, 87, 90-91, 94, 133-135, 157, 164, 173, 177, 180, 187, 189, 197
Franklin, Ky. 137
Franklin, Tenn. 82
Franklin, William B. 65, 68-69
Fremont, John 20
Fry, James B. 71, 119
Fry, John 168
Fry, Speed 19, 26, 72

G

Gaines Landing, Ark. 40
Gallatin, Tenn. 83
Gallop, Colonel 83
Gardner, Franklin 62
Gardner, William 147
Garrard, Israel 91, 94-95
Garrard, Theophilus 19, 22
Georgetown, Ky. 15, 37, 91, 94-95
Gettysburg 62
Gilbert, Charles 35
Gillem, Alvan 139-140, 142-143, 145, 179
Gill, Samuel 17
Gilmer, General 38
Giltner, Henry 89, 93, 96, 105, 143-145, 147
Glenn, Colonel 168
Goode, R.R. 105-106
Goodloe, William 171-172, 180
Graham, Robert 157
Grand Coteau 65-66
Grand Gulf 55-56
Granger, General 37
Grant, H.B. 151
Gray, W.G. 128
Great Hog Swindle of 1864 7-8, 11, 14, 150, 165, 167
Green River 23, 122, 158
Green, Thomas 66-68, 100
Greenville, Miss. 50, 52-53
Gregg, John 56
Gregg, N. 58
Grider, Colonel 88
Grierson, Benjamin 84
Guerrant, Edwin 145-146
Gunn, Winn 192
Guppey, J.J. 48, 68
Gurley, Phineas 176
Guthrie, James 126, 135-136, 201

H

Hackett, Rowland 153
Hagan, James 25
Halleck, Henry 26-28, 32-33, 37, 84, 86, 112, 116-118, 123, 152, 172
Hamilton, May 137
Hammond, J.H. 151
Hanson, Charles 90, 95, 145, 147
Hanson, Richard 110
Hardcastle, Aaron 28
Hardee, William 28, 30, 35
Hardiman, Thomas 85
Harper's Ferry, Va. 17
Harris, Alfred 128
Harrodsburg, Ky. 35-37
Hartford, Ky. 23, 184-185
Harvey, J.B. 16
Hatley, Sherwood 152
Hawes, Richard 37, 96
Hawes, Captain 90
Hazelwood, Crawford 146
Headington, Lieutenant 123-126
Heintzelman, Samuel 93, 117, 123, 132
Helena, Ark. 40
Helm, Emilie Todd 176
Helm, John S. 201
Henderson. D.P. 110
Henderson, John Brooks 109
Henderson, Ky. 123-125
Henn, John 170
Henry, David 138-139
Hicks, George H. 139
Hicks, Stephen 78
Hines, John 128
Hobson, Edward 81-83, 86-88, 91-94
Hodge, George B. 80, 82, 85
Hodges, Albert (A.G.) 76, 173
Hollis, Colonel 137
Holly Springs, Miss. 43, 46
Holmes, Frank 138
Holt, Joseph 101, 110, 121, 127-130, 151, 170-171
Hopkins, James 159
Hopkinsville, Ky. 153
Hornet's Nest 29-30
Horton, Elijah 157
Houston, John B. 10, 110, 160-163, 167, 172
Hovey, Alvin 55
Hunt, S. Thomas 157
Hurlbut 28-29, 82

I-J

Jackson, John 30
Jackson, Miss. 40, 56-57, 59
Jackson, Stonewall 109
Jackson, Tenn. 82
Jacob, Richard T. 82, 110, 120, 162, 168-173, 177-178, 181
Jeffersontown 12, 152
Jeffersonville, Ind. 113, 128
Jeffries, Thomas 128
Jenkins, Capt. 89, 93
Jessee, George M. 139, 158, 189
Johnson, Adam Rankin 137, 139, 199
Johnson, C.K. 183, 188
Johnson, Sam 153
Johnston, Albert Sidney 22, 25-29
Johnston, Joseph 56-59, 80, 84, 136, 180
Jonesboro, Tenn. 140, 143
Jones, J.M. 169
Jones, John 157
Jones, J.R. 137
Jones, Stephen 151
Jones, Thomas 196
Jones, William 87

K

Kalfus, Henry F. 128
Keigwin, Captain 58
Kellogg, Margaret Todd 176
Kentucky Central Railroad 93, 135
Kentucky River 87-88
Keyser, Charles 182
Kilburn, Charles 166
Knights of the Golden Circle 9, 121, 198
Knoxville, Tenn. 26, 34, 37, 80, 87
Konkel 23

L

Lafferty, Thomas 157, 195
Lagrange, Miss. 43
Lake Maurepas 64
Lake Pontchartrain 64
Lake Providence 41, 50, 54
Lancaster, John 141
Landram, William 49, 55, 57
Langlin 23
Lapielle, M. 16
Lauman, Jacob 29
Lawler, Michael 65
Lawton, C.J. 184
Lawton, W.B. 184
Leathers, John W. 137, 195
Lebanon, Ky. 25, 35, 72, 79
Lee, Robert E. 62, 136, 180
Leggett, Mortimer 62
Lesslie 36
Lewers, Thomas 23-25
Lewis, William 124
L'Hommedieu, Major 52
Licking River 95
Lile, James F. 169
Lilly, Wilson 152
Lincoln, Mary Todd 176
Lindsey. D.W. 111
Lingenfelter, John W. 137
Lingenfelter, William 137
Little Rock, Ark. 43-44
Logan County, Ky. 15, 25, 127, 153, 156
Logan's Crossroads, Ky. 25
Longstreet, James 82
Long, William 157-158
Loring, William 58
Louisa, Ky. 86-88, 141
Louisville & Frankfort Railroad 87
Louisville & Nashville Railroad 72, 81, 87, 126, 135, 143
Lownsley, W. 184
Lucas, Colonel 49, 64
Ludington, E.H. 174-175
Lynchburg, Va. 145
Lyon, Hylan 152, 169

M

Magoffin, Beriah 16-22
Magruder, John 69
Mahoney, Major 189
Mallory, Robert 165
Marks, Nathaniel 183
Marshall, Humphrey 37
Marshal, William 157
Martin, H.T. 183, 185
Martin, Robert 89, 105
Martin, Samuel 158
Martin, W.C. 169-170
Mayfield, Ky. 78-80, 152
Maysville, Ky. 89, 94, 157-158, 197
McClellan, George B. 10, 111, 121, 151-152, 159-160, 170-171
McClernand, John 26-28, 30, 42-44, 46, 48, 50, 56-57, 59-61
McCook, Alexander 32, 35-36
McCreery, Thomas 196
McGinnis, George 65-66
McGlassin, W.B. 137
McHenry, John H. Jr. 23-25
McLean, Nathaniel 141, 143, 148, 177
McPheeters, Samuel B. 176
McPherson, James 56-57, 59, 84
Meade, George 62, 138-139
Memphis & Charleston Railroad 33, 77
Memphis, Tenn. 33, 39-40, 44, 50, 79, 84, 193
Mendenhall 31
Meredith, Gen. 157
Merritt, J.E. 126
Middle Creek, Ky. 26
Millersburg, Ky. 94
Miller, Thomas 128
Milliken's Bend 40-41, 43, 46, 50, 54
Mill Springs, Ky. 25-26
Mims, D.A. 86, 141
Miner, O. F. 171
Mires, Colonel 86-87
Mississippi Cavalry 23, 25
Mississippi Central Railroad 40
Mississippi River 40, 42, 44, 54-55, 62, 64
Mitchell, A.J. 128

Monroe, George 91
Montgomery, Bacon 41, 51
Morey, A.J. 194
Morgan, George 42
Morgan, John Hunt 7, 13-14, 34, 81-83, 85-91, 93-96, 100, 105-107, 114, 117, 121, 135, 140-141, 168, 190, 199
Morgan, Lycurgus 170
Morgantown, Ky. 23-25
Morris, John D. 183, 188-190
Morton, Oliver 123, 128
Mosgrove, George 145-146
Mount Alban 59
Mount Sterling, Ky. 79, 86-91, 95-96, 105-106, 134, 198-199
Mudd, John J. 52-53
Mulford, John E. 183
Munday, Marcellus 192
Mundy, Sue 152, 158, 164
Munfordville, Ky. 22, 34, 158
Murfree 147
Murphy, James 158
Murry, Calvin 139

N

Nashville, Tenn. 16, 22, 27-28, 79-80, 83, 111, 112, 148-149, 152
Nelson's Bridge 65
Nelson, William "Bull" 19-20, 23, 30-31, 35
Netter 23-24
New Albany, Ind. 122, 171
New Carthage 54
New Iberia, La. 65, 68-69
Newport, Ky. 165
Nicholasville, Ky. 119

O

Ohio River 11, 18-19, 166, 177, 184
Ord, Edward 64
Orr, John 49
Osterhaus, Peter 55, 58
Owen, R. 47, 64
Owensboro, Ky. 123-124, 184
Owenton, Ky. 36, 189
Oxford, Miss. 46

P

Paducah, Ky. 22, 26-27, 77-79, 84, 112, 137, 152, 157
Paine, E.A. 137
Palmer, John M. 185-188, 190, 192
Paris, Ky. 38, 63, 82, 91, 94
Parsons, Colonel 48
Paul, J.J. 128
Payne, G.S.G. 128
Pemberton, John 55-56, 58-59, 62
Perkin's Landing 51-52
Perryville, Ky. 35-36
Peyton, Dr. J.B. 17
Pillow, Gideon 21, 27
Pittsburg Landing, Tenn. 28-32
Pleasureville, Ky. 157-158
Polk, Leonidas 21, 30, 35
Poole, James 126
Pope, John 16
Porter, David 40, 44, 48, 53-54
Porter, Capt. 24, 112
Port Gibson, Miss. 55-56
Port Hudson 46, 62
Pound Gap 80, 82-83, 87-88
Powell, James 28
Powell, John Pierman 102, 123-126
Prentice, George 139
Prentiss, Benjamin M. 28-30
Prestonburg, Ky. 80, 88, 143
Price, D. L. 188
Price, Sterling 46, 69

Q

Quinby, General 61

R

Randall, Alexander 109
Rankin, James E. 123-124, 126, 158
Ratliff, Robert 90, 144-146
Rawlins, A. 84
Raymond 56-58
Redfield, Major 59
Redford, B.C. 128
Richmond, Va. 117, 122, 144, 178, 180
Robertson, Felix 144-147, 140
Robertson, George 9, 131
Robinson, Stuart 176
Robinson, W. L. 169
Rolla, Captain 138
Rolston, G.W. 169
Rosecrans, William S. 81
Roundaway Bayou 55
Rudd, John 128
Russellville, Ky. 127

S

Saint Louis, Mo. 40, 165, 176
Saint Martinsville 66-69
Saltville Massacre 142-144, 146, 148
Saltville, Va. 42-150, 163, 177, 179, 199
Salyersville, Ky. 88
Samuels, E.H. 137
Sanders, William P. 63
Savannah, Tenn. 28
Sawyer, R.M. 79
Sawyers, Thomas 117-118
Sayre, B.B. 157
Schoeph, Alfred 25
Schofield, A. 173
Schofield, John 72, 75, 79-80, 83-84, 86, 106, 111, 118, 123, 134, 139, 142, 150, 162, 180, 199
Scott, John 176
Scott, John S. 63
Seddon, J.A. 87, 96, 105
Sells, Orange 146
Shacklett, Captain 24
Shanks, Q.C. 184-185
Shaw, William 29
Shiloh Church 28, 30-31
Shipman, Paul 169
Shocker, Harry 146
Shockley, D.W.C. 41
Shreveport, La. 41-42
Sidell, William H. 113, 128
Sill, Joshua 35
Simpson, Andrew 137
Simpson, J.H. 135
Sipple, John W. 159
Skirvin, Joel 137
Slaymaker, Jack 27
Smith, Andrew J. 35-38, 40-42, 47, 50, 60
Smith, Charles 26
Smith, D. Howard 96, 105
Smith, E.C. 147
Smith, Edmund Kirby 34, 37
Smith, Giles A. 54
Smith, J.R. 85
Smith, M.L. 42
Smith, Robert 144
Smith, William 31-32
Soery, Colonel 125
Somerby 23-24
Somerset, Kentucky 25, 117
Sons of Liberty, The 9, 121, 128, 131-132, 137, 198
Speed, Joshua 19, 170
Stagdale, Samuel 159
Steele, Theophilus 183, 188-189
Stevenson, John 196
Stickrod, Henry 128
Stidger, Felix 128
Steele, General 41
Stone, Charles 65
Stoneman, George 84, 91, 174, 177
Sturgis, Samuel 79-80, 84
Suddarth, Samuel G. 170, 173
Sutherland, Capt. 51
Swaine, Wagner 165
Symonds, Henry 11, 156, 164-167, 198
Sypert, Colonel 125

T

Talbott, John H. 128
Taylor, Jesse 26
Taylor, Richard 65
Taylorsville, Ky. 139
Templeton, Lt.Col. 49
Tennessee River 26, 28, 30, 79
Thomas, George 20, 25, 84, 127, 156-157, 159, 180, 186, 190
Thomas, Harvey 127-128
Thomas, Lorenzo 19, 118-120, 149, 178-179
Thomas, W.K. 128
Thompson, A.P. 77-78
Thompson, Charles William 102, 123-126
Thompson, Jack 16
Thornton, W.T. 170
Tilghman, Lloyd 26-27, 58
Tithe, William 157
Todd, R.S. 188
Tomlinson, John 169-170
Townsend, E.D. 121, 172, 173
Travelated, Harvey 137
Trimble, Colonel 145
True, C.J. 71, 88
Tudor, A.B. 169-170
Turley, Sanford 169
Tyler, Major 94

U

Unconditional Unionist Party 7, 9, 76, 111, 121, 131, 170, 190
Union City, Tenn. 78
Uniontown, Ky. 122

V

Vance, Lt. 189
Van Osten, Fred 16
Vaughn, John 144-145, 147
Vicksburg 46, 50, 53-54, 56, 59
Vicksburg Campaign 7, 38-40, 54, 56, 61-63, 69, 190
Vicksburg & Jackson Railroad 41
Vicksburg, Miss. 40, 43-44, 62
Vicksburg, Shreveport, & Texas Railroad 41-42
Virginia Railroad 142
Virginia & Tennessee Railroad 177

W

Wainscott, George W. 137
Walker, Leroy 21
Walker, W.H.T. 57
Wallace, Lew 27-28, 30
Washburn, Cadwallader 65-68
Washburne, Henry 181
Webster, Aleck 85
Webster, J.D. 30
Webster, Mose 85
Wessells, H.W. 183
West Liberty, Ky. 23, 83
West, M.D. 10
Wheeler, Joseph 81
Wherritt, Perry 118
Whilldin, Lt. 41
White River 46
Wickliffe, Charles 138
Williams, John 144
Williams, Rufus 111
Williams, Thomas 50
Williamstown, Ky. 36-37, 137, 157
Willow Springs 56
Wilson, Captain 93
Winchester, Ky. 171
Winchester Pike 63
Wolford, Frank 19, 22, 75, 82, 110-112, 120-121, 162, 168-172, 178, 199
Woodbury, Ky. 23-25
Wood, George 17
Wood, Sterling A.M. 28, 31
Woods, William 126-127
Wooten, B. Grisley 126-127
Wright, General 37
Wright, Colonel 52.
Wytheville, Tenn. 177

Y

Yates, Dick 124
Yates, R.W. 157-158
Yazoo River 40-41, 43, 50, 53-54
Young's Point, La. 52-54

Z

Zollicoffer, Felix 22, 25-26

About the Author

Bryan S. Bush

Bryan Bush was born in 1966 in Louisville, Kentucky and has been a native of that city ever since. He graduated with honors from Murray State University with a degree in History and Psychology, and received his Master's Degree from the University of Louisville in 2005. Bryan has always had a passion for history, especially the Civil War. He has been a member of many different Civil War historical preservation societies, has consulted for movie companies and other authors, coordinated with other museums on displays of various museum articles and artifacts, has written for magazines, such as *Kentucky Civil War Magazine*, *North/South Trader*, and *Back Home in Kentucky* and worked for many different historical sites, and has always fought hard to maintain and preserve Civil War history in the Western Theater. In 1999, Bryan published his first work: *The Civil War Battles of the Western Theater*, which was given good reviews by *North/South Magazine* and *Kentucky Monthly*, which said Bryan Bush's *The Civil War Battles of the Western Theater* "has with his first book created a needed addition to any serious Civil War library." Since then, Mr. Bush has had published *Terry's Texas Rangers: The 8th Texas Cavalry*, *My Dearest Mollie: The Civil War Letters of Brig. Gen. Daniel F. Griffin, 38th Indiana Volunteer Infantry*, *Lloyd Tilghman: Confederate General in the Western Theater*, *Lincoln and the Speeds*, and was a contributor to *Kentucky's Civil War.* Bryan Bush has been a Civil War reenactor for fourteen years, portraying an artillerist. For five years Bryan was on the Board of Directors and curator for the Old Bardstown Civil War Museum and Village: The Battles of the Western Theater Museum in Bardstown, Kentucky.